Scouting the Future

The Public Speeches of William J. Casey

Scouting the Future

The Public Speeches of William J. Casey

Compiled and with Introductions by
Herbert E. Meyer
Appreciation by Leo Cherne
Tribute by Jeane J. Kirkpatrick

Edited by Mark B. Liedl

Regnery Gateway
Washington, D.C.

Library of Congress Cataloging-in-Publication Date

Casey, William J.
    Scouting the future: the public speeches of William J. Casey.
    p.   cm.
ISBN 0-89526-759-4 : $24.95
    1. United States. Central Intelligence Agency. 2. Intelligence service--United States. 3. United States--National security. 4. World politics--1945- I. Title.
    UB251.U5C37 1989
    327.1'2'06075--dc19   89-3482
                                                                          CIP

Published in the United States by
Regnery Gateway, Inc.
1130 17th Street, NW
Washington, DC 20036

Distributed to the trade by
Kampmann & Company, Inc.
226 W. 26th Street
New York, NY 10001

Manufactured in the United States of America
1989 printing

10 9 8 7 6 5 4 3 2 1

Acknowledgements

To Donald Hall and Betty Murphy for their help in the preparation of this book.

Contents

A Eulogy for William J. Casey

Preface

A collection of speeches often reveals more about a person than a biography or even the most powerful of eulogies. It reflects how the person perceives his own strengths, priorities, and even his own place in history. And, as in this collection, when the addresses are actually written by the speaker himself they are even more revealing.

Those who knew Bill Casey will not be surprised by the wisdom and the passion of his speeches. For them, this book will be a reference, to remember the man they knew to be a great patriot, and to continue to learn from him after his death. To those who did not know him, this collection will lift the enigma that shrouded much of his life and his work. There is much to learn from these speeches about intelligence and about America. There is also much to learn about Bill Casey, the public servant who devoted his life to both.

For the scholar, this volume is rich in details of Casey's tenure at the CIA and his concept of the U.S. intelligence mission. For the student of history, it provides inside accounts of U.S. and Allied intelligence operations during World War II, insights into the solid case against Alger Hiss, and Casey's own research on the role of intelligence in the American Revolutionary War.

For journalists, these speeches invite introspection, offering Casey's point of view detached from the politics of the day, the glare of television lights, and the pressure of news deadlines. Casey challenges journalists to weigh more responsibly the tenets of a free press and the need for secrecy in issues of national security.

For all American citizens, his speeches offer an extraordinary view of the world behind the headlines, and an understanding of how intelligence works and why it is vitally important to all of us.

Most strongly, however, I recommend this book to the young people of America — to those who are concerned about the future and whether this nation will remain strong and free. Bill Casey devoted his life to that cause. Although he is gone, his ideals are as timeless as those expressed by other great American patriots. Yet to endure, such ideals must be preserved and promoted by succeeding generations.

Bill Casey understood the tremendous challenges ahead for this nation. And now, the torch has been passed to a generation of Americans who must meet those challenges.

Edwin J. Feulner, Jr.
President
The Heritage Foundation

January 1989

Introduction

In one of the speeches that follow, William Casey remarks that it is "costly and painful to be misunderstood." Perhaps no American public servant of the 1980s was misjudged more than he. To an unsympathetic and ravenous press he was an adversary; the keeper of secrets that must be told; a Cold War spymaster bent on renewing such covert CIA activities as had been zealously exposed during the 1970s. In speech and appearance Casey fit the part. He had not the stage presence suitable for a modern media star. Yet in intellect and vision, he had few equals.

To those who know only the William Casey depicted in the national media, the speeches in this book will seem of another man. Naturally the collection presents his views on the Soviet Union, the importance of intelligence, and other topics one would expect from the Director of Central Intelligence. Beyond that, however, they reveal a broader and far more human William Casey than his public image ever suggested. From these speeches emerges an engaging, witty, scholarly, and remarkably perceptive man. Although some may not agree with his view of the world or his prescriptions for improving it, none can say after reading these speeches that Casey lacked the courage of his convictions, or that his convictions were rooted in anything but altruism.

Several insights into William Casey's character and his tenure as Director of CIA are found in his speeches. Among them is his constant effort to inform the public of the true nature of the intelligence mission. Casey recognized that the public's understanding of intelligence and its image of CIA is limited to clandestine operations and perilous espionage. But as Casey points out in his speeches, the bulk of intelligence work is collecting and analyzing data. Thousands of CIA employees continually sift through messages and information collected from all over the world. Teams of analysts attempt to extract meaning from the data, distinguishing vital from irrelevant, and assessing the political and policy implications. The assessments then are compiled into briefings called National Intelligence Estimates that are delivered to the President and other senior policy-makers. Such political leaders rely on the Estimates to make their national security decisions.

Casey believed that injecting competition into the intelligence assessment process produced better Estimates for national leaders. He bristled at the bureaucratic tendency to find a middle ground when confronted with conflicting assessments of identical intelligence data. In one of his speeches, Casey remarks that the last thing the President needs is "weasel words" that conceal valid differences over the interpretation of ambiguous information. "The President does not need a single best view, a guru, or a prophet. The nation needs the best analysis and the full range of views it can get" (p. 19). Throughout his speeches on this topic Casey challenges intelligence analysts to resist consensus, question the conventional wisdom, and always, to speak their own minds.

Casey's campaign to educate the public on the real business of intelligence involved broadening the intelligence community to include ordinary Americans who have a stake in keeping the nation strong. In several speeches he explains to the business and academic communities how they can become partners in the intelligence mission. Casey believed that the key to successful intelligence, and ultimately to protecting American security, rested in building a national consensus on the need for strong intelligence capabilities. "So while we have made great strides in rebuilding this country's intelligence apparatus, the backing and understanding of the American people is going to be needed to sustain and build on the progress we have made" (p. 27).

Casey believed that by explaining how intelligence works, revealing what is at stake, and showing how every citizen could help, intelligence could become a national concern and commitment. His focus on building such a national consensus helped to breath new life into a CIA that had been nearly destroyed during the 1970s.

William Casey was devoted to his job, but he was driven by his passion for freedom. His speeches chronicle a life of preserving, protecting, and promoting freedom. From his early years in the Office of Strategic Services fighting to liberate Europe from Hitler, to his battles against the modern-day Hitlers with their Marxist brand of totalitarianism, Casey labored for freedom. His grasp of the Soviet threat — expressed eloquently in his October 29, 1983 address to Westminster College (p. 136) — went far beyond Cold War rhetoric. Casey understood the crux of the Soviet threat to be Moscow's absolute rejection and unrelenting assault on fundamental American notions of liberty: "The threat posed by the Soviet Union is the lineal descendent of the same threat Western civilization has faced for better than two thousand years: it is the threat posed by despotism against the...concept that the highest goal of the State is to protect and foster the capabilities and the liberties of the individual" (p. 146). Throughout his speeches Casey seeks to convey this understanding to audiences in nearly every forum.

Casey's passion for freedom extended to the Third World where he advocated bold new directions for U.S. policy. His approach rested on two tenants: first, that Marxism had failed to liberate less developed countries (LDCs), and in fact had wrought misery, famine, and genocide of historic proportions; and second, that the U.S. in the 1980s faced a unique opportunity to help oppressed peoples resisting totalitarian regimes, and to inject free market approaches to LDC economic development that truly would secure freedom and opportunity. He saw in Nicaragua the classic blueprint for Soviet-style oppression, and believed it to be a pivotal test of U.S. resolve to fan new flames of freedom in the Third World (p. 183).

The speeches in this book also illustrate William Casey's tremendous respect for and remarkable knowledge of history. Here, Casey the scholar shines through, but also Casey the realist and Casey the teacher. Several of the speeches in Chapter 8 exhibit his broad and deep understanding of history. And with each of these speeches Casey draws the "lessons learned" from the past and applies them to current affairs. He explains, for example, how the present-day struggle against communism is really the age-old battle against tyranny. He shows also how the lessons of the American Revolution should have dissuaded U.S. policymakers from their chosen course in Vietnam. And he compares the Nazi atrocities of World War II with the communists' exterminations of the modern era in such countries as Cambodia and Afghanistan. His speeches unearth an all-too familiar pattern in the timeless struggle between human liberty and subjugation.

Casey's knowledge of the past propelled him into a search for the future. Here, the speeches reveal yet another insight into the mind of this perspicacious man. In many ways his life's work was, as the title of this book reads, "scouting the future." His job as intelligence chief was to anticipate events. According to Casey, predicting how a particular nation may act is difficult enough, but it is even more difficult when the leaders of that nation themselves have no idea what they will do. Casey often reminded his audiences that intelligence is not infallible. "We do not have a pipeline to God," he remarks in one address, "nor do we have a crystal ball" (p. 18). And yet Casey himself had powers of prophecy that extend far beyond what ordinarily would be considered the intelligence realm.

The breadth of Casey's foresight is demonstrated in his speeches on the subject of technological change. He was acutely aware of the emergence of a new global economy in which America would be challenged as never before. Although his speeches acknowledge that transition always has been a fundamental element of the human condition, what is new, he argues, is the accelerated rate of change in the modern world (p. 106). More than any of his predecessors Casey devoted CIA resources to assessing the long-range policy implications of such rapid change. Casey believed that the intelligence community has a duty and special capability to offer policymakers a vision of the future: "Intelligence is an indispensable tool that enables us to understand the consequences of this rapid movement to a profoundly changed and independent world. It enables us to devise policies which enhance our ability to shape our destiny" (p. 128).

In several speeches the intelligence chief urges the public to join in the effort to "shape our destiny." He outlines key challenges that lie ahead from such diverse issues as rising nationalism, increasing terrorism, and vanishing natural resources. He instructs his audiences on how they can help meet those challenges, and he encourages his listeners to look toward the future while remembering the past and the essential attributes that have carried America this far. "Lofty goals, hard work, and enthusiasm still matter," he remarks in a speech to college students. "Remember your political heritage and the values imparted to you by your families and this college. With perseverance and devotion to duty, you too will pass on the baton so that the opportunities and freedoms you enjoy will be enjoyed by those who follow" (p. 135).

The later speeches in this book reveal the decidedly human attributes of William Casey. Although in earlier speeches he delivers warm and inspiring words to college students and CIA employees, in Chapter 9 Casey the man clearly transcends Casey the Director of Central Intelligence. These speeches suggest the fundamental difference between the real William Casey and his public image. His compassion, strong sense of loyalty, and respect for those who serve the nation are a testimony to his true character. Whether in remarks to his old colleagues from the OSS, in praise of former CIA Directors, or in gratitude to members of government's "silent services" who labor for national security with no public recognition, Casey speaks from the heart. His eulogy to Robert Ames, killed in the bombing of the U.S. Embassy in Beirut, is powerfully moving (p. 292).

A final insight into William Casey that emerges from this book is his enduring optimism. Few officials in the Reagan Administration were attacked more regularly or viciously than was Casey. And yet through it all, he maintained his commitment, and even his sense of humor. On complaints about his mumbling, for example, the intelligence chief responds: "From personal experience I can tell you that mumbling is more in the mind of the listener than in the mouth of the speaker. There are people who just don't want to hear what the Director of Central Intelligence sees in a complex and dangerous world" (p. 289).

One indication of Casey's positive outlook is the number of speeches he delivered to the media. In this book there are several, and in each one Casey candidly offers his perspective in an attempt to build a more constructive relationship with his tormentors. Another measure of the man's optimism is found in nearly every one of his speeches. Although he often sketches a rather gloomy picture of the world he never leaves it as that. His speeches transform such sobering challenges into exciting new opportunities. Perhaps no passage more neatly expresses his philosophy than this from his May 19, 1984, commencement address to the students of Bryant College:

> It is your challenge as this country's future leaders in business and government, in education and the professions, to know and understand world affairs and history, not just for your personal benefit or your company's, but also for the benefit of this nation as a whole. You are embarking on an exciting — though not always an easy — future. Dealing with the world realistically does not mean you cannot or should not have high hopes. As Thomas Wolfe wrote in his novel, *Of Time and the River:* "It's a fabulous country — the only fabulous country. The one where

miracles not only happen but they happen all the time" (p. 135).

It is "costly and painful to be misunderstood," said Casey. "But," he continues, "it is more costly and painful to misunderstand the kind of world in which we have to operate" (p. 17). William Casey understood the world because he lived in a part of it that few others ever see. And while the national media and perhaps much of the public misunderstood him, that concerned him less than the danger that Americans would view the world as they wished it to be, rather than as it truly is.

In an August 13, 1985, speech to new CIA employees (p. 15), Casey describes five characteristics that should be signposts of their careers. In reality these five characteristics describe the essence of Casey's own life. They are: *Devotion, Effort, Ingenuity, Enterprise*, and *Courage*. "Courage," Casey tells his workers, "is the ability to persist with a good idea despite difficulties, setbacks, ridicule, or the indifference of others."

Indeed, William Casey was a public servant of uncommon courage.

Mark B. Liedl

January 1989

Mark B. Liedl is an editor and consultant to The Heritage Foundation in Washington, D.C.

As I Recall Bill Casey

by Leo Cherne

A volume of the speeches Bill Casey delivered while serving as Director of Central Intelligence is important for several reasons. First, it essentially is the only means we have of recapturing the thoughts of this extraordinary man. Second, the volume supplies insights and perspectives on intelligence that challenge popular misconceptions. Except for professionals in the field and scholars who have made intelligence their life's work, few Americans — even the most informed among them — are ever exposed to meaningful discussions of the United States' intelligence mission. And finally, just as these speeches will enlighten Americans who now read them, so too will they aide future historians in evaluating the career and the contributions of Bill Casey.

It may be presumptuous to suggest that one accomplished individual is more complex than another. But having known Bill Casey for some 51 years, and several other Directors of Central Intelligence for shorter intervals, I am persuaded that Bill was the most complex and the least understood of this exceptional group of men.

Two events, the Iranian arms deal and the battle for U.S. aid to the Contras in Nicaragua, dominated the public perception of Bill Casey. These two issues created a public image of the nation's intelligence community that greatly distorts reality and makes more difficult the accurate evaluation that is so necessary if mistakes and misjudgments are to be understood and avoided in the future.

Nothing suffered more in this misinformation process than the answer to the question, "What kind of person was Bill Casey?" Throughout the many years of our friendship I had the opportunity to search for the words that would most capture his essential qualities. Two words most aptly characterize the man: First, Bill was a "scholar," a man devoted

Leo Cherne is Vice Chairman of the President's Foreign Intelligence
  Advisory Board.

1

to books and ideas, the tools of an intellectual. As a scholar, Casey clearly left his mark on the intelligence community. Intelligence as he envisioned it was a far different and greatly expanded undertaking than what had been the norm before he became Director of Central Intelligence. Such an expansion was one only an intellectual could make — an intellectual who, long before his contemporaries, understood that a nation could be threatened by economic dangers as much as by military ones.

Casey profoundly altered the thrust and operating ideas of the intelligence community. His views had been shaped both by his scholarly pursuits and his many years of public service, as Chairman of the Securities and Exchange Commission, as head of the Export-Import Bank, as the Under Secretary of State for Economic Affairs, and as an intelligence officer before, during, and immediately following World War II.

The second word that describes Bill Casey is "patriot." The characterization may be unsettling to some readers and perhaps seems to contradict the notion of "scholar." Patriotism, after all, so readily conjures up flag, pledges, and fireworks, and the aphorism, "Patriotism is the last refuge of a scoundrel." Such are the images, however, that will be engraved on unknowing and unthinking minds. The patriotism that was the hallmark of the bookworm I knew, was one of the least complicated aspects of his life. It was simply a love of country.

Bill's love of country and of its history would propel him on a journey that retraced virtually every step of George Washington's campaign to free America from British rule. Bill studied and searched to find a rationale for every battle of the American Revolution. Where dull plaques are now mounted, his mind explored the landscape and recreated the events. His observations comprise the manuscript of the book *Where and How the War was Fought*, published by Morrow in 1976.

I first met Bill Casey in 1937. Having earned his degree from St. John's Law School, he walked into the offices of The Research Institute of America in the hope of finding employment.

The Institute was not more than a year old, but we were already involved in our third major work, a thorough analysis and explanation of the federal tax laws.

Suddenly, Bill Casey became a tax expert. Only one difficulty dogged him, however, as it did for much of his life. It was the problem people had understanding his speech. Although I knew him for half a century, I have never determined whether his mumbling was the result of indifference or an impediment, or perhaps most likely, simply impatience. Nevertheless, Bill Casey's dictations of complex analyses presented the most severe challenge to any secretary who was assigned to transcribe them.

The Research Institute's volume on federal taxation, *The Federal Tax Coordinator*, was completed during an era of Hitler's increasing domination of Europe and the meeting at Munich with Chamberlain and Daladier, which enabled Chamberlain to returned to England and assure its citizens that he had brought them "peace in our time." Casey's remarkable mental skills had been so evident in his work on the tax project that I was impatient to make him my assistant. With his talents, The Research Institute could embark on the more ambitious project of understanding and explaining a rapidly changing world. This meant analyses of the wide range of New Deal legislation, the historic Supreme Court decision on the constitutionality of that legislation, the changing economy under the New Deal, and in the background, world events.

For us at that time the world was one in which Japan had invaded Manchuria, and Franco was seeking to overthrow a Republican government in Spain, with Hitler, Mussolini, and Stalin sharpening their knives on that bloody whetstone. Munich may have meant peace to Chamberlain, but to Bill Casey and me a more likely outcome was war.

A telephone call from Assistant Secretary of War Louis Johnston brought confirming judgment. He had for some time seen some of the analytic work done by The Research Institute and now was calling to present us with a dilemma. The National Defense Act of 1921 obligated his office to prepare U.S. industrial mobilization plans to be implemented in the event of war. Bernard Baruch had learned in World War I how handicapped the U.S. could be without such plans. But isolationists in Congress had foiled Baruch by refusing to appropriate funds to implement his mobilization plan. And now with a second world war approaching, Louis Johnston faced similar opposition, made no easier by the fact that his boss, Secretary of War Harry Woodring, was also an isolationist. Faced with such a delicate situation, Johnston needed help where he could find it.

Johnston asked that we contribute at least a few of our staff to help rush to completion the mobilization plans his office was preparing. I agreed to spend one half of each week in Washington, D.C., to help in this race against an unknown deadline (Johnston guessed that in one year the war would be upon us). I left Casey in New York in charge of the Institute's analytic staff and its publications.

Within a few months, however, it became clear that more talent was needed for the mobilization project. Casey was thoroughly briefed on the plans as they existed and he began taking large chunks of the work back to New York. There his considerable skills and those of other members of The Research Institute's staff were applied to the task. Plans were devised to organize the entire U.S. economy, differentiating between the economic sectors required for wartime production and those responsible for meeting the peacetime needs of a democratic society. All who worked on these plans agreed that there was no more gifted judge of priorities and allocations than Casey. Our huge body of work, done without a penny of compensation or government reimbursement for any expenditure, was finally completed, by sheer accident on September 1, 1939, the day Germany invaded Poland and World War II began.

Word of the report and of Bill Casey's work reached General William J. Donovan, President Roosevelt's one-man intelligence community. In a matter of months Casey was out of The Research Institute, a lieutenant in the Navy, and one of "Wild" Bill Donovan's prize acquisitions.

Donovan assigned to Casey the responsibility of directing U.S. support for the underground war against Hitler. Although Bill was comfortably positioned in an office in London, he itched to join those he directed behind Nazi lines in what was then fascist Europe. That he did not join them was remarkable. There was a streak of the adventurer in Bill, and a reluctance to ask others to take risks from which he was sheltered.

Casey was never satisfied that intelligence was employing fully the resources of creative minds. His efforts at innovation made him a frequent irritant to his colleagues in British Intelligence. During the enormous intelligence effort to mislead the German High Command about the location of the D-Day landings, Casey insisted that economic intelligence was capable of both identifying the weaknesses in German defenses and magnifying the Nazi's inclination to believe the Allies' disinformation. One of the team of American economists he assembled for this intelligence mission was Walt Rostow. Others who were part of that eccentric company include Arthur Schlesinger, Jr., and Walter Lord, the author of *A Night to Remember* and many other works.

On the last occasion I had to speak with Bill in the office he maintained at the Reagan White House, he expressed regret that his memoirs of his years with General Donovan and the Office of Strategic Services remained incomplete and unpublished. The manuscript did not meet the high standard he had set for it. On my one visit to his hospital room at Georgetown University Hospital, communication with him was impossible. This despite the assistance of his wife Sophia and his daughter Bernadette who shared the 24-hour days to be in his constant company, and who had learned how to coax a response, a random word, through the barrier of his cancer-induced paralysis.

When the publication of Robert Woodward's book *Veil* focused on the author's unsubstantiated conversation with Casey in the hospital, I knew I would find no reliable history in such a work. In order to prod Casey to continue the struggle that living entailed at that time, I urged him to rush his recovery so that he could complete his OSS memoirs. They are now completed, published in 1988 by Regnery Gateway in the book *William J. Casey: The Secret War Against Hitler.*

It is difficult for me to pass by the newspaper and magazine shops found in every airport without thinking of Bill Casey. He could not come within sight of one of these shops without stopping to buy a handful of paperback books. There could not have been a week of his life in which Bill read fewer than half a dozen books. I always felt that the greatest hazard in visiting his home in Rosslyn was the thousands of books stuffed haphazardly into high shelves. I was certain that one day I would read of some poor soul maimed as the shelves and books came tumbling down.

One episode that demonstrated Bill's affection for the written word I recall more vividly than any other of the entire period I knew him. When Soviet tanks entered Czechoslovakia in August 1968, Bill Casey and I were each busy with our altogether different activities, although we both served as members of the International Rescue Committee, an organization that was committed to helping refugees fleeing totalitarian regimes.

As soon as I learned of the Soviet invasion and effort to suppress the "socialist spring" being administered by a Communist leader who was anticipating by twenty years the *glasnost* ' and *perestroika* of Gorbachev, I knew that I would have to head for Europe. Every such event in the past invariably had resulted in violence by the Soviets and a flood of refugees seeking to flee the embattled country. As Chairman of the IRC I undertook to go to Vienna because of the likelihood that large numbers of refugees would seek the safety of Austria. Before I departed, Bill Casey called me to volunteer his services.

Shortly after he joined me in Vienna, we rented a car and a driver to take us to Prague in the hope of establishing contact with protest leaders. We crossed the border without any problems, and on roads that were virtually empty we headed toward Bratislava, the nearest major city. Quite suddenly, hardly 100 feet away, we came upon a watchtower manned by several Soviet soldiers armed with machine guns. We told the driver to slow his pace. It was an unnecessary instruction. Within a minute or two we were surrounded by a company of Soviet tanks, motorcycles, and soldiers.

I spent the next hour or so trying to communicate with the Russian commander of that unit, a fruitless task in light of the fact that I spoke no Russian and he no English. I finally decided to try a tactic that I had long known proved useful to others when apprehended by the Soviet military in similar situations: I demanded to speak with his commanding officer.

It now seemed clear that at least that portion of what I was trying to say was understood.

I walked back to the automobile to share my impressions with Bill, only to find him in perfect comfort ensconced in the back seat reading an Allen Drury novel. For the moment at least, he upset me more than the Russians had. I shouted at him, "Can you tell me how you can sit there reading while all this is going on?" I will never forget him looking up at me with a thin suggestion of a smile and responding. "Do you know of anything more useful I might be doing?"

The spirit that radiated from Bill Casey was a simple compelling one: "Time is not wasted if you have a book in your hand."

Working With Bill Casey

by Herbert E. Meyer

At first blush, the very idea of public speeches by a Director of Central Intelligence may seem odd. Should not the nation's intelligence chief — the official that headline writers are so fond of calling "the Spymaster" or "the Top Spook" — be a shadowy, furtive individual who says as little as possible and who keeps a public profile so low as to be invisible?

Actually, no, for two reasons: First, William J. Casey was a public figure long before President-elect Ronald Reagan named him Director of Central Intelligence at the end of 1980. He served during World War II as a senior officer in the Office of Strategic Services, and wrote and published books on a variety of subjects, ranging from "how-to" tax manuals for lawyers, to a history of the American Revolution. He held top-level government positions including Chairman of the Securities and Exchange Commission, President and Chairman of the United States Export-Import Bank, and Under Secretary of State for Economic Affairs. In short, Bill Casey had been writing and speaking publicly for decades prior to his nomination to the Cabinet as Director of Central Intelligence.

Second, despite the public's fascination — indeed, obsession — with spies and covert action programs, these activities are but a fraction of what modern intelligence is all about. Today roughly 95 percent of the entire U.S. national intelligence budget is devoted to the collection and analysis of information. Any intelligence chief spends the bulk of his time and energy directing the resulting conclusions, judgments, and projections of those who need to have such information. Policymakers are the primary audience, of course. But in Casey's judgment, an informed public is also vital to the health of a democracy. Hence he spoke out publicly for the explicit purpose of making available (in sanitized,

Herbert E. Meyer served as Special Assistant to the Director of Central Intelligence and Vice Chairman of the National Intelligence Council.

7

unclassified form) as much of the intelligence community's conclusions, judgments, and projections as the requirements of national security permitted. He considered it to be part of the Director's job to do this. Moreover, he enjoyed it.

Casey wrote his own speeches. Indeed, one need only skim through them to realize that no one other than Bill Casey could possibly have written these speeches. They contain the kind of personal anecdotes and professional insights that only this man, with his unique background, experiences, and grasp of history, could produce. To be sure, from time to time he did order up speech drafts from various CIA analysts. But no matter how good the drafts were – and some were excellent – he never liked them. "It's my fault," he would say to the disappointed writer. "I just didn't communicate to you what I wanted. I'll just do it myself."

And he would. He would sit at his desk – invariably piled high with top-secret intelligence reports and books he wanted to read – with a cheap felt-tipped pen and one of those long, lined yellow pads that all lawyers need to think, and he would write out his speeches in a bold scrawl that only a very few members of his staff could decipher. (The staff used to joke that if the KGB ever go its hands on one of Casey's speech drafts, it would tangle up their best people for weeks.) Every so often he would tear off the pages he had written and pass them for typing to Betty Murphy, his Special Assistant, or to Debbie Geer, his top secretary.

Other times he would dictate his first drafts to Mrs. Murphy or Ms. Geer. His speech was about as clear as his handwriting, and it was not uncommon for Mrs. Murphy or Ms. Geer to go from one of us who worked nearby to the other, reading a sentence aloud that Casey had dictated and asking our judgment of what a particular garbled word might be. Every so often, one of us guessed right. Mostly we guessed wrong, and when the typed draft was delivered to Casey he would see a word he had never used, mutter something, cross it out and write in the word he wanted. Sometimes, when one of us could not even hazard a guess, the draft would be typed with a blank space, which Casey would dutifully fill in.

Casey took his speechmaking seriously, and he worked hard at it. On some speeches he would devote hours or even days to thinking, drafting, and editing. He would work at his desk, in his car, at home, and on airplanes. When an upcoming speech was especially important to him –

such as his speech at Westminster College in Fulton, Missouri, where Winston Churchill delivered his famous "Iron Curtain" speech in 1946 — Casey would postpone his regular appointments to turn his full attention to drafting and editing. It made for some very long and frantic days at the office for a man with his intelligence responsibilities and workload, and he always blamed himself. "I don't know why I always leave these things to the last moment," he once remarked, looking up from a draft page while his secretaries were typing away at heroic speeds and simultaneously shifting around his appointments calendar. "It just seems to be the way I work. I can't change my habits now." In any case, a speech was never in its final form until whoever was introducing Casey was winding up his remarks and the Director of Central intelligence began striding to the podium.

During his six years as intelligence chief, Casey delivered nearly 100 formal speeches. Of these, seven or eight were to internal audiences, comprised of U.S. intelligence officers. These speeches remain classified. Ninety-three of his speeches were to public audiences. Like any top-level executive, Casey sometimes used the same basic speech on more than one occasion. It is these "repeat" speeches that have been eliminated from this collection. The remaining public speeches in this volume are those which capture the intellectual range and the essence of this remarkable public servant.

Chapter 1

Rebuilding the CIA

INTELLIGENCE IN THE TROUBLED EIGHTIES

As part of his efforts to rebuild the CIA after the 1970s cutbacks, Casey actively recruited key officers who had retired or been forced out by his predecessors. He took special pride in those who agreed to come back and work under his leadership.

Nice to be here. Let me say a few words to introduce myself and set the stage for a dialogue this evening.

Sixteen months ago, President Reagan asked me to be his intelligence chief. It is the job of the intelligence chief to see that a vast flow of evidence is gathered, sifted through, evaluated and analyzed daily, and to forewarn the President of trouble spots — and of the dangers to the United States that lurk there. I have been doing that for these past months, and I can tell you it is an awesome job. Trouble spots abound. Almost all of them present some danger to the interests of the United States. We will talk about some of them later.

In troubled times, Presidents rely more heavily on the country's intelligence services. President Reagan is no different. He took his election as a mandate for a strong intelligence service and has supported the rebuilding of capabilities which had been diminished by the loss of 50 percent of its people and 40 percent of its funding during the 1970s.

There are many reasons I am enormously pleased to be involved in this rebuilding. Intelligence is something I have had a life-long interest

Address to the Association of Former Intelligence Officers, San Francisco, California, May 21, 1982.

in – and dedication to. I got my first taste as an aide to General William Donovan. Then, with David Bruce, I worked in organizing, supplying, and coordinating the French Resistance Forces in support of our landings in Normandy and the liberation of France. And finally, as chief of American secret intelligence operations in sending over 100 deep intelligence missions into Germany itself. Believe it or not, we did use aerial photography and signals intelligence in that operation. After the war, I worked with Donovan, Bruce, Allen Dulles, and Russ Forgan, who succeeded Bruce as CO in Europe, and with General Bill Quinn, who kept the Office of Strategic Services together after Donovan left, in helping President Truman develop the concept and make the case for a peacetime central intelligence service. Later I served on the General Advisory Committee on Arms Control where I learned about counting missiles and monitoring arms control, and on the Murphy Commission headed by Ambassador Bob Murphy who organized and ran our first intelligence network with radio communications to an invading fleet, when he was American pro-consul in North Africa in 1942. The Commission was charged with evaluating our organization and instruments for the conduct of foreign policy and I was asked by President Ford to be one of his intelligence advisors as a member of the President's Foreign Intelligence Advisory Board. So, although I was never in the Central Intelligence Agency, I feel that I was there at the creation and have not been far away since.

There is a rich tradition at the Central Intelligence Agency on which to rebuild. William Donovan met the challenge by scouring our campuses to gather hundreds of the nation's foremost scholars to analyze military, political, economic, and scientific aspects of the great struggle. He reached into the great American melting pot for young men with language skills who would volunteer to go behind enemy lines. He reached out to the financial, advertising, journalistic, entertainment, and industrial communities, both national and international, which he had come to know as a lawyer, to assemble talent to write scenarios for psychological warfare, cover, and deception; and to organize, supply, and run operations on a worldwide scale. He left the country the Central Intelligence Agency as a legacy to ensure there will never be another Pearl Harbor. Bedell Smith and Allen Dulles put flesh and bone on the CIA. Dick Helms and Frank Wisner devoted their professional careers to the creation and development of our human intelligence capability.

Bill Colby took the heat and fought hard to maintain an effective intelligence service in the mid-1970s. George Bush then stepped in and began the long process of restoring confidence and regaining public respect. In doing this job, it means a great deal to me to have known and worked for much of my adult life with all of these founders and leaders of American intelligence and so many of those who supported them: John Bross and Jim Angleton, Ray Cline and Lyman Kirkpatrick, and many others.

It is hard to overstate the damage done to the intelligence service during the 1970s. Unrelenting questioning of the Agency's integrity generated a severe loss of credibility. The credibility is only now being restored. Perhaps more devastating for the long term was the almost unnoticed draw-down of resources that resulted in part from the incessant challenging of the need for intelligence. A larger reason was the budget philosophy that predominated, which asked the question, "What can we do without?" rather than, "What kind of challenges will the United States face over the next ten years – and what kind of intelligence will we need?" The answer to what we can do was always "manpower." With steadily diminishing resources, operations were curtailed, too many good people were lost, analysis suffered.

We have set our goals immediately to strengthen the capabilities of the intelligence community to deal with the complexities of today's problems, and, at the same time, develop new capabilities to meet the challenges of the troubled times we see in the late 1980s and 1990s. We have made a good start and been assured of the President's steady support toward meeting both these goals. Much work remains to be done and we have hundreds of former intelligence officers back on contract to help us: On Tuesday of this week I was in Honduras and met a retiree who gave up fishing and hunting in central Oregon, another who skipped a semester of teaching at the University of Illinois, and a third who left his retirement home in North Carolina to help us teach the Honduran security service to resist intrusion into that country from Cuba and Nicaragua.

So, I'm pleased to meet the San Francisco contingent of AFIO and answer your questions and get your suggestions this evening.

◆ ◆ ◆

OUR GREATEST RESOURCE

Casey did much to instill a sense of purpose and unity at CIA. Casey believed in people. To him, the backbone of intelligence was the rank and file employees who worked countless hours, often with little recognition. Casey went out of his way to acknowledge their contribution. In fact, he shared a special understanding of their work because he had done much of it himself in his early days in the intelligence service.

Here, Casey delivers a gracious and inspiring speech to new CIA employees. The advice he gives them on how to approach their jobs is as much a characterization of how Casey lived his own life.

First of all, let me say that I am delighted to be here as your speaker to applaud your graduation from the Career Training Program. On such occasions it customary for someone like me to say a few things informational, a few things inspirational, and perhaps a few things "congratulational." I hope to do all those things. But most of all, I want to convey my warmest personal congratulations to each of you and to remind you that completion of this program marks only the beginning of your intelligence career. You will find CIA to be a challenging organization; I only hope that our challenges are equal to your expectations.

As many of you know, I began my own intelligence career nearly 42 years ago with an organization known as the Office of Strategic Services – or OSS. OSS was then deeply involved in supporting our forces and our friends in defeating the Axis powers who then controlled all of Europe, much of East Asia, and a good bit of North Africa to boot. General "Wild Bill" Donovan set up, with President Roosevelt's full approval, America's first independent intelligence organization to meet these challenges.

But none of this would be possible without highly motivated officers like you.

The Agency employee is the most valuable resource we have. I want each of you to remember that. I want each of my middle managers to remember that. And I want each of my deputy directors to remember that. Only people can make and move the equipment. Only people can put themselves on the line to obtain the critical information our country

Address at the Career Trainee Graduation Ceremony, Langley, Virginia, August 13, 1985.

needs. Only people with brains and intellectual courage can peer through the uncertainties and fog of international affairs and present clear, concise finished intelligence to our national leaders.

The key to meeting these challenges consistently and well lies in the excellence of our ideas, the excellence of our knowledge, and most especially the excellence of our efforts. Excellence, like quality, cannot be defined apart from the things that have it. Excellence is active. Excellence is curious. Excellence is being adventuresome – taking a risk. Excellence is going the extra mile. Excellence is reaching out. Excellence is inspiring others and challenging them to do better than their best.

Excellence, ultimately, is people and what they do, or create, or achieve. As Edison remarked, "Genius is one percent inspiration, and ninety-nine percent perspiration."

Indeed, when General Donovan established the OSS in 1942, he established an organization that exemplified the highest ideals of exceptional performance and devotion to duty. This tradition has endured through more than 40 years as a core value of the Central Intelligence Agency. Probably no other intelligence organization in the world has achieved as much, or has given of itself so deeply, as has this Agency. Clearly, the history of the Agency is a history of meeting new and greater challenges – and meeting them successfully

You – your class and others like you – will be the intelligence professionals who must meet and master tomorrow's challenges. In your ranks there are a good number of case officers, a sprinkling of analysts, some support – officers, and some technical specialists. Tomorrow's challenges may be very different from those faced by OSS 40 years ago or by CIA today. But the challenges will nonetheless be there – and they will test each and every one of you.

During your time in the CT Program you have no doubt heard how we tout our computers and our high-technology equipment. You have heard us extol our miniature devices, our high resolution cameras, and our sophisticated electronics gear. You have heard us praise our finished analysis and our timely reporting from around the globe. And you have heard us paean the support services such as logistics, medical care, and training. And it is right that we should do this.

We are a family here at CIA. The peculiar nature of our business places an even greater obligation on us to ensure that the cooperative spirit of being a family is firmly established and maintained. We CIA people cannot publicly acknowledge or revel in our successes, or even show publicly the pride in significant individual contributions that is possible elsewhere. We must be aware of this limitation and thus go to extra lengths to ensure that an environment exists within our walls that permits such recognition, and engenders the pride we find in intelligence work and in service to our country. One such celebration is taking place here this morning.

When we have concluded our ceremonies here today, each of you will set off on a new career path. You came to us from many different and varied backgrounds – some of you were economists, teachers, linguists, historians, account executives, and military officers before entering on duty. And, following your graduation today, you will again go your separate ways as operations officers, analysts, support officers, and in many other specialties. But I hope that your common experience in the career training program has made each one of you – first and foremost – an intelligence officer. Whatever direction your career may take, remember always that through great achievements are made by people. Challenges are met – and mastered – by people. And traditions are carried on by people.

Five of the characteristics that should be signposts of your career at CIA are: devotion, effort, ingenuity, enterprise, and courage.

Devotion is a dedication to doing this job that far exceeds even the high standards we require of ourselves.

Effort is the voluntary investment of skills and sweat to make things just a little bit better for everybody else.

Ingenuity is the use of thought and creativity to bring new products or services into being. Sometimes it involves only seeing familiar things in a new way.

Enterprise is the willingness to strive for something new despite the easy temptation of sticking complacently to the status quo.

Courage is the ability to persist with a good idea despite difficulties, setbacks, ridicule, or the indifference of others.

With these five qualities, you will succeed in whatever you do.

◆ ◆ ◆

THE BUSINESS OF INTELLIGENCE

Part of Casey's effort to rebuild the intelligence community involved expanding the scope of intelligence gathering, and broadening the public's understanding of the intelligence mission. Throughout his tenure, Casey spoke to as many business groups as he could. His primary purpose was to use his own credibility with the business community — and his extensive business contacts — to encourage executives who might otherwise have been reluctant to talk with the CIA to share their insights and information with intelligence analysts.

Casey invariably returned from speaking trips with the names of executives he had met, who had agreed to meet with the analysts that Casey promised to send their way. "These guys have been doing business in...for years," Casey would report, naming a country of particular interest and handing over a slip of paper with some executive's name scribbled on it. "Get one of our guys out there and have him find out what these people know." Sometimes the information confirmed a view already held; sometimes it conflicted with CIA views. And, sometimes, the information provided by a business executive tipped off CIA to developments that traditional intelligence sources had not yet revealed.

As the analysts quickly discovered, business executives were not shy about expressing their views on political developments in countries where they operated. While most of these views reflected conventional wisdom, others were fresh and insightful. And — slas — some were absolutely off the wall. Casey took it all in stride. "We don't have to buy every view we hear, but we need to be aware of every view."

From the very start of his tenure as Director of Central Intelligence, Casey poured the bulk of his time and energy into shaping and improving the intelligence community's analytic capabilities. He viewed the National Estimates and other inter-agency analytic products as "the payoff." In this speech, Casey offers a clear sense of what policymakers should expect from Intelligence: "If we can't expect professional analysis which probes and weighs probabilities and assesses their implications, we can expect analyses that assist the policymakers in devising ways to prepare for and cope with the full range of probabilities."

Address to the Annual Meeting of the Business Council, Hot Springs, Virginia, May 9, 1981.

Casey used this speech to signal to the intelligence community that dissenting judgments would henceforth be not only welcome, but actively sought: "The President does not need a single best view, a guru, or a prophet. The nation needs the best analysis and the full range of views it can get. "

One of my associates suggested that I entitle my talk "Misery Loves Company." When I asked him why, he replied that the occasion would bring together the two "devils" of the press — the CIA and the multinational corporation. He went on, "I can see the headlines now: "Casey teaches Robber Barons dirty tricks!" I said, "How do you know it won't be the other way around?"

It is easy and costly and painful to be misunderstood, but it's more costly and painful to misunderstand the kind of world in which we have to operate. Neither intelligence nor the business world yet understand it well enough. All of us are quick to talk about the interdependence of the political world and the interdependence of the global economy. But we are slow to recognize the implications this interdependence has for our respective problems — in terms of economic practicalities, political realities, security requirements, and competitive tactics.

How well has intelligence been doing its job? I was in at the creation of modern intelligence. First with the Office of Strategic Services in World War II. Then with planning the organization of CIA — the first American peacetime intelligence service. Now, about a third of a century later, I've spent four months looking over the American intelligence community that has evolved from that embryo, and talking about how it measures up to today's needs and how it might be improved.

Over the years my predecessors have changed intelligence and made it far more than a simple spy service. They developed a great center of scholarship and research, with as many Doctors and Masters in every kind of art and science as any university campus.

They have produced a triumph of technology, stretching from the depths of the oceans to the limits of outer space. Using photography, electronics, acoustics, and other technological marvels, we learn things totally hidden on the other side of the world. In the SALT debate, for example, Americans openly discussed the details of Soviet missiles. These are held most secret in the Soviet Union, but are revealed by our intelligence systems.

All this has produced a staggering array of information, a veritable Niagara of facts. But facts can confuse. The wrong picture is *not* worth a thousand words. No photo, no electronic impulse can substitute for direct, on-the-scene knowledge of the key actors in a given country or region. No matter how spectacular a photo may be, it cannot reveal enough about plans, intentions, internal political dynamics, economics, and so forth. There are simply too many cases where photos are ambiguous or useless; too many cases where electronic intelligence may drown the analyst in partial or conflicting information. Technical collection is of little help in the most important and difficult problem of all – political intentions. This is where clandestine human intelligence can make the difference.

We started a clandestine intelligence service in OSS. Over the years it has proved itself and has served the nation well. It also has received slings and arrows which it did not deserve. I am personally dedicated to supporting it and strengthening it.

Of late a good deal of the criticism of our intelligence has been leveled at analytical function. The necessity of analysis is obvious. Collection is facts. Just as houses are made of stones, so is collection made of facts. But a pile of stones is not a house – and a collection of facts is not likely to be intelligence.

Much of the criticism is based on unrealistic expectations of what an intelligence service can do. We produce good current intelligence. We also produce good intelligence on military and economic capabilities. But if one reduces all intelligence analysis to the predictive function – and then looks for a 1,000 batting average – no intelligence organization will measure up. We are interested in foreknowledge, but we do not have a pipeline to God. Nor do we have a crystal ball. In short, the CIA does not have powers of prophecy. It has no crystal ball that can peer into the future with 20-20 sight. We are dealing with "probable" developments.

Also, it is one thing to deal with something that is knowable – but unknown by us. It is another thing to deal with something that is unknown – and unknowable. Often intelligence is expected to predict what course a country will take – when the leaders of that country themselves don't know what they will do next.

If we can't expect infallible prophecy from the nation's investment in intelligence, what can we expect? We can expect foresight. We can expect a careful definition of possibilities. We can expect professional analysis which probes and weighs probabilities and assesses their implications. We can expect analyses that assist the policymakers in devising ways to prepare for and cope with the full range of probabilities. The President does not need a single best view, a guru, or a prophet. The nation needs the best analysis and the fullest range of views it can get.

The process of analysis and arriving at estimates needs to be made as open and competitive as possible. We need to resist the bureaucratic urge for consensus.

We don't need analysts spending their time finding a middle ground or weasel words to conceal disagreement. Their time needs to go into evaluating information — searching for the meaning and the implications of events and trends — and expressing both their conclusions and their disagreements clearly. The search to unify the intelligence community around a single homogenized estimate serves policymakers badly. It buries valid difference, forcing the intelligence product to the lowest or blandest common denominator. The search for consensus also cultivates the myth of infallibility. It implicitly promises a reliability that cannot be delivered. Too frequently, it deprives the intelligence product of relevance and the policymaker of the range of possibilities for which prudence requires that he prepare.

The time has come to recognize that policymakers can easily sort through a wide range of opinions. But, they cannot consider views and opinions they do not receive. The time has come to recognize that CIA, military intelligence, and every other element of the intelligence community should not only be allowed to compete and surface differences, but be encouraged to do so.

The time has also come to recognize that the intelligence community itself has no monopoly on truth, on insight, and on initiative in foreseeing what will be relevant to policy. For that reason, we are in the process of reconstituting a President's Foreign Intelligence Advisory Board. It will be made up of strong and experienced private individuals with a wide range of relevant backgrounds.

In addition, we are asking a wide variety of scientists, scholars, and other experts to serve on advisory panels and to address special problems. We contract with think tanks and a wide variety of business corporations to do specialized research for us. To get all the intelligence we need, we've got to go beyond the formal intelligence organizations. We've got to tap all the scholarly resources of the nation.

We will need to do even more of this in the future to cope with the intelligence requirements of our increasingly complex and dangerous world as it generates new threats. In the OSS, we were doing pretty well if we knew where the enemy was and how he was redeploying his forces. For the first twenty years of a peacetime intelligence, most of the effort went to understanding the production and capabilities of weapons. It is only in the last decade that it has dawned upon us that we have been threatened and damaged more by subversion and economic aggression than by military force. We will still devote a large slice of our effort to military estimates and rely very heavily on them in formulating our defense budget and force structures. But they will have to be supplemented by increased efforts to assess economic vulnerabilities and technological breakthroughs. We also have to identify social and political instabilities — and how they can be or are being exploited by propaganda, subversion, and terrorism. To meet these challenges fully, we will not hesitate to call upon the expertise in the private sector for assistance.

So much for the kind of intelligence capabilities we have and need to develop. Let me now give you some of the specifics of the problems we face.

Our first priority is still the Soviet Union — its military capability and economic strength. It has been the number one adversary for 35 years. It is the only country in the world with major weapons systems directly targeted at the United States which could destroy the U.S. in half and hour. For that reason alone, it remains the number one target.

Given the complexity of today's world, however, there are many other problems of concern to intelligence. For example: nationalism, terrorism, and resource dependency.

The tide of nationalism is running strong in the less-developed countries of the world. There is hostility and negativism toward free enterprise. There are potential dangers here for American, European, and even Japanese multinational corporations. Local politicians cannot always manage this distrust of foreigners. Free enterprise from abroad suddenly appears as foreign domination or neo-colonialism. It is difficult to predict when and where this hostility will break out — as it does periodically.

Nationalism is not new. Its manifestations range from restrictive policies to outright expropriation. What is new today is that it is accompanied by global economic distress. This is caused by the explosive growth in energy costs in both the industrialized countries and the less-developed ones.

The enormous cost of fueling economic activity is forcing the less-developed countries into austerity and no-growth policies. They are running out of credit. They cannot meet the very high interest rates required. All this intensifies instability.

One form of instability that we are likely to see more of around the world is terrorism – hijacking, hostage-taking, kidnapping, assassination, bombing, armed attack, sniping, and coercive threats. These are all mindless acts of violence designed to create a political effect, regardless of the innocence of the victims.

Last year also marked the first time that a large number of deadly attacks were carried out by individual nations. This is a dangerous development. It is one thing for a demented individual or a private group of fanatics to resort to terror; for a nation to resort to it with all the resources it can command is another – and much more serious – matter.

It is a grim story. What do we do about it? At CIA, international terrorism has been high on the list of intelligence priorities for some time. Defensive tactics are taught to key personnel serving abroad. Many business corporations have been searching for defensive measures to protect their people. What must be done is to adopt a firm policy and develop a strategy for dealing with terrorism before a crisis situation arises – then the terrorists hold all the cards. Terrorists have got to learn that there is little or no payoff where Americans and American interests are involved.

Lastly, a word about resource dependency. Roughly a decade ago, we received a jolt. Shifting geopolitical patterns, coupled with rising Third World nationalism, sharply tempered our expectations. The oil crisis of 1973 was the first time we could actually see and feel the crushing impact of international "non-military warfare" strike us squarely where it hurts the most – in our pocketbooks and in our life-styles.

That crisis still haunts us with a new reality. Others, well away from our borders, can now place their hands on our economic throttles and on our economic throats. International tensions and threats are not limited to military ones.

Looking at the world more broadly, what do we see as we look around the world:

◆ We see a Soviet Union rapidly building its military strength while ours has been declining.

◆ We see the U.S. falling behind in economic competitiveness as the Japanese and Germans give, invest, and innovate more, and Koreans, Singaporans, Taiwanese, Brazilians, and Mexicans increasing their share of the world market as ours diminishes.

◆ We see political and economic instability in the Middle East, Africa, and Latin America where we get the fuel and minerals to keep our economy going.

◆ We see the Soviet Union with its Cuban, East German, Libyan, and Syrian proxies demonstrating remarkable ability to exploit instabilities by well-orchestrated subversion and paramilitary operations conducted with guerrilla fighters that they train, equip, and direct.

◆ And we see large numbers of tanks and guns stockpiled in Syria, Libya, and Yemen on the fringe of the Arab peninsula and transported to Nicaragua and Cuba, Angola and Ethiopia, *and used* in Chad and Lebanon, El Salvador, and Guatemala.

I am not here to frighten you. I am here to say that the world is full of economic, political, and military dangers which need to be taken seriously and watched closely. And that the outlook is not all black.

The USSR has fallen into a hornet's nest in Afghanistan. After eighteen months, Afghan freedom fighters confine Soviet troops to a half-dozen cities and to their barracks at night.

The Soviets are rightly concerned that developments in Poland could unravel the communist system; also that suppression would entail heavy economic and political costs, as well as bloodshed and prolonged resistance from militant Poles.

The Soviet economy is gasping under its inherent inefficiencies and its burden of enormous military expenditures; also, its many billions each year to Cuba and Vietnam, cut-rate oil to East European satellites, and huge worldwide expenditures for propaganda and subversion.

Here in the U.S., Congress has taken its first action to revitalize and make our economy competitive again and to restore our military strength. That will restore confidence around the world among our allies. I believe the new tone has brought new *vigor* to our friends and new *caution* to those inclined to adventure in far-off places. As Learned Hand said: "Freedom imposes a burden." We Americans willingly shoulder that burden today as our forefathers did in the past.

Let me now conclude with a quick word about accountability. It is often said that intelligence is not accountable. Nothing could be further from the truth. Intelligence has always had to answer fully to the President and in varying degrees to Congress, the National Security Council, the Office of Management and Budget, and the Intelligence Oversight Board. In the past few years, we have witnessed an expanded intelligence oversight role for the Attorney General and the Courts.

Today our relations with the two permanent congressional intelligence committees are excellent. We are responsive to their concerns, as we should be. In turn, their attitude is one of "what can we do to help you accomplish your mission?" Our response has been to ask them to help us protect necessary secrecy, with such legislation as may be appropriate.

The first bill along these lines was passed by Congress last October. It deals with intelligence oversight and how it is to be exercised. For us, it means that we have to report important activities at most to two instead of eight committees. Congress realized that it is very difficult to keep something secret when up to 200 people have to be cut in on it. It's down to about 20 now.

The second legislative bill that would help us is not yet passed. It is designed to protect the secret identities of intelligence officers and agents under cover. It is really outrageous that dedicated people engaged or assisting in U.S. foreign intelligence activities can be endangered, and are endangered, by a few individuals; individuals whose avowed purpose is to destroy the effectiveness of intelligence activities and programs duly authorized by Congress. This has got to be stopped.

Third, we need an exemption from the Freedom of Information Act (FOIA). There is too much information released that should remain secret. This law is a poor law because it allows *anyone* to request information on the activities of our intelligence agencies. FOIA also costs intelligence agencies millions of dollars and ties up people who could — and should — be doing intelligence work.

Recently, we spent $300,000 to meet one FOIA request. It was from Mr. Philip Agee, a renegade from the CIA who goes around the world exposing those he thinks are CIA people.

If the KGB wrote us (and we assume that they do), we would have to respond in ten days. Do we really want to turn the CIA into a purveyor of information for the world rather than a supplier of intelligence to our policymakers?

Secrecy is essential to any intelligence organization. Ironically, secrecy is accepted without protest in many areas of our society, from income tax returns to crop futures. Physicians, lawyers, clergymen, grand juries, and journalists all have confidential dealings protected by law. Why should national security information be entitled to any less protection?

◆ ◆ ◆

BUILDING A NATIONAL CONSENSUS

Once more Casey reaching out to business leaders. In this speech he gives a broad view of the challenges facing the country, and how a newly invigotated intelligence service is working to meet those challenges. As in the preceding speech, Casey instructs his audience on how they – and the American public – can help the CIA to do a better job. "So while we have made great strides in rebuilding this country's intelligence apparatus, the backing and understanding of the American people is going to be needed to sustain and build on the progress we have made."

Casey ends the speech with an extensive discussion of leaks and their devastating impact on national security. He calls for a broad-based, concerted effort to halt them.

Gentlemen, I am very honored and grateful for this opportunity to be with you tonight. Business and community leaders are important in the process of building a national consensus on policy issues affecting our national security and, quite frankly, I look for opportunities to get my perspective across to audiences like this one. Tonight I would like to talk

Address to the Denver Chief Executive Offiers, Denver, Colorado, July 30, 1986.

to you about a few of the threats and challenges confronting the United States that have been weighing heavily on my mind and, I suspect, on yours as well. I would also like to talk about this country's intelligence capabilities and how people like yourself can make and are making such an important contribution to our mission.

Just a few decades ago, the United States dominated the world economically, politically and militarily; and the United States and the Soviet Union were the international players that mattered. That day is long past. The number of players has proliferated, issues have become bewilderingly complex, the pace of change and technological advance almost overwhelming, and the world much smaller and far more interdependent. And this, in turn, has revolutionized the world of intelligence.

The Soviet Union, of course, remains the principal threat to U.S. security and the primary concern of U.S. intelligence. But the nature of this threat has changed dramatically since the days when Russia was largely confined to the Eurasia land mass. The Soviet leadership remains committed to building a military force that could fight and win a nuclear war. Moscow is relentlessly expanding a large arsenal of nuclear weapons aimed at the U.S., Europe, and East Asia. New missiles and missile-carrying aircraft and submarines have been developed, tested and deployed in amazing profusion.

By 1980, Soviet strategic offensive forces already had caught up, and in some key areas surpassed those of our own. One sobering example: the Soviets are now protecting their land-based missile force by making it mobile. A mobile U.S. intercontinental ballistic missile will not be deployed until the 1990s at best.

Perhaps even more alarming, the Soviets are in the midst of a major long-term missile defense program – their own "Star Wars," if you will – involving some 10 research and development facilities and thousands of scientists and engineers. They long ago deployed an ABM system around Moscow. We are the newcomers on the block, although you would never know it by listening to Soviet propaganda condemning the President's Strategic Defense Initiative as "destabilizing."

Due in large part to our extraordinary technical collection capabilities, we have done a pretty good job of staying on top of Moscow's tremendous effort to erode the strategic nuclear balance in its favor. But as we proceed further into the current arms control dialogue with Moscow, the demands for high-quality intelligence on Soviet plans and actions will be extraordinary. I want to assure you that we are not resting on our laurels. We are working on promising new collection systems, and devoting enormous resources to monitoring current Soviet capabilities and assessing the characteristics of Soviet weapons that may not be deployed for ten to fifteen years.

That's the challenge for intelligence. In a more general sense, it's going to be extremely important that this nation develop a hard-headed, disciplined approach to arms control. We cannot allow Gorbachev's full court propaganda press to stampede us into accepting new agreements that merely allow the Soviets to consolidate their gains while cutting off our own opportunities to modernize our strategic offensive and defense forces.

I have been talking in a strategic military context, but the main threat from the Soviets probably lies elsewhere. The West once again is engaged in a critical struggle with totalitarianism. This time it is in the form of Marxism-Leninism, and the primary battlefield of this struggle is not on the missile test range or at the arms control negotiating table but in the countryside of the Third World.

In the aftermath of our sad experience in Vietnam, the Soviet Union began to test whether the U.S. would resist foreign provoked and supported instability and subversion elsewhere in the Third World. It developed an aggressive strategy which avoids direct confrontation and instead takes maximum advantage of Third World surrogates like Cuba, Vietnam, Libya, and Nicaragua to obtain Soviet objectives....

In this regard, it will come as no surprise to any of you that I believe the stakes in Central America are huge and historic. A Soviet military base on the American continent dividing North and South America is being put into place – a toehold of Soviet military power and subversion that could endanger the Panama Canal in the short term and Mexico in the somewhat longer term. Right now the Sandinista army with Cuban helicopter pilots and combat direction and a half billion dollars of sophisticated Soviet weaponry is going all out to destroy the Nicaraguan resistance before new assistance can reach it. In the meantime, the Sandinistas are sticking to their blueprint of building an all-powerful state security apparatus the strongest armed forces in Central America and in developing a center for exporting subversion and terrorism to the region....

The new money recently voted by Congress will make it possible to further turn up the heat on the Sandinistas by steadily expanding the number of resistance troops in the field and by opening new areas of operation. But we should not kid ourselves. The Soviets and their Sandinista clients will not give up their toehold without a determined fight. We are only at the beginning of this struggle and we have to resist that old American tendency to expect instant and easy success. A more protracted commitment is necessary and this means convincing Congress and the American people that now is the time to counter Soviet subversive involvement in the Third World. Given the nature of insurgent conflicts, the cost to Moscow and its allies of countering an insurgence is considerably greater than the cost to the West. By requiring Moscow to counter multiple insurgencies, the risk and cost to the Soviets are increased substantially, and alternatives to Soviet domination can be kept alive in several Third World arenas.

I told you I wanted to discuss the state of U.S. intelligence. Thanks to the support of the President and Congress, I can tell you that our intelligence system today is more robust than at any time in our history and in far better shape than six or seven years ago. We have made enormous progress across the board in collection and analysis. Anyone who left us more than three or four years ago would not recognize the place. We have restaffed the clandestine service and our analytical cadre. We have significantly increased both the quality and quantity of collection and analysis. Resources in support of military operations have been greatly increased. We have rebuilt our capability on the Third World, significantly improved our work on the Soviet Union, and created the capability to tackle new intelligence problems.

But the world moves on without regard for past achievements. We still are worried about our ability to keep pace with new Soviet weapons programs as they keep expanding and the Soviets turn more and more to measures intended to deny us critical information. While our capabilities against terrorism, narcotics, technology transfer, subversion, and a long and steadily growing list of other new challenges have improved by leaps and bounds, they are stretched to the limit and often beyond. And still we, of all organizations, must try to hold in reserve resources to monitor countless wars and crises, and still look to the future.

So while we have made great strides in rebuilding this country's intelligence apparatus, the backing and understanding of the American people are going to be needed to sustain and build on the progress we have made. I am not just talking about passive acceptance or support. We have learned that no matter how strenuous our own internal efforts, we cannot approach our job with a strictly in-house mentality. If we don't tap the impressive sources of expertise outside our building, our own capital stock of knowledge and imagination will rapidly deplete. We have worked hard to rebuild our bridges to the academic community following the bad old days of the Vietnam era. We submit many of our important assessments for review by outside academic experts who work with us on a consultant basis.

But there is another important source of outside expertise we are using more effectively – the private business sector. In addition to the commercial information services we subscribe to, the publications we purchase, the databases we receive or compile, and our own people overseas, we listen closely to what the business community has to tell us. We find U.S. businessmen – whether they be manufactures, bankers, or commodity dealers – ready and willing to share their insights with us on subjects ranging from high-technology developments in Europe and Japan, to Third World debt problems, to Soviet grain purchase, and many more.

We know they're out there dealing with their foreign counterparts every day and have access to information and ideas that the government cannot get in any other way. We have reorganized our component responsible for being in touch with the business community and we are devoting some of our best talent – and a lot of it – to the endeavor. In sum, we view this relationship as essential to our mission and we want to ensure that it remains a strong one.

Before I sit down, let me lay down just one more marker. I am sure you have all heard about the Reagan Administration's recent efforts to deal with an old national security problem that is becoming increasingly intolerable. I am talking about the deliberate leaking of sensitive classified intelligence information from the executive branch of our government, and the replaying of that information by the media.

I don't have time tonight to go through the whole chamber of horrors on leaks. To cite just one example that you are no doubt generally familiar with, we lost a very sensitive and valuable communications intelligence source when *Newsweek* divulged the source of messages last March about the bombing at the West German nightclub in which two

U.S. servicemen were killed. And the unkindest cut of all was when the media subsequently tried to blame the leak on the President, whose comments two weeks later on that subject were deliberately vague and made, in any event, long after the damage had been done.

And there doesn't seem to be any relief in sight. We know, for example, that a well-known investigative journalist has collected extensive information for a book on the downing of a Korean airliner. He says his book will make it clear that the Soviets were totally responsible. No doubt it will but we don't need that kind of help. The publication of previously unreleased details about our communications intelligence capabilities will be an enormous windfall for the Soviets that will enable them to take effective countermeasures against us.

Another example of what we're up against is the investigative teams the *New York Times* and *Washington Post* have formed to compete with each other in publishing exciting or controversial stories on this country's intelligence effort, and they profess to be bewildered when we do not express enthusiasm and gratitude for this effort to tell what they call "the real story" of intelligence.

We know we can't throw rocks around in a glass house. Our first priority must be to tighten discipline within our government and, believe me, we are doing just that. We are putting into place mechanisms to aggressively investigate apparent cases of leaking within the government and to take punitive and legal action against guilty government employees. People have lost their jobs in recent months.

But, of course, the leak itself is just one side of the equation. We have to do a much better job than we have in the past of convincing the American people and the media of their own responsibility to protect intelligence sources and arguments. We can, and do, lose sensitive collection systems that cost billions of hard earned tax dollars. Agents can, and do, die as a direct result of leaks and our allies can, and do, lose faith in our abilities to protect information they pass to us. Just a few weeks ago, the intelligence service of one of our closest allies told us they can no longer pass us advance information on terrorist activities. They have had enough of reading about their most sensitive, well-protected information in the U.S. media. And when sources and methods are compromised in areas such as counterterrorism, the direct result easily can be dead American tourists and other ordinary citizens.

But don't just take my word for it. Let me quote a more prominent
American public figure on this issue: "The necessity of procuring good
intelligence is apparent and need not be further urged. All that remains
for me to add is that you keep the whole matter as secret as possible.
For upon secrecy success depends in most enterprises of this kind, and
for want of it, they are generally defeated."

That was George Washington speaking. You know it's truly amazing
how good most of Washington's advice was and how well it has stood
the test of time. It's also true that a lot of his advice has not been easy
to follow and I suppose this is a good example. But it's advice that I
believe this nation and its elected and appointed officials have to act on.
In this dangerous world we live in and in this modern era of intelligence,
the stakes have become entirely too high to keep sweeping this problem
under the rug.

As Director of Central Intelligence I am charged by law with protecting the sources of information that enable this country to protect its
citizens in an increasingly unfriendly world. And I am sure you are going
to be hearing about more efforts. You will also hear charges that this administration is attempting to intimidate the media and undermine First
Amendment rights. I know I can count on you to put such shrill reactions into perspective. I have been a practicing journalist myself and no
one values more than I the First Amendment and the enormous privilege
of living in a country that has a free press. The media also need to be
reminded that the men and women of CIA are in a dangerous, difficult,
and not particularly well paid profession because they want to ensure
that their children and grandchildren will continue to enjoy that
privilege.

But national security is also a constitutional right and privilege. Obviously what's needed is some balance and accommodation. The government and the media must work together to ensure that sensitive intelligence sources and methods are not published. At the very least the
media should cease seeking secrets as an end in itself and should exercise careful judgment in printing leaked information. That's really all
we are asking. And once again people such as yourselves can be of enormous help in forging a national consensus that will support such a modest
but critical objective.

◆ ◆ ◆

THE STATUS OF U.S. INTELLIGENCE

Casey's rebuilding program included strengthening the dialogue between the intelligence and academic communities. In this speech to college students, he notes the importance of that relationship, and challenges the students to help develop solutions fo rthe future.

At the intellectual heart of this speech is Casey's analysis of the West's "real ace-in-the-hole" in its competition with totalitarianism: its "technological ingenuity, its entrepreneurial talents, and its free market economics." Again, this was the kind of issue to which Casey devoted more time and effort than generally realized. Note his disclosure that he had organized a team of CIA analysts "to identify Western technologies that can be brought to bear on Third World resources and markets" to stimulate or support development.

As he did so often, Casey used a public speech to hammer home the "lessons learned" from history, and to apply them to current events. Speaking here of Central America, he points out that "History shows that a combination of nagging insurgent military pressure and progressive withdrawal of domestic and international support is what brings down or alters an unpopular government. This process already is underway in Nicaragua."

President Shultz, students and faculty, ladies and gentlemen, it is a particular honor as well as a special pleasure for me to bring to this campus, to this center, and to this community, the deep gratitude and great respect which the American intelligence community has and will always have for John Ashbrook. Enshrined in the minds and memories of our people as well as in our archives is the valiant and successful fight which Congressman John Ashbrook waged on the floor of the House of Representatives to enact the Intelligence Identities Act of 1982. Without John's courage and zeal that law would not have carried. You will recall that renegade Americans seeking to destroy the nation's intelligence capability were revealing the identities, locations, and addresses of officers and agents serving our nation around the world. Each person named in the publications they sent around the world became a potential target, along with his family and colleagues, for assassination or other

Address to the John Ashbrook Center for Public Affairs, Ashland College, Ashland, Ohio, October 27, 1986.

forms of terrorist attacks. Dick Welch, our station chief in Greece, was fingered by these traitors and assassinated in the driveway of his home as he was getting out of his automobile. We owe it to John Ashbrook that our officers and agents now enjoy legal protection from this kind of dastardly criminal activity and that this kind of information is no longer published in any regular organized form. We will never forget John Ashbrook. I also wish to express my esteem to Fred Levison and Ed Loesy and thank them for their support of the Ashbrook Center. Finally, I thank my old comrade-in-arms and 40 years of politics, Cliff White.

Over the last six years, the Reagan Administration has made a concerted and, I believe, successful effort to rebuild this nation's intelligence capabilities. One of the things of which I am most proud is the manner in which we have strengthened our dialogue with the academic and business communities of our country. We have learned that if we do not tap the impressive sources of experience outside government, our own capital stock of knowledge and imagination will rapidly deplete. Speaking engagements such as this one, the numerous joint conferences our analysts hold with their academic counterparts, and the outside review and critique to which we submit many of our most important assessments all keep us sharp and open to new ideas. I have already spent a stimulating hour with the fellows of the Ashbrook Center and I look forward to more questions and answers upon completion of my remarks.

I have been asked to talk today about the status of U.S. intelligence. That is a fairly broad topic. Perhaps the best way to tackle it is to spend a little time discussing the kind of world and the nature of the conflict our nation faces and how this determines the mission of intelligence in support of United States policy.

You students of Ashland College have the privilege of receiving a first-class liberal education. I know you have been exposed during the course of your studies to the two great irreconcilably opposed ideas about the relationship between the individual and the state. The conflict between state despotism, and the notion that the highest goal of the state is to protect individual freedoms and creativity, has dominated Western history for millennia. Do not make the mistake of putting this conflict in the past tense. The current competition between the United States and the Soviet Union is the latest chapter of the same conflict that pitted Athens against Xerxes and the Persians, and Medieval Europe against Genghis Khan and the Mongols.

Unfortunately this is a history lesson that is not always sufficiently appreciated. It is important that our nation understand just how different the Soviets are from us in their history, culture, and outlook.

Look at the Daniloff affair. That fact that the Soviets were incapable of making a distinction between journalism and espionage, but perfectly capable of indulging in the most blatant form of hostage-taking, tells me that we are dealing with a *fundamentally* alien and *totally unpalatable* value system that threatens our own cherished institutions. Look at the KAL-007 shootdown. We should *not* get bogged down in the question of whether or not the Soviet Air Defense Command knew for a fact that it was shooting down a civilian 747. All we need to know is that the Soviet system was perfectly capable of shooting down a large unidentified aircraft on the *mere suspicion* that it *might* have been engaged in espionage.

I apologize for starting out on such a philosophic note, but ladies and gentlemen, it is simply impossible to understand why this country needs a strong intelligence capability if we don't understand why we are engaged in a competition with the Soviets in the first place and what the real nature and historical context of the contest is. A thousand years of Russian history – reinforced only recently by Marxism-Leninism – tells the Soviet leadership that conflict is inevitable, that the contest for global supremacy is unending, that one side will win and the other lose, and that God, or as good Marxists say "the forces of history," will ensure Russian victory.

So what does this outlook mean for U.S. national security and for our intelligence mission? It means, among other things, that the Soviet leadership remains committed to building a military force that could fight and win a conventional or nuclear war. Since the end of World War II, the Soviets have maintained a sizeable edge in conventional manpower and firepower in Europe. And some time ago, the Soviets began to relentlessly expand a large arsenal of nuclear weapons aimed at the U.S., Europe, and East Asia....Perhaps even more alarming, the Soviets are in the midst of a major long-term missile defense program – their own "Star Wars,"...and they are embarked on a civil defense program featuring a hugely expensive and ambitious underground construction and transportation facility to ensure the survivability of their national leadership during a nuclear war. In missile defense, we are the newcomers on the block, although you would never know it by listening to

Soviet propaganda condemning the President's Strategic Defense Initiative as "destabilizing." It is hardly surprising that the Iceland talks floundered on Gorbachev's insistence that President Reagan back away from SDI. Given the Soviets' impressive strategic gains, they have every reason to want to cut off our government's plans to develop its own strategic defense.

The CIA's original intelligence mission was the prevention of a surprise attack on the U.S. – another Pearl Harbor. Thanks in large part to our extraordinary technical collection capabilities, we are doing a pretty good job here. But we do have our hands full. Moscow continues, through camouflage, concealment, and other measures to deny us critical information we need to assess the current strategic balance or to verify any future arms control agreement. This means we must devote enormous resources and a wide variety of human skills and specializations to develop new intelligence collection capabilities and accurately assess Soviet nuclear arms control strategies and the characteristics of Soviet weapons that may not be deployed for another ten to fifteen years. Much of our budget, time, and attention will continue to be dedicated to this core problem.

There was a day when understanding the military capabilities of our principal adversary was practically our only mission. That day is long past. The world has changed tremendously since the immediate post-World War II era when the U.S. and Soviet Union were the only players that mattered. The number of players has proliferated, issues have become bewilderingly complex, the pace of change and technological advance almost overwhelming, and the world much smaller and far more interdependent. And this, in turn, has revolutionalized the world of intelligence.

Cuba has in our time become the largest country in the world. Its government is in Havana, its administration is in Moscow, its army is in Africa, and its people are in Miami. For most of CIA's history, Asia, Africa, and Latin America were relatively neglected areas. The Iranian revolution made it painfully clear that the longer term interests and security of this country can be directly at stake in the Third World. In the wake of our sad experience in Iran, we have significantly expanded our effort to monitor and anticipate instability and unrest in countries of key importance to the U.S.

Once again we have our hands full. Much of the Third World is in crisis. One needs to look no further than just beyond our southern border to see a cross-section of the problem: crushing debt, a growing disequilibrium in food supply, rapid population growth, and explosive urbanization. But unfortunately, the threat to Third World stability does not come solely from such inherent developmental problems. It comes as well from overt and covert activities aimed at subverting or destabilizing governments friendly to the U.S. In fact, ladies and gentlemen, I believe that the primary battlefield of this age-old struggle with totalitarianism is not on the missile test ranges but in the countryside of the Third World.

In this vital area, the Soviet Union has been busily testing whether the U.S. will resist foreign provoked and supported instability and insurgence in the Third World. It has developed an aggressive strategy which avoids direct confrontation and instead takes maximum advantage of Third World surrogates like Cuba, Vietnam, Libya and Nicaragua to obtain Soviet objectives. This enables Moscow to deny involvement, label such conflicts as internal, and warn self-righteously against outside interference.

This creeping imperialism has, in my view, two primary targets: the oil fields of the Middle East, which are the life line of the Western Alliance; and the isthmus between North and South America. Afghanistan, South Yemen, Ethiopia, as well as Cam Ranh Bay in Vietnam, and Mozambique and Angola in Southern Africa, bring Soviet power much closer to the sources of oil and minerals on which the industrial nations depend, and put Soviet naval and air power astride the sea lanes that carry those resources to America, Europe, and Japan.

Time and time again we have watched the Soviets and their surrogates move in to exploit and instigate social and economic discontent. They gain an insurgent base, expand it with trained men and military arms, drive out investment, and wait for another country to fall. Since 1972 Moscow has added five new client states in the Third World and threatens more than a dozen other regimes via cross-border military operations, insurgencies, and subversion.

It is not a very pretty picture. Marxist-Leninist policies and tactics have unleashed the Four Horsemen of the Apocalypse. Throughout the Third World we see famine in Africa, pestilence through chemical and biological agents in Afghanistan and Indo-China, war on three continents, and death everywhere. In those occupied countries in which Marxist regimes have been either imposed or maintained by external forces, there has occurred a holocaust comparable to that which Nazi Germany inflicted in Europe some 40 years ago. Some four million Afghans, more than one-quarter of the population, have had to flee their country. In Cambodia, two to three million people, something like one-quarter of the pre-war population, have been killed in the most violent and brutal manner by both internal and external Marxist forces.

Now for the good news. The pendulum of history slowly but surely is swinging away from Soviet Marxism as a model for Third World countries, and toward the concepts of democracy and free market economics. There was a day – not too long ago – when Soviet-style collectivism was widely seen as the panacea for Third World social and economic ills. No one – not even the Soviets and their friends – believes this today. About all Moscow still has going for it is a proven formula for subversion and an undiluted willingness to use raw power to shore up and protect its unpopular client regimes. In short, the Soviets increasingly find themselves on the defensive: supporting high-cost, long-term efforts to maintain in power the repressive regimes they have installed or co-opted in places like Afghanistan, Angola, Ethiopia, Cambodia, Mozambique, Yemen and Nicaragua. Right now, well over 300,000 resistance fighters have taken up arms against the well over 300,000 Soviet, Vietnamese, and Cuban troops occupying these countries.

This role reversal could turn out to be one of the great historical turning points of our lifetime. But it will work out this way only if the indigenous Third World forces resisting Marxism-Leninism, together with the U.S. and the West, can act to take advantage of this open "window of opportunity" to advance democracy.

How do we do this? First, we need to understand that two can play the same game. Just as there is a classic formula for communist subversion and takeover, there also is a proven method of overthrowing repressive government that can be applied successfully in the Third World.

Nicaragua, where a Soviet military base dividing North and South America is being put in place, is a good example. The new money recently voted by Congress will make it possible to further turn up the heat on the Sandinistas by steadily expanding the number of resistance troops in the field and by opening new areas of operation. I am not talking about matching the Sandinistas weapon-for-weapon or of achieving a classic military victory. History shows that a combination of nagging insurgency military pressure and progressive withdrawal of domestic and international support is what brings *down* or *alters* an unpopular government. This process already is underway in Nicaragua. The insurgents have made large gains among a people unhappy with Managua's recent collectivization and resettlement programs, as well as the Sandinistas' mandatory military draft and anti-church policies.

Both we and the Soviets have a lot at stake in the Third World. But nowhere is this more true than in Central America. The Sandinistas, with a lot of Soviet and Cuban help, have build an all-powerful state security apparatus, the strongest armed forces in the region and, perhaps most disturbing, have developed a center for exporting terrorism. The Libyans, for example, have been supporting the Sandinista government in Nicaragua to the tune of something like $100 million a year. Young men from Latin America are being sent to Libya for training in the terrorist camps there and then are brought back to be planted among the population in Central America, Venezuela, and Ecuador. If the Sandinista regime consolidates itself, we can expect Managua to become the Beirut of the Western Hemisphere.

And of course, there is no way a country can immunize itself from such an infection. Already hundreds of thousand of Nicaraguans and Salvadorans have fled their countries and headed north. Can anyone doubt that as soon as it becomes apparent that the communists are about to complete their conquest of Nicaragua, another signal will be flashed and millions of people will leave Central America, and ultimately Mexico, to cross the border into the United States?

There is nothing inevitable about this scenario. I am convinced that with only very modest military assistance from the West, the anti-communist liberation movements now underway in Nicaragua and the Third World can continue to develop and eventually restore freedom and bring democracy to those countries. But this country's strategy in the Third World must go beyond supporting freedom fighters.

Marxism-Leninism may be intellectually, morally, and economically bankrupt, but we are not. In addition to doing what we can to support indigenous resistance to Soviet-backed repressive regimes, we have to come to grips with the core developmental problems of the Third World and how the West's technological ingenuity, entrepreneurial talents, and free market economics can be brought to bear. This, of course, is the

West's real ace-in-the-hole and here we have only just begun to scratch the surface.

I can assure you that we are going to do more at CIA. We have moved the huge general issue of the Third World stability and freedom up to one of our front burners. We are seeking to exploit Soviet vulnerability but we are moving on a broader front as well. For example, we have a team of analysts working to identify Western technologies that can be brought to bear on Third World resources and markets. Our need for people with language capabilities, some experience and knowledge of foreign culture, and for Third World economists and social scientists has never been greater.

As I have already made clear, the intelligence profession indeed is a lot different than it was just ten years ago. We've been drawn into other non-traditional areas of collection and analysis at a breathtaking pace. I am talking about the kind of international issues that are imposing increasingly difficult challenges to our society. This list is long — international terrorism, industrial competitiveness, the proliferation of nuclear, chemical and biological weapons, international finance, trafficking in narcotics and stolen blueprints and other forms of stolen technology, just to mention a few.

I'm proud of the manner in which we have moved smartly to extend our reach to develop new collection techniques, hiring and training new kinds of analysts, and utilizing emerging technologies. But in our business we can't afford to stand still. The KGB and its allied intelligence services and front organizations constitute a worldwide apparatus that is working to steal our technology, damage our reputation, divide us from our friends, and destabilize, subvert, and overthrow governments friendly to us. CIA is the only organization in the West with the range, the resources and the capabilities necessary to deal effectively with this challenge. We, more than any other organization in the West, have the information, expertise and resources to do in-depth research across the broad spectrum of international, political, economic, military, and demographic developments and produce careful assessments of the problems we will face now and beyond the year 2000.

Some of our new recruits will be charged with unraveling the puzzle of how the Soviet Union and some other countries are setting up hundreds of dummy corporations in order to illegally acquire some of our most sensitive new technology. Others will be given the job of charting the convoluted road map of international drug dealing. Others will be charged with the task of exposing and countering the huge Soviet espionage and propaganda apparatus. Many will be given the task of developing new methods of gathering, analyzing and interpreting data. There is, in fact, an endless parade of new challenges.

This is, in other words, an exciting time to be working in intelligence. We are optimists who are trying to open wide that window of opportunity I've alluded to. But I don't want to leave anyone out of the fun. It's an exciting time to be an American. I hope a few of you will end up in intelligence work. Most of you won't. But all of you, one way or another, are going to be involved in the problems I've addressed. And all of you are going to have the opportunity to be a part of the solutions. Your generation's intellectual curiosity and entrepreneurial spirit, its patriotism and, yes, its understanding of history will go far in determining how our nation fares in the opening years of the 21st century.

*   *   *

Chapter 2

How Intelligence Really Works

AMERICAN INTELLIGENCE YESTERDAY, TODAY, AND TOMORROW

Intelligence is a process. And like all processes, this one is made up of a series of steps, each of which must be taken – in the correct order – to produce a successful product. Casey was especially frustrated by criticism of intelligence that reflected a critic's failure to understand the process. In this speech he spells out how intelligence works.

There was a time only forty years ago when William J. Donovan, a New York lawyer, was a one-man CIA for Franklin Roosevelt. His World War I Congressional Medal of Honor and his nickname of "Wild Bill" implanted on him the image of a swashbuckling adventurer. In reality he was a mild, softspoken intellectual, whose deepest interest was intelligence.

As the outstanding investigative lawyer of his time, Donovan had learned how to gather a huge array of facts, sift, and analyze them, assess their meaning, arrive at a conclusion and present it vividly. He persuaded President Roosevelt that it would be critical in fighting a war and

Address to John M. Olin Distinguished Lecture Series, Brown University, Providence, Rhode Island, October 15, 1981.

preserving the peace to develop and apply this ability on a worldwide scale.

By the time Pearl Harbor came, Donovan had gathered hundreds of the finest scholars in America and had them processing geographic, scientific, political and military information in the Library of Congress. Two years later, Donovan had scoured our campuses and mobilized thousands of the finest scholars in America. He had assembled what had to be the most diverse aggregation ever assembled of tycoons and scientists, bankers and foreign correspondents, psychologists and football stars, circus managers and circus freaks, safe crackers, lock pickers and pickpockets, playwrights and journalists, novelists and professors of literature, advertising and broadcasting talent. He drew on the great American melting pot to create small teams of Italian Americans, Franco-Americans, Norwegian Americans, Slavic Americans, and Greek Americans.

What did he do with this array of talent? He used it to create intelligence networks behind enemy lines, to support the resistance forces that oppression always creates, to bring disaffected enemy officers over to our side, to dream up scenarios to manipulate the mind of the enemy in deception and psychological warfare programs.

But above all he created a machinery to evaluate, sift and analyze.

Intelligence has many facets. It is a very uncertain, fragile, and complex commodity:

> First, you have to get a report.

> Then you have to decide whether it's real or fake.

> Then, whether it's true or false as you find out what other intelligence supports or contradicts it.

> Then, you fit it into a broad mosaic.

> Then, you figure out what it all means.

> Then, you have to get the attention of someone who can make a decision.

> And then you have to get him to act.

The highest duty of a Director of Central Intelligence is to produce solid and perceptive national intelligence estimates relevant to the issues with which the President and the National Security Council need to concern themselves. When Bedell Smith took office as Director of Central Intelligence, he was told that President Truman was leaving in twenty hours to consult with General MacArthur at Wake Island and that he would want seven intelligence estimates to study on the plane. Smith assembled the chiefs of the intelligence community in the Pentagon at 4 p.m., divided them and their staffs into seven groups, and told them they would work all night and have their assigned estimate ready for delivery at 8 a.m. President Truman had his estimates as he took off for his discussions with General MacArthur.

Over the years, and particularly during the last decade, a lot of criticism has been levied at our national intelligence estimates.

Much of the criticism is based on unrealistic expectations of what an intelligence service can do. The CIA does not have powers of prophecy. It has no crystal ball that can peer into the future with 20-20 sight. We are dealing with "probable" developments.

If we can't expect infallible prophecy from the nation's investment in intelligence, what can we expect? We can expect foresight. We can expect a careful definition of possibilities. We can expect professional analysis which probes and weighs probabilities and assesses their implications. We can expect analyses that assist the policymakers in devising ways to prepare for and cope with the full range of probabilities. The President does not need a single best view, a guru, or a prophet. The nation needs the best analysis and the full range of views and data it can get.

The process of analysis and arriving at estimates needs to be made as open and competitive as possible. We need to resist the bureaucratic urge for consensus.

We don't need analysts spending their time finding a middle ground or weasel words to conceal disagreement. The analyst's time needs to go into evaluating information – searching for the meaning and the implications of events and trends – and expressing both their conclusions and their disagreements clearly. The search to unify the intelligence community around a single homogenized estimate serves policymakers badly. It buries valid differences, forcing the intelligence product to the lowest or blandest common denominator. The search for consensus also cultivates the myth of infallibility. It implicitly promises a reliability that cannot be delivered. Too frequently, it deprives the intelligence product cannot be delivered. Too frequently, it deprives the intelligence product of relevance and the policymaker of the range of possibilities for which prudence requires that he prepare.

Above all, the policymaker needs to be protected from the conventional wisdom. Let me give you some horrible examples.

Before there was a CIA, Senator Brian McMahon and Lewis Strauss, then a member of the Atomic Energy Commission, performed one of the most important intelligence missions in the history of our nation. Together, they insisted that we had to develop a program to monitor and detect all large explosions that occurred at any place on the earth. We had to have that intelligence.

The first chance to perfect such a system was offered by tests which we were planning to conduct in the vicinity of Eniwetok in the spring of 1948. A detection system was devised by the end of 1948 but the Air Force found itself short of funds to procure instrumentation for the monitoring program. About one million dollars would be required to complete it, and contracts had to be let at once if the instruments were to be ready in time. Lewis Strauss, a great patriot and Chairman of the Atomic Energy Commission, volunteered to obligate himself for the million so that the contracts could be made firm immediately. This effort was launched in the nick of time, and in September it established that an atomic explosion had occurred somewhere on the Asiatic mainland and at some date between August 26 and 29, 1949.

Had there been no monitoring system in operation in 1949, Russian success in that summer would have been unknown to us. In consequence, we would have made no attempt to develop a thermonuclear weapon. It was our positive intelligence that the Russians had exploded an atomic bomb, which generated the recommendation to develop the qualitatively superior hydrogen weapon, to maintain our military superiority.

On January 30, 1950, President Truman made the decision to build the bomb. We were able to test our first hydrogen bomb in November 1952. The Russians tested their first weapon involving a thermonuclear reaction the following August.

Had we relied on the conventional wisdom about Soviet nuclear capability, the Russian success in developing thermonuclear weapon capability in 1953 would have found the United States hopelessly outdistanced, and the Soviet military would have been in possession of weapons vastly more powerful and devastating than any we had.

Early in 1962, John McCone, newly arrived as Director of Central Intelligence, saw reports coming in about the arrival of anti-aircraft weapons in Cuba. What are they there to protect, he wondered. There are no targets there now, he concluded, so they must intend to bring something there which will need to be attacked and hence will need to be defended. Thus, he was many months ahead of anyone in Washington in predicting the possibility that Moscow might base offensive missiles in Cuba. When Cuban refugees brought reports that large missiles were being brought in and installed, McCone considered this confirmation of his tentative forecast, while everyone else in Washington dismissed them on the basis that the Soviets would never do anything so foolish – until the U-2 pictures could not be denied.

To protect against the conventional wisdom, CIA, military intelligence, and every other element of the intelligence community should not only be allowed to compete and surface differences, but be encouraged to do so. Policymakers can easily sort through a wide range of opinions, but they cannot consider views and opinions they do not receive.

The time has come to recognize that the intelligence community has no monopoly on truth, on insight, and on initiative in foreseeing what will be relevant to policy. For that reason, we are in the process of reconstituting a President's Foreign Intelligence Advisory Board. It will be made up of strong and experienced individuals with a wide range of relevant backgrounds.

To get all the intelligence we need, we've got to go beyond the formal intelligence organizations. We've got to tap all the scholarly resources of the nation and the perspectives and insights you develop from your activities around the world. We're geared to do that in open and direct contact with the campuses, the think tanks, and the business organizations around the country.

We will need to do even more of this in the future to cope with the intelligence requirements of our increasingly complex and dangerous world as it generates new threats. In the OSS, we were doing pretty well if we knew where the enemy was and how he was redeploying his forces. For the first twenty years of a peacetime intelligence, most of the effort went to understanding the production and capabilities of weapons. It is only in the last decade that it has dawned upon us that we have been threatened and damaged more by coups and subversion and economic aggression than by military force. We will still devote a large slice of our effort to military estimates and rely heavily on them in formulating our defense budget and force structures. But they will have to be supplemented by increased efforts to assess economic vulnerabilities and technological breakthroughs. Increasingly, priority attention will go to the need to identify social and political instabilities – and how they can or are being exploited by propaganda, by subversion, and by terrorism.

So much for the kind of intelligence capabilities we have and need to develop.

Now, let me say a few words about what we face. Our first priority is still the Soviet Union. It has been the number one adversary for 35 years. It is the only country in the world with major weapons systems directly targeted at the United States which could destroy the U.S. in half an hour. For that reason alone, it remains the number one target.

Less lethal but perhaps more dangerous is the threat of worldwide subversion and insurrection and tiny wars of so-called national liberation. Over the last five years we've seen the combination of Cuban manpower, Libyan money, and Soviet arms and transport substantially seize and thoroughly threaten the African continent from Angola to Ethiopia and across through the Sudan and Chad to the Western Sahara.

We've seen the same forces take over Nicaragua and threaten to Castroize all of Central America. We see the crossroads and the oil resources of the Middle East threatened from Iran and Afghanistan from the east, Syria from the north, Yemen from the south and Libya from the West – all literally stuffed with Soviet weapons.

There are many levels at which the Soviet Union challenges us today.

First, there is the strategic arena in which the increasing accuracy and power of Soviet missiles thoroughly threatens the survivability of our own land-based missiles. This has led to a Presidential decision to accelerate the strengthening of our air and sea retaliatory capability and to basically defer the decision on the basing of the more powerful land-based missiles until we can better evaluate the role that anti-missile defense and versatile cruise missiles can play in maintaining our deterrent capability.

Secondly, on the Central European Front, Soviet and Warsaw Pact forces vastly outnumber NATO forces and tanks, planes and troops.

Thirdly, in the ability to project miliary power over long distances, the Soviets, together with their Cuban proxies, have demonstrated their capability in Angola and in Ethiopia, while the rapid deployment force we have recently created remains untested.

In numbers, experience, and freedom to act, the ability of the Soviets to subvert other governments and propagandize in other countries is unrivalled. A few years ago the United States was providing twice as much military equipment to Third World countries. Today the Soviet Union is providing 50 percent more equipment to a larger number of Third World countries – and military advice and influence go along with these relationships. The Soviets, along with their Eastern European satellites, and Libya, Cuba, and the PLO, engage in the widespread training of guerrilla fighters and terrorists, and sometimes use them to destabilize governments and thus lay the ground for their support of revolutionary violence.

Large and specialized segments of the KGB and the Soviet military intelligence known as the GRU, together with trade and scientific delegations roaming the advanced world, are acquiring Western technology and using it to build the military threat that we have to defend against, and to reduce the drain which that process imposes on the Soviet economy at a rate which we only recently have begun to realize.

This is the range of the threat, so much of it new and beyond the traditional range in capabilities of Western intelligence, which we are now called upon to deal with.

A strong defense and ability to exercise influence in the world requires a strong industrial basis.

We need to ask ourselves tough questions about where our economy and where our companies are headed. For example, what will the increasing globalization of the automobile industry do to the industrial base on which we must depend for national defense? As the auto industry becomes globalized our need to keep the sea lanes open will become more critical.

How will the attrition of our computer and semi-conductor industry, under the impact of the drive the Japanese have mounted to capture this market, undermine our defense capability? How will it impact our ability to make our way in the world through the manufacture of machinery and equipment that will be increasingly controlled and guided by microprocessors?

If the French, Germans, and Japanese, and less developed countries like Korea and Brazil, convert more rapidly than the United States from fossil fuels to nuclear energy, how rapidly will lower power costs in those countries be converted into important competitive advantages in manufacturing costs? How will the instabilities in southern Africa on the one hand and seabed mining on the other affect the structure of our world mineral markets and impact our manufacturing industries?. . .

What will count here and around the world is a renewal of confidence in our people and among other nations in the strength of purpose and the reliability of the United States to do what needs to be done to make our own society stronger and more efficient, and to work with our friends and allies in support of freedom and justice.

◆ ◆ ◆

ANALYSIS AND ASSESSMENT

Casey recognized that intelligence is much more than espionage or covert action. As he outlines in this speech, "the heart of it is knowing what information we need to protect our country and its interests in the world, where and how to get it, how to put it together, and what to make out of it." The media's focus on espionage and covert action to the virtual exclusion of analysis used to really bother Casey. "Those guys don't understand," he would mutter after reading yet another wildly inaccurate or distorted story in the newspapers. Then he would shrug his shoulders and turn the meeting back to the subject at hand, which usually involved an intelligence analysis of some country, region, or issue.

Ladies and gentlemen, I am very pleased to be here with the Commonwealth Club again. Judge Grant did quite a job of research. She didn't tell you that she and I were in the OSS together. She was under age. She also forgot to mention that I was once a notary public.

I thought I'd talk about what you pay for and what you get in our American intelligence community. There are a lot of false impressions about intelligence. Intelligence is much more than espionage, or

Address to the Commonwealth Club of California, San Francisco, California, May 21, 1982.

codebreaking, or cameras in the sky, or collecting signals and electronic impulses. The heart of it is knowing what information we need to protect our country and its interests in the world, where and how to get it, how to put it together, and what to make out of it. Then you have to get it used in developing and implementing our own policies, in helping our friends and allies defend themselves, and in blunting hostile propaganda and subversion directed at the United States and its friends and allies.

My predecessors, foremost among them John McCone, who I am happy to see here at the head table, have created a great apparatus of scholarship and technical marvels to collect and process a vast flow of information from all over the world. But our intelligence service had fallen behind badly for having lost 50 percent of its manpower and 40 percent of its funding during the 1970s. It is hard to overstate the damage done to the intelligence service during the 1970s. Unrelenting questioning of the Agency's integrity generated a severe loss of credibility. That credibility is only now being restored. With steadily diminishing resources, operations were curtailed, too many good people were lost, and analysis suffered.

We have set our goals immediately to strengthen the capabilities of the intelligence community to deal with today's more complicated world, and, at the same time, develop new capabilities to meet the challenges of the troubled times we see in the late 1980s and 1990s. We have good progress and have been assured of the President's steady support toward meeting both these goals.

Analysis, and its assessment in National Intelligence Estimates, is the bottom line of the intelligence process. Intelligence analyses must be linked to the policy process. It must answer a question the policymakers have asked, are about to ask, or should have asked. Poorly drawn or incomplete analysis is a disservice to the policymaker and an unforgivable waste of an enormously complex and costly collection system. Collection, after all, is only facts, and just as houses are made of stone, so collection is made of facts. But a pile of stones is not a house, and a collection of facts is not intelligence. It is analysis and assessment that make it intelligence.

My highest responsibility is to produce sound national intelligence estimates on issues relevant to our national security. We have taken steps to assure standards of integrity and objectivity, relevance and timeliness, accuracy and independence to the national estimate process.

The time it takes to give the President an estimate on a timely topic has been drastically streamlined. Days and weeks are no longer spent in compromising and semantics to paper over divergent views. It is my responsibility to make the estimate and to protect the President from conventional wisdom by ensuring that estimates reflect the substantiated judgments held by any of the components of the intelligence community. We have brought a lively competition in the estimative process. The chiefs of all intelligence components (the NSA, the DIA, the State Department's Intelligence and Research component, the Armed Services, Treasury, FBI, and Energy) meet as a Board of Estimates in the National Foreign Intelligence Council. This involves them personally in the substance of estimates to make them better, to see that different views are fully reflected, to give the policymaker not some diluted consensus but a range of real and specific expectations. After all, a policy to deal with a future which cannot be precisely foreseen must be sufficiently broad and flexible to provide for a range of concrete possibilities.

We have instituted an aggressive program to take advantage of the expertise of outside scholars and researchers in recognition that intelligence people have no monopoly on the truth. We are reaching into the think tanks, the academic institutions, the science labs, and the business community for a wide assortment of experts to address special problems for us and to get different perceptions.

Now, what do we see out there. The Soviet Union presents the largest danger and is still our number one priority. We see a frightening buildup of all military forces with the latest technological advances. But we are no longer just worried about Soviet military capability – though it remains the only country able to threaten the destruction of the United States. We are now alarmed at the ability the Soviets have shown to project their power abroad through worldwide subversion and insurgency. A large part of enhanced influence in the world comes from the adept use of proxy forces, arms sales and military advisers around the world.

Recently, we had our cartographers prepare a map to show the Soviet presence in its various degrees of influence. They colored in red on a map of the world the nations under a significant degree of Soviet influence. Close to 50 nations were in red. Ten years ago, only 25 nations would have been colored in red. In the ten years between 1972 and 1982, four nations have extricated themselves from Soviet grasp and 23 nations have fallen under a significantly increased degree of Soviet influence or insurgency supported by the Soviets or their proxies. It is, in my opinion, no coincidence that the eleven insurgencies now under way throughout the world supported by Russia, Cuba, Libya, and South Yemen happen to be close to the natural resources and the choke points in the world's sea lanes on which the United States and its allies must rely to fuel and supply their economic life. It is not hard to understand how this has come about. Time and again we have watched agents of the communist apparatus move in to exploit underlying social and economic discontents, which are plentiful throughout the world. They gain a base, then expand it with trained men and military arms. With this help, local insurgents sabotage economic targets and drive out investment. This further heightens political and economic discontent. As discontent grows, more people go over to the insurgents, which makes them bolder and stronger.

El Salvador provided an example of how we can help these beleaguered nations defend themselves. The training of El Salvadoran troops and officers in the United States imparted new capabilities to the government army. The success of the recent elections in El Salvador came largely from developing new intelligence sources and showing the El Salvadoran army how to use intelligence to break up guerrilla formations before they could attack provincial capitals in order to stop the voting. This resulted in the American television audience seeing in living color Usulatan, the provincial capital nearest Nicaragua, with its streets empty and its inhabitants huddled behind closed doors as guerrillas fired their rifles at doorways. Then, a minute later, this television audience saw in the rest of the country long lines of people patiently waiting in the hot sun to cast their vote. That contrast in a few minutes wiped out weeks of distortion and propaganda about what has been happening in Central America.

Today, El Salvador has a new government and a vote of the people has overwhelmingly rejected the insurgents, organized, supplied and directed from Nicaragua and Cuba, in their attempt to stop the election. Next door in Honduras, a democratically elected civilian government, to which the military are fully subordinated, presides over a free and open society. Nicaragua can't stand this contrast to its own militarized and totalitarian society in which opposition forces, free expression, civil liberties, and human rights are being stamped out. So instructions have gone out, and communist and extreme leftist elements in Honduras have begun to hijack airplanes, plant dynamite in buildings and otherwise lay the groundwork for revolutionary violence in their determination to see that free democratic government does not succeed in Central America.

Subversion and insurgency exploit instability. We have established a Center for the Study of Insurgency and Instability which uses a wide range of techniques and methodologies to provide advance warning of instability and potential for destabilization, in order to protect us from being caught by surprise as we were in Iran. The small and weak countries in which insurgencies can be fostered and developed to overthrow governments do not need and cannot handle expensive and sophisticated weapons for which virtually all of them clamor. What they need is light arms to defend themselves against externally trained and supported guerrillas, good intelligence, good police methods, good communications, training in small arms and their use in small unit actions, and mobility to keep up with the hit-and-run tactics of guerrilla forces. We can introduce an element of stability into the Third World by helping small countries develop those skills and capabilities, for a fraction of our foreign aid budget. Governments facing civil war cannot achieve economic and social progress until they are able to control internal disruption.

We face another monster known as international terrorism. The Soviet Union has provided funding and support for terrorist operations via Eastern Europe and its client nations like Libya and Cuba. With at least tacit Soviet approval many groups have trained together in Cuba, Libya, Iraq, South Yemen, and Lebanon. Even if the Soviet Union withdrew all patronage, terrorist activity would certainly continue, perhaps unabated. Terror has other independent patrons, currently the most prominent being Libya. Terrorist training camps are the largest industry in Libya, next to oil. International terrorism has taken on a life of its own. When enough terrorists are armed and trained, they must kidnap and rob to get money for what has become a big business. They need to assassinate and blow up things to get the media spotlight needed to recruit, keep up morale, and make propaganda for their causes.

This terrorism, from headquarters in Beirut in Lebanon, Tripoli in Libya, and Aden in South Yemen, ranges across borders into five continents. Working with the intelligence services of friendly nations, we are developing a network to track terrorist organizations and train local quick reaction and rescue forces to fight terrorism worldwide.

Another threat is in the exploitation of indigenous religious, political, and other regional tensions. The most immediately dangerous may by the Shia and Sunni Moslem tensions running through Iran, Iraq, Syria and other states on the Persian Gulf, which could bring heavy Soviet influence into the oil regions of the Middle East. Similar tensions exist to be inflamed and exploited between Arabs and Jews, between moderate and radical Arabs, and between blacks and whites in Africa. The Russians and Cubans are poised to exploit tension between Gringos and Latinos in this hemisphere if the Falklands and other latent territorial disputes get out of hand.

There are lower level threats springing from an awesome range of special Soviet capabilities. Only recently have we established how the accuracy, precision, and power of Soviet weapons, which we must now counter with budget busting appropriations, are based on Western technology, and to a far greater extent than we had ever dreamed. The Soviet political and military intelligence services, KGB and GRU, have for years been training young scientists to target and roam the world to acquire military technology from the U.S., Western Europe, Japan, and anywhere else. They have acquired technology worth many billions by purchase, legal and illegal, by theft, by espionage, by bribery, by scientific exchanges, and by exploiting our open literature and our Freedom of Information Act. We need to sensitize and protect our scientists, engineers, and sales forces against technology pickpockets, dummy customers, and forged papers used to funnel sensitive equipment and knowledge behind the Iron Curtain. A year ago we established a Technology Transfer Center to identify and help fight this hemorrhage of our research and development.

Moscow's skill in propaganda continually puts us at a disadvantage. While our intelligence has shown the Soviets carrying off the biggest peacetime military buildup in history, deploying over 200 missiles targeted at the capitals of Western Europe, and using chemical and bacteriological weapons against freedom fighters and women and children in Afghanistan and Indo-China, they have succeeded in painting the United States as the threat to peace.

This is accomplished through their political and intelligence apparatus in a far-flung and many-sided campaign of what they call active measures. Our intelligence can identify the distortions of these active measures but to develop the necessary instruments and links to expose and rebut them, the private sector in the free world will have to carry much of that load. This is a challenge to everyone who believes in the values of a free and open society.

In the final analysis, all these threats boil down to a struggle for the hearts and minds of men. The courage of the Afghan freedom fighters, supported by arms and training provided by other nations, escalates the price and deters armed insurrection everywhere. The world has seen the communist system fail in Poland. The once proud call of Lenin, "Workers of the world unite," today makes those in the Kremlin tremble. Many Third World countries have tried the communist model and discovered that it doesn't work. The Soviets have been kicked out of Egypt, Sudan, and Somalia. But to hold their people, leaders in these harassed countries needed to show that ties with the West do yield economic benefits. Even a modest Western presence enhancing their trade and production and creating some jobs is all that they need to point to. Here the American private sector can play a far more significant role than government aid. What is needed in the Third World is not steel mills and power plants but entrepreneurial activity suited to the prevailing level of economic opportunity. That's the vision which President Reagan projected at the Cancun Summit. We now need private sector leadership to encourage and show American small and medium-sized businesses how to move offshore and involve themselves in the world.

The intelligence community has focused attention on the enormous economic problems which the Soviets are facing at home. Assessments have been produced on Soviet economic dependency on Western trade, on Soviet military use of Western technology, on the need for Western credits and energy markets to save the Soviets from devastating hard currency squeeze in the years immediately ahead, and on how forces in the global economy are likely to impact our competitive position, our balance of payments, our capital formation, and the industrial base on which our national security must rest. These are some of the ways intelligence can protect both our national security and economic interest from threats emanating from external sources.

One concluding thought: as a nation we have a propensity for shooting ourselves in the foot. One of these self-inflicted wounds, close to my heart, leaves us the only country in the world which gives foreign intelligence agencies and anyone else a legal license to poke into our files. I question very seriously whether a secret intelligence agency and the

Freedom of Information Act can co-exist for very long. The willingness
of foreign intelligence services to share information and rely on us fully,
and of individuals to risk their lives and reputations to help us will continue to dwindle away unless we get rid of the Freedom of Information
Act. Secrecy is essential to any intelligence organization. Ironically,
secrecy is accepted without protest in many areas of our society.
Physicians, lawyers, clergymen, grand juries, journalists, income tax
returns, crop futures – all have confidential aspects protected by law.
Why should national security information be entitled to any less protection? I'm not asking for any retreat from our commitment to protecting
essential liberties but only to bear in mind, as Justice Goldberg once
said, that "while the Constitution protects against invasions of individual
rights, it is not a suicide pact."

◆ ◆ ◆

THE FIRST LINE OF DEFENSE

*At least twice a year, Casey would organize what he called a
"worldwide briefing." In essence, these briefings were reports from the
Director of Central Intelligence on how the world looked to American
intelligence at the time: key trends, developments, problems and opportunities that we saw looming before the country and its key policymakers.*

*The effort and energy devoted to shaping these briefings was
monumental. Casey himself would outline a draft briefing, based on National Estimates and other analytic products that had come across his
desk since the previous briefing. Then he would meet, singly or in
groups, with the National Intelligence Officers (the intelligence
community's senior analysts, who together formed the National Intelligence Council, and who are responsible for geographic regions of the
world and for special issues such as general-purpose military forces,
strategic forces, counterterrorism, and economics). The NIOs then
would prepare sections of the briefing as assigned by the Director of
Central Intelligence. The sections would be blended together into a
(theoretically) seamless piece of work. Casey would then take this comprehensive draft and work it some more. Invariably he would order*

Address to the Mid-America Club, Chicago, Ilinois, April 4, 1984.

revisions, and when completed he would revise the revisions. Meanwhile, production schedules for National Estimates would be blown, and the new schedules blown as well.

In short, Casey viewed production of these worldwide briefings as an essential, integral part of managing intelligence. In his view, by organizing our perceptions for policymakers we organized them for ourselves. Thus the exercise served to point us toward our own intelligence research program.

The briefings would then be given to the President, Vice President, senior national security policymakers and military officials, and to Congress. In sanitized form, the briefings would be given to foreign leaders who met with Casey on visits to Washington, or to leaders Casey met with on his overseas travels. And as a man who liked to get the most for his money, Casey would use the material gathered for these briefings (edited and sanitized to remove classified material) to convey to the public a sense of what our government was seeing and thinking as it looked beyond our borders.

It's not easy to cover all the things I'd like to talk about to such a distinguished audience. But I thought the way I'd approach you is to tell you briefly what American intelligence sees out there around the world and then briefly describe how we go about serving as the nation's first line of defense. I have to be fairly general and after that, I'll have time to answer your questions and go into things more deeply as far as I can without being either indiscreet or insincere.

As we look out there, the Soviet Union still dominates our interests. As great Kremlin watchers, we see Chernenko as the third of three aging and sick leaders. He's a transitional leader; whether he dies tomorrow or two years from now really makes little difference. The CIA buried Chinese Chairman Mao some twenty times before he finally died. That's a very good example about the hazards of predicting when anyone might cash in.

What we do know for sure is that the Soviets have a large and growing arsenal of nuclear weapons which are aimed at the United States and Western Europe, and at East Asia, Japan, China, as far as Thailand and Malaysia. On top of that, new missiles and missile-carrying planes and submarines are being designed, developed, tested, and deployed in amazing profusion. It takes us ten years to come up with an airplane, and during that period of time, they'll have ten to twelve new missiles with varying capabilities. This is compounded by the fact that over the last decade the Soviets have improved their capabilities for missile defense while we've done little or nothing. Recently, we've seen alarming signs of radar deployments which go beyond the 1972 treaty limiting missile attacks. We've seen the testing of interceptors and other activities which could give them a running start if they decided to break the treaty and establish a nationwide missile defense. That, of course, could heavily tip the strategic balance against us and I'd say they've got a four to five year head start.

On the European front, the Warsaw Pact forces outnumber NATO in troop strength, tanks, guns, and planes. These weapons are being deployed in an increasingly aggressive way and backed up with long-range missiles which could reach the European capitals. Yet the main threat may be elsewhere. Khrushchev told us as early as 1961 that the communists would win, not through a nuclear war, which would destroy the world, not through a conventional war, which could still lead to nuclear war; but through national liberation wars in Africa, Asia, and Latin America. We didn't believe that in 1961 any more than we believed Hitler when he told us just how he would go about taking over Europe.

Since then the Soviets have developed Cuba as a base and source of manpower. During the 1960s and during the early 1970s, we saw them send weapons one thousand miles away to link up with Cuban troops in Angola, Ethiopia, South Yemen. Then we saw Vietnam, Angola, Ethiopia, South Yemen, Iran, and Nicaragua taken over by regimes hostile to the United States and faithful to the Soviet line.

This process established Soviet power:

- ◆ In Vietnam, along China's southern border, outflanking the Chinese, and astride the sea lanes through which Japan's oil comes from the Persian Gulf.

- ◆ In Afghanistan, 500 miles closer to the warm water ports of the Indian Ocean and to the Straits of Hormuz, through which comes the oil essential to Western Europe.

- ◆ On the Horn of Africa overlooking the passageway of Suez, which connects the Mediterranean Sea and the Indian Ocean.

- ◆ In southern Africa, rich in minerals, which the industrial nations must have.

♦ In the Caribbean and Central America on the very doorstep of the United States.

This is a continuing process of creeping imperialism which seems to be moving into other areas of strategic significance: Chad, Honduras, Guatemala, Sudan, even Thailand. The most effective thing the Soviets do in implementing this technique is through the creative and effective use of proxies. This is not exactly new in history. Romans used men from conquered countries to fight their enemies. Later, Swiss and German mercenaries were available to the highest bidder all over Europe, the British army had its Ghurkas, and the French their Foreign Legion. The Soviets have brought a new dimension to this. They use the Cubans, the East Germans, the Libyans, the Vietnamese, the North Koreans, and the PLO in quite a different role.

These Soviet proxies act in peace as well as war. Their role is as much political as military. Different proxies have specialized functions. Of the more than 40,000 Cubans in Africa, 80 percent are soldiers on active duty. Vietnam has the fourth largest army in the world. This keeps China and Thailand worried and solidifies the Soviets' position in Kampuchea. Just this week, Vietnamese troops crossed the border into Thailand and the Chinese sent them an artillery message far to the north at the other end of Vietnam.

That's the way these low-intensity conflicts go. North Korea, Libya, Cuba, South Yemen, East Germany, and Bulgaria trained the security forces that organized block watchers in these occupied countries to protect the governments from their people. They also run training camps for terrorists and insurgents to destabilize and create the basis for overthrowing governments around the world.

Terrorism has become a weapon system used by sovereign states to destabilize other governments and intimidate them in their foreign policy. As practiced today, international terrorism has obliterated the distinction between peace and war. Major terrorist organizations and a great many more "mom and pop shops" are hired by Iran, Syria, Cuba, Libya, and other radical governments. U.S. facilities, emissaries, and personnel here and around the world are a major target and this is a growing challenge for our intelligence capabilities.

Narcotics flow into the United States from South America, the Golden Triangle of Southeast Asia, Thailand, Afghanistan, Pakistan, and

Iran. These narcotics come in container ships, small ships, and aircraft; they even come in stomachs through customs in airports. We see some of the huge amounts of money from this activity going into destabilizing political and terrorist activities.

On top of these acts of violence, we also need to cope with nuclear proliferation, technology transfer, and Third World debt – an international problem which could undermine political stability of some of these countries as well as our own security and prosperity. Finally, perhaps the most critical and most difficult intelligence challenge we face is the assessment of Soviet technology and science and its potential for military and strategic surprise. We do this every two years. We just completed one in-depth study. We believe we're still ahead in most of the twenty critical technologies we look at as having a military strategic significance. But they've pulled ahead or alongside in some of our margins, and lead times tend to shrink across-the-board. It is only in semiconductor and computer areas that we really have a ten to fifteen year lead time; but this could disappear quickly. (I'll cover that in a moment.) One thing we see is that the ability of the Soviet military-industrial complex to acquire and assimilate Western technology far exceeds anything we previously estimated.

During the late 1970s, the Soviets got about 30,000 samples of production equipment, weapons, and military components, and over 400,000 technical documents both classified and unclassified.

The majority of the stuff they acquire is of U.S. origin, with an increasing share of it coming through Western Europe and Japan. This truly impressive take is acquired by both legal and illegal means. We estimate that during this period, the KGB and its military equivalent, the GRU, and their surrogates among the East Europeans' intelligence services – the Poles, Czechs, East Germans, and so on – illegally stole about 70 percent of the technology most significant to Soviet military equipment and weapons programs. So the net effect is that the Soviets have been shortcutting, saving time, saving R&D, and acquiring things they wouldn't otherwise acquire to develop in their weapons systems the precision and accuracy that has forced us to approve budget-busting funds for our military programs.

Some examples:

♦   The Soviets had our plans on the C-5A transport plane before it flew.

- Soviet trucks which drove into Afghanistan came from a plant out-fitted with $1.5 billion of modern American and European machinery.
- The gyros and bearings in their heavy missiles were designed in the U.S.
- The radar in their AWACS is ours.
- Their space shuttle is a virtual copy of our initial shuttle design, and the list goes on and on.

Just how do the Soviets get so much of our technology?

First of all, they comb through our literature, they buy through legal trade channels, they religiously attend our scientific and technological conferences, and send 40-year-old scientists over here to study while we send 20-year-old students of poetry and literature to Moscow. Between 1970 and 1976, the Soviets purchased some $20 billion in Western equipment and machinery, much of which had potential military applications.

They use dummy firms in sophisticated international operations to divert and steal Western technology. We've identified some 300 firms operating in more than thirty countries engaged in these technology diversions. Most diversions occur by way of Western Europe, which is why we have made such a strong effort to enlist the help and support of our European allies in combatting these technology losses and diversions.

U.S. microelectronic production technology is the second most significant industrial technology acquired by the Soviets since the end of World War II. With this help, they have systematically built a modern microelectronics industry. The Zelenograd Science Center is the Soviet equivalent to Silicon Valley built literally from scraps of Western technology. All Soviet monolistic integrated circuits are copies of U.S. designs. They even copied the imperfections contained in some of the U.S. samples!

This is very serious business. The West must organize to protect its military, industrial, commercial, and scientific communities, keeping two objectives clearly in view: First we must seek to maintain our technological lead time over the Soviets in vital design and manufacture know-how. Second, manufacturing, inspection, and most importantly, automatic test equipment, which would alleviate acute Soviet deficiency in military-related manufacturing areas, must be very strictly control-led. That's a tough task.

On our side, we've had a fair number of successes in frustrating the Soviet technology theft. We've penetrated some of these phoney tech-nology firms and we've been able to stop a lot of their activities and diversions. I will just mention one.

Late in 1983 and early in 1984, West German and Swedish Customs seized several advanced VAX computers and thirty tons of related equip-ment that were being smuggled into the Soviet Union by perhaps the most notorious of these illegal smuggling trading programs headed by a man named Richard Muller. This turned out to be just the tip of the iceberg. We'd rather stop them in Stockholm and Hamburg in order to prevent equipment from going into the Soviet Union. That stuff had been sent to those destinations by breaking it up into components sending some through South Africa, some through Switzerland, some through Germany, some through Sweden, and so on. But we found out that much larger quantities of computing electronic equipment has been success-fully diverted into the Soviet Union through activities of the Muller firm, by others like that firm, and the Western manufacturers who have dealt with them. So this a very wide-spread activity.

Now I'd like to take a little time to comment on the apparatus which American intelligence has developed to meet this broad array of challen-ges I described so briefly. My predecessors have enlisted photography, electronics, acoustics, seismic reading, other technological marvels, to gather facts from all corners of the earth. These capabilities have and are being enhanced as new technologies and new intelligence require-ments emerge. As a result, we will be receiving four times as many photos, signals, and reports in four or five years as we're receiving now. To sift and evaluate and get practical meanings on this veritable Niagara of facts, we need to recruit and develop dedicated people.

We have scholars and scientists of every discipline, in the social and physical sciences, as well as engineers and specialists in computers and communications. We have them in a profusion which I think is un-matched by any university. We work hard to tap scientists and businessmen who roam the world with their professional capabilities, for the information which comes their way and for the insight and un-derstanding they develop.

It's necessary to distill the sweeping array of data acquired by clandestine reporting commonly known as spies, that is obtained in overt discussions by military attaches, by diplomats around the world, by contacts with businessmen and scientists, scholars, and openly conducted here in the United States. All this is distilled into intelligence assessments on specific issues and problems.

Where appropriate it's addressed in National Intelligence Estimates, which are relevant to the decisions which the President and his colleagues are called upon to make. For these National Intelligence Estimates, the chiefs of the components which we call the American intelligence community – Defense Intelligence Agency, the National Security Agency, CIA, the Army, the Navy, the Air Force, and the Marine Corps intelligence staffs, as well as the FBI, and the intelligence arms of the Department of State and Treasury – comprise a board of review. They are charged with contributing information and the judgments developed by our analysts.

We take great care to make sure that these estimates are no longer what they used to be, kind of a compromised consensus. So we make efforts, and I think we're successful in presenting our intelligence as a range of alternatives rather than what used to be a watered down, compromised opinion.

All these tasks can't be done without getting the assistance of people around the world who share our values and want in one way or another to help in this work. To get that kind of help, it is essential that the American intelligence community maintain its reputation for integrity, competence, confidentiality, reliability, and security. I think that the quality of the intelligence we produce manifests the loyalty and dedication of our people. Large numbers of Americans are now interested in joining our ranks – demonstrating that we do maintain that kind of a reputation despite a steady drumbeat of criticism from the media.

With few exceptions, the highly publicized charges made against the CIA and other intelligence agencies during the mid-1970s turned out to be false. The charges were on the front pages and their repudiations were buried away when few people would notice. Now this kind of ordeal and problem was terminated in the late 1970s by leaders in the Congress, and the Chairman of the Intelligence Oversight Committee who spoke up to declare that the intelligence communities had been libeled and unfairly treated. Out of this process came a congressional oversight process which has assured that special intelligence activities are known and scrutinized by elected legislatures responsible directly to the people.

Still despite this, intelligence gets a lot of flack. Everything imaginable is charged to secret intelligence activities. Its purposes and activities are widely distorted and misrepresented.

I submit that the intelligence function is so critical to our present security and to our national interests that it must be defended; and the people who put their careers on the line to carry out its functions have made it clear that they expect their leaders to defend them, their skill, their record of accuracy, and their integrity. So for that reason I'd like to tell you just a little about the people who meet this sweeping challenge every day.

I'll start by telling you what they say about themselves. I think their quality and character is epitomized in a CIA Credo in which they declare their mission and the standards that they demand of themselves. It says:

We are the Central Intelligence Agency.

We produce timely and high quality intelligence for the president and government of the United States.

We provide objective and unbiased evaluations and are always open to new perceptions and ready to challenge conventional wisdom.

We perform special intelligence tasks at the request of the president.

We conduct our activities and ourselves according to the highest standards of integrity, morality, and honor and according to the spirit and letter of the law.

We measure our success by our contribution to the protection and enhancement of American values, security, and national interest.

We believe our people are the Agency's most important resource. We seek the best and work to make them better. We subordinate our desire for public recognition to the need for confidentiality. We strive for continuing professional improvement. We give unfailing loyalty to each other and to our common purpose.

We look to our leaders to stimulate initiative, a commitment to excellence, and a propensity for action; to reward and protect us in a manner which reflects the special nature of our responsibility, our contribution, and our sacrifices; and to promote among us a sense of mutual trust and shared responsibility.

We derive our inspiration and commitment to excellence from the inscription in our foyer: "And ye shall know the truth and the truth shall make you free."

The people in the CIA have survived one of the most rigorous screening processes known to man — the highest skill requirements, the toughest intelligence and psychological testing, severe medical clearances, security clearances, and polygraphs. This gives us high confidence that those who get through this obstacle course are smart, clean of drugs and alcohol addiction, healthy, and psychologically able to cope. The record is that since the beginning of the CIA there are some 83,000 people who have worked for us. The bad apples who really let the country down and embarrassed or disgraced themselves and damaged the organization are very few and far between.

Last year we had 153,000 inquiries for employment; we selected 23,000 applicants for interviews; of those, 10,000 were actually considered for employment; 4,000 got through all the screening and all the tests satisfactorily, and only 1,500 made it through the entire screen process and entered on duty. That's a very tough selecting process. And after obtaining their security clearances they have to go back and pass it again and again.

Those who obtain career status — and their families — live with any number of security responsibilities, heavy travel, and away-from-home demands, heavy pressure and timing requirements, and many other constraints. Last year they forfeited 97,000 hours of annual leave and worked untold hours of uncompensated overtime. That's not something you'd find in your ordinary organization. Finally, I think this is really perhaps the most important point: throughout their career they know that there is no public recognition or public acclaim for their achievements and that criticisms, justified or not, have to be tolerated in silence.

These are the people our national leaders turn to when something needs to be done well and fast. Perhaps the satisfaction is perverse, it may be subtle, but it is real. I think it's found in the knowledge that intelligence is our first line of defense, for our security and future as a nation.

That satisfaction is heightened by understanding the perils represented by nuclear weapons, by international terrorism, by deliberate destabilization, by subversion and support of revolutionary violence around the world. I think there is a satisfaction in being called upon for constant vigilance and readiness to cope with these threats. The bond of trust and sharing of responsibility among these people flourishes from realizing how success affects our safety and from feeling the human and economic cost of each little granule of information that falls into their hands, and for knowing how the value of all that hangs finally on the care and depth, breadth and precision with which those nuggets of intelligence and information are evaluated, analyzed, and interpreted to their practical use. It is by confronting all of this in its multiple dimensions, and meeting that responsibility in different ways at various levels that the effectiveness, the quality, and skill that characterizes our people and organization are demonstrated. That's how that quality is developed and maintained.

Now finally I'd like to say that this is not our intelligence service – it's yours. It works for our common security and well being. There's a lot of things you can do to help it: You could speak up when our work and purposes are misunderstood and misrepresented; explain and share your knowledge and insight when our offices contact you for valued information; direct promising young people looking for a challenging and honorable career to our recruiters; and some of you could continue to develop the relevant technology and creative capabilities for the better, faster, and deeper collection, processing, and analysis of information, as some of you have in the past, and without which we could not keep up with the demands of this world.

* * *

Chapter 3

Secrecy in a Free Society

LAW AND INTELLIGENCE

This is the first of many speeches in which Casey — himself an attorney — talked about the relationship between the law and intelligence. Like the head of any large U.S. government agency, he grappled often with legal issues. Unlike many other agency heads, Casey enjoyed this sort of thing. And while the issues themselves were constantly changing, his view remained constant: One never did anything that was not legal. Acting illegally was not only wrong, but unnecessary and stupid.

Thank you, Dr. Thornton, for your most gracious introduction. You mentioned Nathan Hale. It is true that there is a statue of Nathan Hale at the CIA Building in Langley but I am thinking of having that replaced by a statue of Hercules Mulligan. After all, Nathan Hale got caught trying to get into British occupied New York. That's not the example we wish to emulate. In contrast, Hercules Mulligan operated throughout the Revolutionary War as a tailor in New York City measuring British officers for uniforms. The bits of information he gleaned from them were sent on horseback out to Setauket, Long Island, carried across Long Island Sound by row boat, again carried by a rider on horseback across Westchester County, then across the Hudson, and then down to Washington's headquarters in Morristown, New Jersey. Hercules Mulligan functioned throughout the war, was never caught, never broke his

---

Address to the Eighty-Ninth Commencement Exercises of the New York
School of Law, New York, New York, June 7, 1981.

cover, and rests today, still well covered, in the churchyard of Trinity Church facing Wall Street.

You have kindly asked me to address a few words to you to mark an occasion both you and I will have cause to recall with pride – receiving a law degree from one of this city's finest and most venerable law schools.

It is an honor to speak at this law school which has been launching so many fine lawyers in our profession for almost a century. I welcome you to our profession. Today is an occasion of joy. With the training and disciplines brought to you by a distinguished faculty, your visits to the busy courts nearby and your own study, you are rich in the opportunities and challenges generated in our complex and dynamic country both here and around the world. The great prize for your journey to the Bar is a license to contribute and participate actively in virtually every aspect of a free society, a society in which the greatest success and satisfaction comes from devising innovative and effective ways to serve others.

You may be curious to know what a lawyer is doing as Director of Central Intelligence

To start with, the law, very properly, plays a significant role in defining, authorizing and restricting the activities of the CIA. I see many other affinities between the professions of law and intelligence-gathering, at least as they are practiced in the United States: Both confront the paradox of being at the same time seekers of truth and partisans in a cause. Both are trained in an adversarial mode of thinking, and rewarded for aggressiveness; yet both must fight by the rules, respecting the rights of individual citizens and upholding the law and the Constitution. Even while using an adversary's own tactics to defeat him, neither may ever lose sight of what distinguishes the lawful from the lawless. Both are also engaged in a fiercely competitive business with high-risk stakes, where important issues of public concern often hinge on the outcome.

Lawyers and intelligence officers both spend much of their time in the process of discovery. In both professions, the elusive truth emerges only by an arduous accumulation of facts, and by weighing and shifting contradictory and incomplete evidence. In intelligence as in law, distortions of the truth caused by preconceptions, unexamined assumptions, and plain wishful thinking can be fatal to success. In both fields of endeavor, realism joined with skepticism is the beginning of wisdom. I am interested in enticing more lawyers as intelligence officers because they have in common the need to convert analysis into a practical judgment on how best to provide *now* for uncertainties and possible developments which only the future will precisely disclose.

Both professions have been criticized at times for serving the immediate exigencies of the client at some cost to the higher values they are charged with defending. Yet in the end, despite human errors of judgment and an occasional lapse displayed by lawyers as well as intelligence officials, society has come to recognize (perhaps reluctantly) that both are indispensable to safeguard the integrity and independence of our national institutions. As law is essential to democratic society, intelligence is essential to national security.

Recognition of the need for intelligence concerning the intentions of our adversaries is as old as the nation itself. During the War of Independence General Washington observed:

> The necessity of procuring good intelligence is apparent and need not be further urged. All that remains for me to add is that you keep the whole matter as secret as possible. For upon secrecy, success depends in most enterprises of the kind, and for want of it, they are generally defeated.

During the first 165 years of our nation's history, however, we were able to exist behind the security of wide oceans and friendly borders and the need for intelligence was episodic. The world changed drastically for America in general, and for the fledgling intelligence community in particular, on December 7, 1941, and for better or worse, it will never again be the same. The United States no longer enjoys the splendid isolation that its oceans and borders once provided, and it must now exist in a world in which the minimum period of warning in the event of nuclear attack is counted in less than 20 minutes.

As a result, we have today a national intelligence community made up of more scholars in the social and physical sciences than any campus can boast. It uses photography, electronics, acoustics, and other technological marvels to gather facts from the four corners of the globe and inform the public, as we saw in the SALT debate, of the precise capabilities of weapons on the other side of the globe which the Soviets keep most secret.

George Washington, wherever he is, and people in other countries, must find it puzzling that our government permits any person, including an officer of an antagonistic intelligence service, to apply for documents from our intelligence records and demand lengthy legal justification if they are denied.

A law that is grounded in the presumption that all government records should be accessible to the public, unless the government can justify in detail a compelling national security rationale for withholding them, *unwarrantedly* disrupts the effective operation of an intelligence agency.

Thus for reasons of security as well as efficiency, there is a strong current of opinion in this administration — and I believe in the Congress and the public — in favor of some modification of the Freedom of Information Act and other questionable burdens imposed on intelligence and other government activities. I wish to emphasize that this does not represent a retreat from our government's historic and cherished commitment to protecting essential liberties. But we should bear in mind, as Justice Goldberg once said, that "while the Constitution protects against invasions of individual rights, it is not a suicide pact."

Today, we live in an extraordinarily challenging world. Protected though we may be by military might and economic strength, we are vulnerable without an effective intelligence service. We need it to help us judge the capabilities and intentions, and monitor the activities, of those with interests adverse to ours, to evaluate changing economic and political trends worldwide, and to anticipate danger before it threatens.

Your generation is the first in this century to grow entirely to maturity in a world where the United States is being actively pressed to defend its role as the foremost economic and industrial power in the world. We now face competition from others in the free world, but we are still very much a great nation and power. Any country that can successfully engineer a feat like the flawless launch and recovery of the Columbia space shuttle has adequate resources and resolve to retain its position as leader of the free world. We all can take great pride in that magnificent achievement.

We nevertheless must recognize that we are now challenged as never before by military and commercial competitors of unprecedented strength. We can not rest on past achievements. We have permitted our own resources, both material and spiritual, to be drawn down. In the private sector, we have allowed an alarming decline in productivity and hence in our ability to compete in world markets. In the governmental sector, we have continually exhausted our reserves and then borrowed to cover the shortfall, compounding the inflationary pressure on interest rates and sapping public confidence in the government's ability to control expenditures.

These trends must not be allowed to continue. We must trim the fat and revitalize our institutions.

Critical to this are the human resources in which this nation has always been so rich, young people with good minds and good educations, with energy and enthusiasm and the confidence to tackle the difficulties ahead of us. Those fortunate enough to be trained in the law have a special opportunity to give themselves to public service because there are so many ways they can contribute. The substantial number of attorneys serving in key positions in government is ample evidence of the many possibilities it offers to bright young lawyers.

You will not get rich working for the government. There you will quickly enjoy a degree of responsibility and freedom which young attorneys rarely find in the private sector. But, also in private practice you can find the deep personal satisfaction of being able to work directly and specifically for the public good. The client's interests may always be framed broadly to include that objective, for in the last analysis the client is the public.

This is nowhere clearer than in the field of national security law. Here one is always aware that losing a lawsuit could entail the surrender of national secrets, or that giving ill-considered advice could result in grave personal consequences for others laboring in the national interest. It is privilege to work for such a client, to whose welfare so many are deeply and personally committed. So I hope to welcome some of you to public service — and I'd like to urge you to always remember that it is one of the glories of America that public service can be rendered in the private sector as well as in the public sector.

◆ ◆ ◆

PROTECTING SOURCES AND METHODS

As the traditional trickle of news leaks increased to a torrent during the Reagan years, Casey's concern about such leaks also grew steadily. Indeed, as years went by the effort to staunch the flow of leaks became one of Casey's major undertakings. What bothered him was not the domestic political damage these leaks caused — he recognized and accepted that sort of thing as the normal, if regrettable, price of democracy — but rather the national-security damage these leaks caused. As the nation's intelligence chief, he saw this damage close-up, every day, and he found it intolerable.

In the spring of 1983 Casey began to speak out publicly about the need to stop leaks; it was a theme to which he would return time and again during the years to come.

When I was asked to address you on my views concerning journalism, I thought it an unusual opportunity for a Director of Central Intelligence. I am reminded of a shogun in old Japan who was riding across his kingdom when he came upon one of his samurai, bloodied and woebegotten. The shogun asked him what had happened. My Lord, I am just back from doing battle with your enemies to the East," answered the warrior. To which the shogun replied, "But I have no enemies to the East." The samurai paused and then said, "You do now!"

As I look around the world today, I am certain I don't need any more adversaries. My purpose here tonight is not to create any new ones. Some tension is inherent between the press and the intelligence community but we want to minimize tension and maximize cooperation. Journalists are committed to finding out the most they can about us. We are committed to protecting legitimate secrets. That does not mean our relationship boils down to "It's our job to protect secrets and a reporter's job to uncover them." That would put us in a position analogous to a tourist and a pickpocket. The tourist should not have to protect the wallet from the pickpocket.

As Director of Central Intelligence, my primary responsibility is to provide the most accurate, timely analysis of foreign developments to

Address to the Edward Weintal Prize Ceremony, Georgetown University, Washington, D.C., April 13, 1983 our national leaders. That must sound familiar to those of you in the press. Journalists are also responsible for accurate, timely analysis. To fulfill my responsibilities, I must also see to it that the intelligence community develops the broadest possible range of sources of information. Again this must sound familiar. We value and use information, observation, and analysis provided by embassy personnel, military attaches, and the world press. We maintain large research organizations and an around-the-clock news room and editorial organization to analyze the flood of information from all sources and make it useful to policymakers.

I am required by law — the National Security Act of 1947 to be specific — to develop the means to protect intelligence sources and methods. This is a serious responsibility and one I do not take lightly. Journalists take seriously their right to maintain the confidentiality of their sources — and have gone to jail rather than expose them.

Under our political system, I carry out my responsibilities as Director of Central Intelligence under the close scrutiny of the press — certainly a unique position among the intelligence chiefs of the world. But while intelligence should not be divorced from public opinion, neither should it be overly concerned with the daily shifts, the ups and downs, of public criticism or praise. This is more properly the concern of the elected representatives. Elected officials, whether in the White House or in Congress, must stay closely attuned to the public's wishes. We in intelligence must be responsive to the President and Congress. We receive the public's direction through them. That is why we welcome congressional and presidential oversight. That our actions are reviewed and approved by the public's representatives gives them a legitimacy they would not otherwise have in our open society.

The press has an enormous impact on public opinion and, therefore, on policy decisions. Surveys show that most Americans receive news concerning their government from the media; two-thirds of our citizens listen exclusively to television for their news. Thus, journalists exercise considerable power and influence. That power must be accompanied by a strong sense of responsibility. I am *not* persuaded that a journalist must print any alleged intelligence information he or she receives because "someone else will print it anyway." Nor am I convinced by the argument that if a reporter obtains some information, it is then correct to assume our adversaries' intelligence organizations must also have it. These are facile justifications.

The 1970s were a very trying period for us in intelligence. The intense scrutiny by the press, while harmful to morale, did have one valuable result – the establishment of new, and the strengthening of old, oversight procedures. Again, I want to emphasize that we welcome this; it makes us stronger. The press is another means of ensuring checks and balances, *if* reporting is accurate and fair. But I would ask you to keep in mind that irresponsible exposure in the press of alleged intelligence operations – correct or incorrect – creates very real problems for us.

We must protect our sources and methods and often cannot correct inaccurate stories. False stories or partial truths send wrong signals to those who might choose to work with us. Allied intelligence services question cooperating with us out of fear their own programs could be compromised. Our own officers are also affected. An intelligence officer will not take necessary risks if he or she fears the sources or programs they are responsible for could be exposed in the press. And, as you know, timidity whether by a reporter or an intelligence officer breeds failure.

This is not to say there can never be a dialogue between intelligence and the press. I have witnessed admirable restraint and judgment by journalists. The American press, unlike the Australian press, did not sensationalize the absolutely false allegations that CIA had been involved in the illegal activities of the Nugan Hand Bank. Nor, as far as I am aware, has any U.S. newspaper ever reprinted the long lists of alleged intelligence agents published in the infamous *Covert Action Information Bulletin*. I have been gratified by the readiness of journalists to carefully consider withholding publication of information which could jeopardize national interests, and by their skill in reporting a story in a manner which meets the public need as they perceive it, yet minimizes potential damage to intelligence sources. The trick is to recognize the potential for damage and to consult on how it might be minimized. We are anxious to do this. And since my appointment as Director, I have seen a growing understanding by the press of our efforts to improve the quality, timeliness, and reliability of the analysis we provide to our national leaders.

Unfortunately, inaccurate stories still appear; some of which damage our credibility and ability to function at the highest level of performance. Recent stories that the CIA was reluctant to get involved or take seriously the investigation into the shooting of the Pope and that the President was dissatisfied with our role are untrue. I have to wonder what the motivations are for these stories. Likewise, I think the press sometimes exhibits a very selective perspective. Meaningful analysis of the recent executions of 15 labor, bar association, and other community leaders in Suriname and this regime's growing ties to Cuba did not occur until about a month after the first reports of the slaying. Would the same delay have occurred if such violations had taken place, for instance, in El Salvador? In February of this year, when five men in Miami were convicted of conspiring with Cuban government officials to smuggle drugs into southern Florida, I was surprised there were no reports in such national newspapers as the *New York Times* or *Washington Post* despite the fact one of the men testified that the Cuban government planned to "Fill up the United States with drugs."

An example of good reporting is *The Wall Street Journal*'s articles on yellow rain. They were the only major national newspaper to treat this important issue in a hard-hitting manner. In general, the press has adequately and fairly reported on technology transfer. But press reporting concerning the alleged dispute between DIA and CIA analysis of the rate of increase in Soviet military spending was overblown. I believe the press has not conveyed the force, scope, and intensity of the Cuban threat in the Caribbean and Central America. This has not received the indepth, extensive reporting it deserves. The connection between the narcotics trade, terrorism in the destabilization of governments and organizations, and support of insurgencies is a story which can bring Pulitzer Prize. The media do extensive reporting and analysis on the Soviet missile and conventional military threat which we spend hundreds of billions of dollars to counter. But the big story out there is what could be the more lethal process which in less than a decade has positioned Soviet power on the southern flank of China, on both sides of the oil fields in the Middle East, at choke points in the world sea lanes, and at our very doorstep in the Caribbean and Central America.

I find a continuing misunderstanding of what we in CIA are trying to accomplish when we review former and current employees' manuscripts before publication. We are not attempting to prevent unflattering or unfavorable comments from being published. We are only concerned that classified information be protected. It is true that sometimes the process takes longer than we or the author may like. Reviewing a 600-page novel filled with references to fictionalized intelligence operations can be a laborious process. Nearly 75 percent of all manuscripts we have reviewed have been cleared without objection. Most manuscripts are reviewed in fewer than thirty days; some in a matter of hours to accommodate a press deadline. This is not the perspective that readers find in press accounts. I would hope that the same skepticism applied to the statements of public officials be applied to those few disgruntled former employees peddling their books. These authors may not be in a position to judge whether an intelligence source or method needs protecting. I also would hope that a reporter's skepticism would extend to those with tales of impropriety – the whistleblowers. Some of these people may have legitimate complaints, but they are obligated to first bring their stories to the appropriate oversight committees or internally to their inspector general. Unless the whistleblower first follows these proper routes of criticism, he or she cannot be considered a responsible citizen nor should the reporter take their tale at face value.

Within the constraints imposed by my legal responsibilities to protect legitimate secrets, we do make attempts to respond to queries from the press. Every question posed by a reporter that comes into my public affairs office at CIA is thoroughly researched before possible responses are considered. I am sure newsmen and women feel they receive more "unable to help" and "no comment" responses from us than from any other government agency and it must be frustrating for them. But we do try to contribute to the accuracy of a story whenever we can.

I appreciate the opportunity to speak to you tonight. If there is one thought I would like to leave with you it is that we in intelligence and journalists share the common responsibility of protecting sources. Perhaps this tie can lead us to a better understanding of each others concerns. We would both benefit.

◆ ◆ ◆

INTELLIGENCE AND THE PRESS:
STRIKING A BALANCE

What is most striking about Casey's frequent speeches to press groups like this one is not merely the content of his speeches, but the very fact that he made them. Despite the torrent of national security leaks – and the vicious personal attacks to which he was subjected – Casey continued to search for a workable relationship between the press and the intelligence community.

For obvious reasons, the damage done to our national security by unauthorized leaks is more visible to the intelligence chief than to any other senior official. As the years went by, Casey became disturbed, worried, appalled, and finally furious by the extent of this damage. Moreover, as Director of Central Intelligence he was legally charged with protecting U.S. intelligence "sources and methods" – and thus responsible for doing something about the problem of leaks. In this speech Casey offers his perception of the proper relationship between the press and intelligence.

Good afternoon. It is a privilege and a pleasure for me to be with you today to discuss national security and the media. National security has many dimensions but I will focus on one element – intelligence – which impacts military forces and weapons acquisition, terrorism and regional conflicts, diplomacy and arms control, and virtually every other aspect of our foreign and defense policies.

The work of the American intelligence community is much like yours. We both work at the collection and proper presentation of accurate information that leads to informed judgments. Our officers overseas, like your correspondents, work day and night to obtain vital information. Like many skilled journalists, CIA analysts send hours poring over reports from many different sources in order to present facts in the context of broader events and issues.

Neither you nor the CIA can do its job without having sources and methods of collecting information, which often must remain unidentified to the public. I am required by law to protect the sources and methods by which we collect intelligence. This is a serious responsibility and one

Address to the American Society of Newspaper Editors, Washington, D.C.,
April 9, 1986.

I do not take lightly. You in journalism take just as seriously the confidentiality and protection of your sources.

Our country has invested time, effort, and talent over many years and spent many billions of dollars to develop methods of collecting the information needed to assess missiles and other weapons aimed at the us, to determine the intentions and vulnerabilities of our adversaries, to develop effective defenses and countermeasures, to protect our citizens and installations around the world from terrorist attacks, and to assist our diplomats. Good intelligence sources are critical to our national security, including our hopes of effective arms control and the safety and liberty of our citizens. Secrecy and confidentiality as to how and through whom we collect information is essential to our effectiveness.

We must classify and restrict the circulation of information about how and where we collect intelligence, and of the reports and assessments based on that intelligence if they might reveal or compromise our sources or methods. The KGB and other hostile intelligence services spend billions of dollars each year in their effort to acquire this information. The unauthorized publication of this restricted information hands to our adversaries on a silver platter information that their spies, their researchers, and their satellites are working 24 hours a day to uncover and use against us.

In recent years, publication of classified information by the media has destroyed or seriously damaged intelligence sources of the highest value. Every method of acquiring intelligence we have – our agents, our relationships with friendly intelligence and security services, our photographic and electronic capabilities, the information we get from communications – has been damaged by the publication of unauthorized disclosures.

Stories in both the print and electronic media have shown, sometimes in great detail, how to counter capabilities in which we have invested billions of dollars and many years of creative talent and effort. This, time and time again, has enabled those hostile to us to abort huge investments, to conceal and otherwise deny us information critical to our defense, and to deprive us of the ability to protect our citizens from terrorist attack. Leakers are costing the taxpayers millions and even billions of dollars – and, more important, putting Americans abroad as well as our country itself at risk.

We need to protect our sources and methods, but we do not wish to limit you in any way from getting the information the public needs and should have. I believe we are all working toward the same goal – maintaining the best and most free country in the world. We fully support and admire your commitment to inform the public, and the dedication and ingenuity with which you meet that commitment.

But we do believe we all have responsibilities we must balance. We have a very delicate and difficult balance to strike. I think Mrs. Katherine Graham got it right in a very thoughtful and constructive speech she made on terrorism and the media at the Guildhall in London last December.

She told how a television network and a columnist had obtained information that we were reading the messages of people arranging the bombing of the U.S. Embassy in Beirut. Shortly after their public disclosure that traffic stopped. This undermined our efforts to capture the terrorist leaders and eliminated a source of information about future attacks.

Mrs. Graham went on to say, I quote:

> This kind of result, albeit unintentional, points up the necessity for full cooperation wherever possible between the media and the authorities. When the media obtains especially sensitive information, we are willing to tell the authorities what we have learned and what we plan to report. And while reserving the right to make the final decision ourselves, we are anxious to listen to arguments about why information should not be aired. [The media] want to do nothing that would endanger human life or national security. We are willing to cooperate with the authorities in withholding information that could have those consequences.

I submit these principles apply with the same force to costly intelligence capabilities as they do to targets threatened by terrorism.

I have experienced and witnessed admirable restraint by journalists. I have been gratified by the readiness of many of you to carefully consider our own interest, sometimes withholding publication of information which could jeopardize national interests or, more frequently, treating or presenting a story in a manner which meets the public need, yet minimizes the potential for damage, and finally, your readiness to consult on how damage might be minimized. We are always ready and available on short notice to help on that.

I hasten to add, however, that the most effective way of preventing these types of leaks is to increase discipline within the government. That's where the primary responsibility rests. The inability to control sensitive information is destructive of the morale of people who do keep secrets, as well as damaging to our security. During the last several years, the President has emphasized the special obligation federal workers have to protect the classified information with which they are entrusted. We have increased our efforts to uncover those who violate this trust. And we are studying whether new laws are needed to deal with federal employees who decide on their own to disclose classified information.

When our intelligence assessments reach the media, whether authorized or not, we are frequently asked to produce the evidence which supports our judgments. Sometimes we can, but much more often we cannot without jeopardizing our sources and teaching our adversaries how to deny information in the future.

If we can't reveal our evidence or disclose our sources, why should policymakers or the public trust intelligence assessments? Our primary credibility comes from the accuracy and reliability and integrity of the people and the process by which they are produced. Our intelligence products are the work of career professionals based on information from a wide variety of sources and the most sophisticated and advanced technology in the world: photography, space satellites, electronics, acoustics, communications collectors, seismic, and other sensors.

Our national intelligence estimates are the result of long hours of preparation and debate by analysts from the DIA, CIA, NSA, Army, Navy, Marines, and Air Force intelligence and other components of the intelligence community. Their work is reviewed by the chiefs of each of these components sitting as the National Foreign Intelligence Board and charged with seeing that the relevant information and judgments held by their organizations are available. As the Board's chairman, I see that any substantiated dissenting or alternative view is reflected so that policymakers have the benefit of the full range of opinion in the intelligence community.

In a world where the Soviet bloc spends lavishly on new weapons and works aggressively to expand its control and influence at the expense of free nations, and where sovereign states, like Libya, use terrorism as an instrument of foreign policy, it is increasingly essential that the public learn what sorts of challenges their government is facing.

We make extraordinary efforts to respond to requests from both the executive and legislative branches to sanitize or declassify intelligence information and assessments in order to make them available to the public. Perhaps the best example of the intelligence community's contribution to the public debate on important issues of national security has been the DIA's annual publication, *Soviet Military Power*, which is closely coordinated by CIA. Last summer the intelligence community at the request of the White House and Congress, sanitized and presented in open testimony our assessment of Soviet strategic forces.

More frequently, CIA material is declassified for use in other government publications, such as the State Department's White Papers on Terrorism, and two recent publications by the Defense Department on Soviet acquisition of Western technology. Whenever intelligence is used as the source for unclassified publications, it is important that we stay within the evidence to maintain our integrity and to protect the policymaker.

This orderly and cautious approach to the public use of intelligence is guided by the highest authorities and involves the close participation of intelligence professionals. When we promise our sources confidentiality, we in many cases literally hold their lives in our hands. As we respect the right of the press to gather and publish news and applaud your exposure of waste, corruption, and other misconduct, we hope you will respect our right and duty to keep the nations's legitimate secrets. Among the thousands of editorials about the failings and shortcomings of government employees, I can recall few, if any, that took a public servant to task for illegally revealing classified information. Yet classified leaks are at least as damaging as the cost overruns, conflicts of interest, and other types of malfeasance so properly criticized by the press.

We are eager to develop better understanding and closer cooperation between you in the working press, who perform such a vital function in our society, and the intelligence community, which plays and essential role in protecting this nation.

America needs a free, vigorous press and it needs a superior intelligence service. We are both serving our country in vital and fundamental matters.

◆ ◆ ◆

HALTING UNAUTHORIZED LEAKS:
THE NEED FOR SECRECY

One of Casey's favorite aphorisms was, "The hardest thing to prove is something that's self-evident." The notion that unauthorized leaks damage U.S. security is a case in point. Either you cannot prove it at all, or you cannot prove it without make the damage worse. As he says in this speech, "It is difficult to discuss the specific damage to this nation's ability to protect itself without confirming the accuracy of information which has been delivered through the media, thus removing any doubts that remain in the minds of the KGB or the terrorists."

In this crucial but little-noticed speech, Casey removed any lingering doubt that journalists who lived off leaks had become a special target. The Director of Central Intelligence was out to stop them. To "regain control" over national secrets, Casey proposed a four-step program: 1) To "tighten discipline" among U.S. government employees who use classified information. 2) To improve cooperation between the media and the government on stories which put intelligence sources and methods at risk. 3) To establish that restrictions on the misuse of sensitive and properly classified information "cannot be violated with impunity." 4) To enforce and perhaps tighten laws Congress has enacted to protect classified information.

That at least some journalists who live off leaks would attempt to somehow retaliate against Casey – for example by smearing him so thoroughly that in the future no senior U.S. official would dare stand up to them – is self-evident. It is, therefore, impossible to prove.

Although I haven't been here for fifteen years, I've spent lots of time at a PLI podium and I'm glad to be back to speak to you today about the extremely delicate and critical relationship between the media and our national security. The responsibility to protect intelligence sources and methods which the National Security Act explicitly places on the Director of Central Intelligence makes this a matter of great and continuing interest to me. I want to be very careful and precise in addressing it because too frequently, when I speak of the damage from publishing clas-

---

Address to the Communications Law Conference of the Practicing Law Institute, New York City, November 14, 1986.

sified information, I find myself accused of wanting to demolish the First Amendment and trying to muzzle our free press.

To head off that reaction, let me say that I cherish the First Amendment and admire the diligence and ingenuity of the working press. I applaud exposure of waste, inefficiency, and corruption by the media and in the courts. I salute and support ferreting out and publishing the information the people need to be well informed about events around the world as well as the activities of their democratic government. In this, I speak from forty years of experience as a friend and supporter of the media and an active principal in publishing and broadcasting.

Unauthorized disclosures of classified information have become a cancer which undermines presidential authority to conduct foreign policy, our national security process, and our intelligence capabilities. It is sapping the morale and ethic of those in government who do respect and comply with our security regulations.

In recent months, publication of classified information by the media has destroyed or seriously damaged intelligence sources of the highest value. Every method we have of acquiring intelligence – our agents, the assistance we get from other security services, our photographic and electronic capabilities, the information we get from communications – has been damaged by the publication of unauthorized disclosures.

Stories in both the print and electronic media have shown, sometimes in great detail, how to counter capabilities in which we have invested billions of dollars and many years of creative talent and effort. This, time and again, has enabled our adversaries to abort huge investments, to conceal and otherwise deny us information critical to our defense, and to deprive us of the ability to protect our citizens from terrorist attack. Leakers are costing the taxpayers millions and even billions of dollars – and more important, putting americans abroad, as well as our country itself, at risk.

Our country has invested many years of effort, the talent of hundreds of thousands of our citizens, and billions of dollars of intelligence. And the nation has gotten an excellent return on its investment. We have and continue to develop methods of collecting the information needed to assess missiles and other weapons aimed at us, and determine the intentions and vulnerabilities of our adversaries so that we can respond with effective defenses and countermeasures, protect our citizens and installations around the world from terrorism, and assist our diplomats and policymakers by telling them the cold hard truth about events around the world that affect U.S. interests. Good intelligence is critical to our national security, critical to our hopes of effective arms control, and critical to the safety and liberty of our citizens.

American intelligence collects information through a variety of advanced technological systems, through the cooperative efforts of our allies, and also through sensitive dealings with people around the world who want to help us, sometimes at great risk. If the details of how we collect intelligence are publicized or can be deduced through the information these sources provide, the agents will be arrested and perhaps executed, our adversaries will take steps to neutralize our technical collection capabilities, and our allies, as they lose confidence in our ability to protect their information, will refuse to share it with us. Secrecy and confidentiality about how and through whom we collect information is essential to our effectiveness.

To protect our national security and our intelligence sources, we must classify and restrict the circulation not only of information about how and where we collect intelligence but of the reports and assessments based on that intelligence if they might reveal or compromise our sources and methods. The KGB and other hostile intelligence services each year spend billions of dollars trying to acquire this information. But the authorized publication of restricted information hands such information to our adversaries on a silver platter.

Damage to national security from broadcasting secrets in news far exceeds that resulting from espionage. Make no mistake about it, the publication of these secrets helps those who work against our nation's interests — be they Soviets, terrorists, or drug dealers. It is vital that the public understand what is going on, why it is happening, and what needs to be done about it.

We have clearly reached the point where we must address this risk to our fundamental security. We can no longer tolerate unauthorized disclosures that increasingly debilitate sources of intelligence which Congress appropriates billions of dollars to develop and maintain. Such unauthorized disclosures deprive us of the ability to identify and defend against the tens of thousands of devastating warheads which are targeted at us and our allies, and protect the organized and determined terrorist gangs and narcotics rings that threaten innocent citizens all over the world.

It is difficult to discuss the specific damage to this nation's ability to protect itself without confirming the accuracy of information which has been delivered through the media and removing any doubts that might remain in the minds of the KGB or the terrorists. I can say that some of our sources have not been heard from after their information has been published in the U.S. press. Others have decided that cooperating with the United States is too risky. Leaders and intelligence services of our closest allies have told us that if we can't tighten up, they will have to pull back on cooperation with us because they have had enough of reading the information they provide in the U.S. media.

Four steps are necessary to regain control over our national secrets: We must tighten discipline among U.S. government employees who use classified information. We must develop better cooperation between the media and the government on stories which put intelligence sources and methods at risk. We must establish that restrictions on the misuse of sensitive and properly classified information cannot be violated with impunity. And we must enforce and perhaps tighten laws Congress has enacted to protect classified information.

The first step is to increase discipline within the government. The inability to control sensitive information is destructive of the morale of people who do keep secrets, as well as damaging to our security. Federal workers have a special obligation to protect the classified information with which they are entrusted. Efforts to uncover and discipline those who violate this trust need to be strengthened.

The government official, military officer, or contractor employee who has been cleared for access to classified material is responsible for keeping the secrets he is given. There is no room for doubt about this. Each person who is cleared must sign a nondisclosure agreement which spells out his or her responsibilities in significant detail. When these individuals discuss classified information with unauthorized persons, there is little likelihood that they do not understand what they are doing. Still, we have allowed an atmosphere to develop where many believe there is little risk and no penalty for violating the trust placed in them by their nation.

Within the government, the effort to stop and penalize the unauthorized disclosure of classified intelligence has been weak and fragmented. It needs to be tightened up and speeded up. Unauthorized disclosures need to be identified as soon as they are published. Investigations must be swift and thorough. Disciplinary action appropriate to the violation needs to be applied to deter others from similar violations. The FBI has established a unit of specialized people to improve this process and in recent months more leaders in federal service have been identified and removed than any like period I can recall.

Too much information is classified. We will work to reduce the body of classified information, but that can't be done overnight. It will take time. In acting against unauthorized disclosures we should focus on really damaging and critical disclosures.

Even as we improve discipline within the government, the media will continue to come into possession of information which, if published, can jeopardize lives, damage national security and the international relationships and reputation for reliability of our nation. Many media professionals recognize a responsibility to weigh these dangers before rushing into print or onto the air waves.

Ben Bradlee, in an op-ed piece in the *Washington Post* of June 8, 1986, said: "We do consult with the government regularly about sensitive stories and we do withhold stories for national security reasons, far more than the public might think. The *Post* has withheld information from more than a dozen stories so far this year for these reasons." We give Ben Bradlee high marks for that, but we can't fully agree when he goes on to say: "We don't allow the government – or anyone else – to decide what we should print. That is our job."

No one can tell a publisher what he must print. On the other hand, Congress has enacted legislation which makes it unlawful to disclose or publish certain categories of information – and the media, like everybody else, must adhere to the law.

The First Amendment to the Constitution is cited to make the point that the media should be the sole judge of what may or may not be printed on national security matters. The public's right to know is not absolute. Where national security and foreign policy are at issue, the First Amendment permits determinations by appropriate governmental authorities that certain information should not be released into the public domain. This is what the classification system is all about. When the sanctity of classified information is protected by a duly enacted criminal statute, those who would publish or otherwise disclose proceed at their own risk.

In the *Pentagon Papers* case, the Supreme Court ruled that the First Amendment outlawed prior restraint, but Justice Douglas and Justice

White, in concurring opinions, supported the law imposing criminal penalties on the publication of information on communications intelligence.

That statute was passed shortly after World War II to protect classified information about communications intelligence from being "knowingly and willfully" published or in any other way made available to an unauthorized person. Congress carefully limited the application of this prohibition to communications intelligence, which it called "a small degree of classified matter, a category which is both vital and vulnerable to almost a unique degree." Our reading of Japanese and German communications had brought victory in World War II much earlier and saved many thousands of lives and Congress clearly regarded communications intelligence as one of our best chances to learn about other nations' military plans and of warnings of military attacks against us.

Today, as media disclosure deprives us of our best source of warning of terrorist and other threats, we cannot justify failure to use a statute enacted by Congress to protect this sensitive and irreplaceable communication information. Justice Byron White wrote in his concurring opinion of the *Pentagon Papers* case that the language in the communications statute is "precise". He warned that "newspapers are presumably now on full notice of the position of the United States and must face the consequences if they publish."

I believe it will be necessary for the Congress in their next legislative session to consider more explicit restrictions on unauthorized disclosure of other types of properly classified information.

Legislation of this type would not be unusual or precedent-setting. In recent years, Congress has recognized the need for statutory protection of national security information, and has acted accordingly. In 1980, Congress passed the Classified Information Procedures Act to protect against disclosures of classified information by defendants in criminal trials, through "graymail" or otherwise.

In 1982 Congress passed the Intelligence Identities Protection Act that protects our intelligence officers and sources overseas. This occurred after the efforts of a small group of Americans to destroy the ability of our intelligence agencies to operate clandestinely by disclosing the names of covert intelligence agents, led to the murder of a CIA station chief in Greece.

Because existing statutes were enacted at different times to address different specific purposes, we have a patchwork of statutes applicable to certain kinds of disclosures in certain circumstances – diplomatic codes, atomic energy restricted data, agent identities, and information concerning communications intelligence.

Last year the District Court in the *Morison* case held that the espionage statutes are not limited to classic espionage in the sense of disclosures to foreign agents but are applicable to unauthorized disclosures to the press.

There has been a great hue and cry that *Morison* is not a spy. That's bunk. Nobody said he was a spy. He was convicted of violating a section of the law which prohibits the disclosure of classified U.S. government information to unauthorized persons. That's exactly what he did. We will see what happens on appeal.

While I believe the *Morison* decision to be a correct and appropriate interpretation of the law, I recognize that it has stirred up an enormous amount of debate and controversy about the proper reach of the espionage statues. I believe the national interest would best be served by a new statute which unequivocally expressed Congress's intent to punish unauthorized disclosures of classified information.

What is needed is a bill making it a criminal offense willfully to disclose classified information to persons not authorized to receive such information. The bill should not be a strict liability statute, but should apply to persons who intentionally disclose classified information, knowing or having reason to know that the information is classified. Certainly it should apply to government employees and others with authorized access to classified information; that is, individuals who voluntarily undertake a "trust" relationship with the government. If classification to protect national security is to have any meaning, it should apply to information which can be shown to have been willfully and knowingly taken and published from papers properly classified.

◆ ◆ ◆

RESPONSIBLE JOURNALISM: LIVES ARE AT STAKE

Of all the allegations made by The Washington Post*'s Bob Woodward in his book* Veil, *published in the fall of 1987, none generated more public uproar than Woodward's allegation that Casey himself was responsible for the attempted assassination in Beirut on March 8, 1985, of the Shiite terrorist Sheikh Mohammed Hussein Fadlallah. On that date a car packed with high explosives was driven to a Beirut suburb about fifty yards from Fadlallah's high-rise apartment. The bomb went off killing eighty people and wounding scores more; Fadlallah himself was unhurt. Woodward alleged in* Veil *— as he had earlier alleged in his newspaper — that Casey, in violation of U.S. law prohibiting assassination, personally had "ordered" the car-bombing, which in Woodward's version of events was staged by Saudi Arabia at the U.S.'s (that is, at Casey's) behest.*

This speech — delivered publicly more than one year before publication of Veil *— shatters Woodward's version of events. To grasp just how, it is necessary first, to outline the key points Casey makes in this speech and, second, to outline the key points as written in* Veil.

Here's what happened as Casey tells it:

1) Woodward called the CIA's press officer and claimed to have information that the Agency, in effect, was responsible for the car-bombing.

2) Woodward was told that the story was untrue.

3) Further, he was urged — begged — not to print such an allegation on the grounds that, if published, some people would assume it to be accurate; that among these people could be Mideast terrorists who might then retaliate against the U.S. or against U.S. citizens. It is here that Casey warned Woodward that if he went forward with the allegation he (Woodward) "might wind up with blood on his hands."

4) Woodward published the allegations in the Washington Post, *on May 12, 1985.*

5) One month after publication (on June 14, 1985) a U.S. civilian aircraft — TWA Flight 847, en route from Athens to Rome — was hijacked with 153 people on board. The plane wound up in Beirut, and in the course of a 17-day ordeal the hijackers murdered a U.S. Navy sailor

Address to the American Jewish Committee, Washington, D.C., May 15, 1986.

*who was on board, Robert Stethem. In announcing their murder of Mr.
Stethem, the hijackers claimed publicly to be retaliating for the supposed
U.S.-sponsored car-bombing the previous month.*

Now, here's the way Woodward recounts these events in Veil:

*1) He called the CIA's press officer and claimed to have information
that the Agency, in effect, was responsible for the car-bombing.*

*2) He was urged — begged — not to publish the story on the grounds
that it would trigger retaliation; this was when Casey himself warned
Woodward that he might "have blood on his hands."*

*3) One month later TWA Flight 847 was hijacked. During the course
of this 17-day ordeal a U.S. Navy sailor, Robert Stethem, "was killed."*

As any reader of Veil *will discover, Woodward's account of these
events is not as straightforward as this summary suggests. The material
itself is scattered throughout the text in bits and pieces, and to fully grasp
Woodward's account a reader needs to flip back and forth from page to
page and even from chapter to chapter.*

*Nevertheless, when the whole of Woodward's account is pulled
together and matched against the Casey speech the gap that emerges is
rather striking:*

*1) Woodward does indeed report that he was urged — begged — not to
publish his story. But he fails to mention that the CIA's press officer,
and then Casey himself, both denied that the U.S. had anything whatever
to do with the assassination attempt.*

*2) Woodward's account of the TWA Flight 847 hijacking is uncon-
nected to his account of the Fadlallah car-bombing. Indeed, the two accounts appear in different chapters of the book.*

*3) While Woodward does report that Mr. Stethem "was killed" during
the course of the hijacking ordeal, he doesn't report that the murderers
said publicly that their vicious act was in retaliation for the alleged U.S.-
sponsored car-bombing the previous month.*

4) Thus the account in Veil *leaves the casual reader unaware that
Casey's warning to Woodward — that he would wind up with blood on
his hands — turned out to be tragically prophetic.*

*Of course, these differing accounts still leave unanswered the key
question: Did Casey violate the law by ordering up the assassination of
Fadlallah? This brings us to the final distortion of Woodward's version.*

*In his 1986 speech, Casey reports that following publication of the al-
legations by Woodward in the* Washington Post, *these allegations were*

investigated by the House Select Committee on Intelligence. Moreover, reports Casey, the committee – the majority of whose members, to put it mildly, were not among the Director's biggest fans – publicly concluded that "no complicity of direct or indirect involvement can be established with respect to the March 8 bombing in Beirut."

Yet in his book – published more than one year after the car-bombing, public release of the House Select Committee report, and Casey's own public speech – Woodward chooses not to include this key finding.

How, then, was it possible for Woodward to get away – at least for a while – with such a monumental lie? Part of the answer is in the manner in Veil *was launched by the publishing company, Simon and Schuster. Simon and Schuster short-circuited the normal process of distributing advance copies to members of the press and to those individuals with sufficient knowledge or expertise to comb through the text and uncover whatever distortions or inaccuracies there might be. While Simon and Schuster justified its extraordinary decision to forego the normal checking-for-accuracy procedures on grounds of wanting to prevent leaks (!), in fact the company's objective was to remove any possibility that the book's distortions and inaccuracies would be uncovered and the book therefore discredited.*

Alas, the publisher succeeded. When Veil *was sprung on the public with one of the most extensive, and costly, sales blitzes in publishing history, no one in a position to refute Woodward's allegations had read it. And by the time such people had read* Veil *– and to their dismay found scores of distortions and inaccuracies in addition to the ones surrounding the Fadlallah car-bombing episode – the publicity blitz was over, and the damage done.*

Ladies and gentlemen, it's a great privilege for me to be speaking before the 80th anniversary the Annual Meeting of the American Jewish Committee. This afternoon I have been asked to speak to the problem of international terrorism – a scourge that increasingly is beginning to dominate our lives and times. But before I begin, let me say that it is a special privilege to appear before a group that has done so much itself to fight this epidemic of violence. I know that Rabbi Tanenbaum and the American Jewish Committee have been at the forefront of the effort to mobilize a broad national constituency in this country in support of the Administration. Let me tell you that those of us inside government need your help and appreciate your efforts. Terrorism is a cancer that is spreading. In 1983 we recorded about 500 international terrorist incidents; last year the number increased to about 800. The United States and its friends and allies continue to be the primary targets. The number of persons killed or injured in 1985 exceeded 2,200 – more than any other year, more even than the terrible toll in 1983 when the U.S. and French contingents of the peacekeeping force in Lebanon were bombed. The rising casualty rate reflects the increased use of large bombs by terrorists as well as greater willingness to harm innocent bystanders through indiscriminate attacks.

The capability of the terrorist to kill, maim, kidnap, and torture his victims has been enormously enhanced by state sponsorship. Libya, Syria, and Iran use terrorism as an instrument of foreign policy. They hire and support established terrorist organizations, of which there are many around the world. These countries make their officials, their embassies, their diplomatic pouches, their communications channels, and their territory a safe haven for these criminals available to plan, direct and execute bombings, assassinations, kidnappings, and other terrorist operations.

They have operated largely in the Middle East and in Europe. Today they are now spreading their wings into this hemisphere. The threat to U.S. facilities, personnel, and interest is particularly high in Colombia, Ecuador, and Peru where strongly anti U.S. terrorist groups are active.

The link between Libyan - and Cuban-sponsored terrorism and Nicaraguan-sponsored terrorism is large and growing larger. For some years, the Libyans have been supporting the Sandinista government in Nicaragua with something like $100 million a year. You'll remember how Nicaraguan-supported insurgents in El Salvador killed our Marines at a cafe in the capital of that country.

We now see Nicaragua training young men for violence and subversion, sending them into South America – into Colombia for the attack on the Palace of Justice in Bogota and as far south as Chile. Young men from Latin American countries are being sent to Libya for training in the terrorist camps there and then brought back to be planted among the population in Central America, Venezuela, and Ecuador. If the Sandinista regime consolidates itself, we can expect Managua to become the Beirut of the Western Hemisphere.

There is a Soviet connection and support for all this. While some refer to that connection as shadowy, it seems very real to me. The states I have just mentioned are not necessarily close allies of Moscow, but they share a fundamental hostility to the West. The Soviets, who hold no moral objections to the use of terrorism and see much of the unrest it creates as ultimately beneficial to their foreign policy objectives, do not participate in any international efforts to block terrorism or to join in multilateral efforts to combat it. In backing revolutionary causes against established governments, it is largely a matter of indifference to the Soviets whether terrorist tactics are used as long as the groups that commit these acts attack non-Soviet or non-bloc targets. And Soviet support for international terrorism comes packaged in a variety of ways ranging from direct training of terrorist personnel to political backing and funding for states actively engaged in sponsoring terrorism.

The East Europeans, almost certainly with Soviet knowledge and support, provide safe havens, transit privileges, and movement of weapons bombs for terrorists. Bulgaria's state trading organization "Kintex" – which is essentially a state smuggling operation – and Czechoslovakia's comparable organization "Omnipol," are among the most prominent companies whose weapons eventually have appeared in terrorist hands.

Let me now turn to the problems that U.S. intelligence analysts and counterterrorism policymakers face as they seek to tackle the problem of international terrorism. You've all heard an endless stream of commentary calling for a much greater intelligence effort against terrorism. I couldn't agree more. But it is also important for you to know that we have made a remarkable amount of progress over the past few years.

In order to prevent terrorist plans or disrupt their activities, we need information about them. But the very nature of terrorist groups and their activities makes this task extremely complicated. Terrorist groups are very small, making penetration a very difficult task for police or intelligence agents. Moreover, the operating life of any single group of terrorists is often no more than a few years. Likewise, typical terrorist leaders have a relatively short business life.

So how do we go about it? First, we are acquiring as much information as we can about terrorist groups including *modus operandi*, organizational structure, personnel support, financial and communications arrangements, and their relationships with other groups or state sponsors. Much of this is just hard research, compiling a large data base and attempting to fill in the gaps. It is not very glamorous and people who do it do not capture the headlines. But it is the foundation upon which the U.S. counterterrorism effort rests. Continuing collection and analysis enables us to improve our ability to detect trends in terrorism operations, upgrade security in areas most likely at risk, and determine vulnerabilities of terrorist groups. We have put in place a system of rapid communications to gather assessments, have reports tested by experts throughout our government, and pass conclusions and warnings quickly to the point of the threat.

Action based on our intelligence, along with that of other friendly countries including moderate Arab governments, has been taken to prevent a great many planned terrorist attacks around the world. The rate of effective warning is increasing, rising to 26 during the month of April this year.

Sometimes we fall just heart-breakingly short of success, as was the case with the Berlin nightclub bombing last month. You have heard the President's statement outlining the evidence for the Libyan complicity in the Berlin bombing. We also have compelling evidence of Libyan involvement in attempts to attack other U.S. targets, several of which were designed to cause maximum casualties similar to the Berlin bombing:

◆ France expelled two members of the Libyan's People's Bureau in Paris for their involvement in a planned attack on visa applicants waiting in line at the U.S. Embassy.

◆ France subsequently expelled two disgruntled Fatah Force 17 members recruited by Libya to conduct another operation against the United States in Paris.

◆ In early April, a Libyan-inspired plot to attack the U.S. Embassy in Beirut was aborted when the 107 mm rocket exploded on launch.

◆ Turkish police in late March arrested two Tunisians in Istanbul who claimed they were planning on behalf of the Libyans to use explosives against a U.S. target in Turkey; the operation was planned to inflict heavy casualties.

All in all, nearly fifty Libyan diplomats have been expelled recently from Spain, Italy, France and West Germany. In fact, so far this year we have reports of well over 35 Libyan-associated threats, including surveillance of planned attacks against U.S. personnel and facilities in Europe, Africa and Asia.

Together with the intelligence and security services of friendly countries, we have developed a worldwide counterterrorist network which functions through intelligence exchanges, training and technical support, and joining operations. The terrorists are everywhere, moving silently across borders and striking with as much stealth and surprise as they can manage. This apparatus must be able to follow them, pass word on their movements, pick them up or abort their plans, or otherwise defend against them.

We have become increasingly effective in this and our capabilities are improving. I take this occasion to further a necessary dialogue on how we can overcome what I consider the greatest single impediment to protecting our interests and our citizens from the scourge of international terrorism.

In recent years, publication of classified information by the media has destroyed or seriously damaged intelligence sources of the highest value. Every method we have of acquiring intelligence – our agents, our relationships with other security services, our photographic and electronic capabilities, the information we get from communications – has been damaged by the publication of unauthorized disclosures.

In recent weeks and months, a flood of information and misinformation has appeared in print and on the air waves. You've all seen it. Before the President spoke to our people and told them about the conclusive evidence that we had about Libyan direction of the attack on allied soldiers in the Berlin nightclub, major newspapers and news magazines published that Libyan communications were being read. The Libyans stopped using those communications and this is bound to put other peaceful citizens in jeopardy. This is a severe problem we must address if our fight against terrorism is to succeed.

This is a delicate and critical problem, and I want to be very careful and precise in addressing it. Let me first say that I yield to no one in my respect for the media and the people who work for them and for their function in our society. It has been my own personal activity in newspapers, books, magazines, and electronic broadcasting that has given me the capital to run a personal deficit for more than ten years in order to serve our country. I respect the diligence and ingenuity of the working press in gathering and publishing news and applaud its exposure of waste, inefficiency, corruption and other misconduct. In short, I speak from thirty years of experience as a friend, participant, and supporter of the media.

I have two points that I feel I must make at this time in order to discharge the obligation specifically placed on me by the law of our land to protect intelligence sources and methods. Put very simply, they are, first, that the media like everyone else must adhere to the law. Second, all of us have responsibilities to balance in carrying out its mission.

In the face of the new terrorism, now is the time to mutually address those responsibilities together in a serious and measured way. Congress, shortly after it established the National Security Agency to gather signals intelligence, in 1950 enacted a law which prohibits the publication of information about communications intelligence. There has been widespread violation of that law over recent weeks and months. Much damage has been done. Kay Graham, the publisher of the *Washington Post*, in a recent very thoughtful and constructive speech cited the kind of damage which we have sustained. She told how a television network and a columnist had obtained information that we were reading the messages of people arranging the bombing of the U.S. Embassy in Beirut. Shortly after this public disclosure, that traffic stopped. This undermined our efforts to capture the terrorist leaders and eliminated a source of information about future attacks.

Where there already has been public disclosure about communications intelligence, the law has been violated but the milk has been spilled. I would not, therefore, at this time favor action for these past offenses. But I strongly believe that if we are to protect our security as a nation and the safety of our citizens in this age of international terrorism and intercontinental missiles, the law now on the books to protect a very narrow segment of information – that dealing with communications intelligence – must be enforced.

There are other large areas of information about our intelligence, our national security, and our relationships with other nations which can and frequently should be published without violating any law. But there are situations in which many of us believe there is a responsibility, before rushing into print or onto the air waves, to weigh and consider the danger to life and limb of our citizens and others, and to the international relationships and the reputation for reliability of our nation.

The temptation to go beyond the facts and piece together and stretch fragments of information in order to make a publishable story, and sometimes in order to sensationalize, is a dangerous thing. It can and has cost lives. It can wrongly impair reputations and disrupt relationships critical to our national interest. Let me illustrate with a true story: During 1985, a well-known reporter called the information officers at the Central Intelligence Agency and told him he had a story that we had helped the security service of a friendly nation stage a car bombing of the headquarters of a terrorist organization which had resulted in death or injury to a large number of residents and passers-by in the neighborhood. Our officer told the reporter that his information was incorrect and that the CIA had no knowledge of and no involvement, direct or indirect, in the attack. He was also told that if he charged U.S. involvement, he might wind up with blood on his hands. The story was run in his newspaper. It got around the world and created a false impression of U.S. involvement in the bombing.

The House Select Committee on Intelligence investigated the matter and concluded that "no complicity of direct or indirect involvement can be established with respect to the March 8 bombing in Beirut." But this came too late. A month after the misleading story was published to the world, terrorists hijacked a TWA plane and its 153 passengers and took them to Beirut. When the hijackers shot and killed an American serviceman, they claimed it to be in retaliation for the bombing in Beirut in which the reporter had involved the CIA after the CIA's spokesman had denied to him any involvement, direct or indirect, in the bombing.

In putting this story together, the reporter had talks with officials in the executive branch and staffers of the Congress about collateral matters including our long-term practice of providing training and technical assistance to the security services of other countries in order to improve our capabilities and cooperation on counterintelligence and counterterrorism. This kind of assistance goes back many years. We are doing more of this to cope with today's intensified terrorist threat. This does not make us responsible for the consequences of law enforcement activities in other countries.

The reporter justified publishing the story by taking the view that this longstanding training somehow made us responsible for a particular action of the organization even though we had no knowledge of the action and no contact with those who carried it out.

This is a tragic story. There is enough blame for everyone involved to share. Government officials talked more than the rules permit on classified matters. The reporters ignored accurate information with which they were carefully, clearly, and honestly provided. They stretched the implications of scraps of information they gathered. We at the CIA either did not have time or were not fast enough in bringing the matter to the attention of management at the newspaper.

We all must do better. This is a dangerous and unpredictable world in which all of us must move with caution and responsibility. Certainly any responsible person would want to exercise special care to avoid setting in motion this kind of sequence of events.

In conclusion, I would like to emphasize that all of us have a very serious challenge in coping with a rapidly growing terrorist threat. We are eager to develop better understanding and closer cooperation with organizations like yours and others in the private sector who can make a contribution to developing polices and educating our people about this dangerous development.

I particularly applaud and encourage the interest and efforts of my good friend Rabbi Tanenbaum and of this organization to implement the public education aspects of Vice President Bush's Task Force report on combatting terrorism.

* * *

Chapter 4

Meeting the Challenges of a Rapidly Changing World

THE IMPLICATIONS OF STRUCTURAL CHANGE

Casey viewed CIA-sponsored conferences like this one on Structural Change as vital to the business of intelligence. He encouraged analysts to conceive such conferences, and made clear that when a good idea for a conference emerged, the money would be available.

Good morning, ladies and gentlemen, and welcome to this conference on the Economic and Security Implications of Structural Change. We thank all of you for spending the time these two days to share your ideas and thoughts with us.

Structural change can mean many things and I'm reminded of that as I note old friends on the program with whom I've had the privilege of working on different kinds of structural change.

There's Leo Cherne with whom I worked 45 years ago in analyzing a *proficient* structural change called industrial mobilization. In a few short years it brought the American economy out of the Great Depression and converted it into a prolific producer of weapons of war.

Then there's Charlie Kindelberger who, when we worked together with the OSS in London forty years ago, was producing another kind of structural change. He was dissecting the German war economy to select the bridges and the synthetic oil plants for the Allied Air Forces to knock

Address to the Conference on Structural Change, CIA Headquarters,
  Langley, Virginia, June 3, 1985.

down to immobilize German tanks and planes. Then a few years later, when we worked together on the Marshall Plan, he had switched gears to play a major role in reconstructing Europe.

Then there's a youngster named Pete Peterson who, when we were in the Nixon Administration fifteen years ago, did the first in-depth analysis in the American government to assess the implications of the Japanese trade and technology surge which had by then developed in part from economic and tax policies to which our keynote, Leo Cherne, had contributed as an economic advisor to Douglas MacArthur.

These activities and others in which many of you have been involved as actors or students have produced profound changes in the past few decades – changes on a scale that used to take centuries to unfold. Many of these changes are sparked by advances in technology, and the pace of that advancement keeps accelerating.

Some examples of this process come to mind: Following the vigorous growth and "economic miracles" of the Marshall Plan years, our West European allies have recently been experiencing painful combinations of sluggish growth, chronically high unemployment, and political conflict in depressed regions. Several factors underlie these adjustment problem:

- ◆ Lack of labor mobility.
- ◆ Disincentives for business to fire outmoded labor.
- ◆ The burdens of social spending and unemployed.
- ◆ The need for capital formation.

On the other hand, despite wartime devastation and population pressures, Japan and the newly industrialized countries of East Asia have accomplished one of history's most dramatic transformations in springing out of developing-country status.

In Japan, a different form of structural adjustment is needed – but it is a structural problem all the same:

- ◆ Excessive domestic savings relative to investment continue to force Japanese industry into export markets.
- ◆ Japanese domestic growth not related to foreign sales is lagging.

Along with the strength of the dollar, these make up the broader context of our problems with Japan.

I, for one, am not satisfied that we in government have focused on the problem of structural change and approached it as systematically as we should, in a way that leads to realistic policy options. I think it is and will continue to be one of our priority issues.

There are obvious constraints on what the intelligence community can realistically do in this area. Our priorities are often pulled by current policy needs, but we have got to do a better job of analyzing long-term issues – of not missing the forest for the trees in producing current intelligence.

For this reason, I strongly feel we need to take careful measure of the structural changes taking place in the world today, as well as the need for a feasibility of alternative forms of policy response and adjustment. Let there be no doubt about it, these changes and/or the absence of an appropriate policy response can and do affect the national home. They affect our ability to deal with countries overseas. And they will affect how this country fares over the next quarter-century.

An undertaking on this scale needs to have some order imposed on it. We need to know what the important questions are. We need to have enough of a grasp of the implications that we can set our priorities for analyzing them. We need to understand how the various parts of the problem interact. That is what I personally hope this conference will achieve.

And so, in welcoming you this morning, let me also challenge you. The issues and problems before you are not simple, and no simple answers should be forthcoming. But over the course of the next two days, I look to this distinguished group to shed some light on the many dimensions of structural change – on what they mean, and what we need to analyze and understand about them.

I think you will find the program an interesting one. I look for thorough exchanging of ideas, not a consensus. I want you all to speak candidly.

◆ ◆ ◆

THE GLOBAL POLITICAL CLIMATE AND THE MULTINATIONAL COMPANY: WHAT'S ON THE HORIZON?

Casey believed that the impact of economics, technology, and science on national security affairs was all too often underrated or even ignored. He beefed up the intelligence community's collection and analytic efforts in these fields, and insisted that military and political judgments be based on a grasp of these matters. In this speech he provides a clear summary of his (broad) perspective.

It is easy and costly and painful to be misunderstood, but it's more costly and painful to misunderstand the kind of world in which we have to operate. And we have not understood it as well as we must.

We have been quick to talk about the interdependence of the global economy and been slow to respond to it's imperatives or even recognize implications for our economic policies, our security requirements, our management practices and our competitive tactics.

From World War II until the early 1970s almost all our economic policies assumed a closed economy. The United States was the policy unity, the primary trading market. The outside world was only a complication to policy and a fractional add on to the market. If exports exceeded imports, then one might adjust one's estimates to account for what was called "net exports." And in discussions of monetary policy the term "Eurodollars" might occasionally be uttered. But by and large these were matters left to the experts and did not intrude into most policy discussions, whether in government or in the press.

Today it has become essential to think of the United States as an open economy. Any policy measure is now seen to have an immediate impact on money and trade flows, an impact that may either reinforce or, more often, vitiate the original policy move.

We now appreciate that any additional monetary or fiscal stimulus will have little effect on employment but will have an immediate effect on the position of the United States in world economy. In particular, the immediate effect of attempting through monetary means to stimulate the economy is likely to be an immediate depreciation of the exchange rate.

Address to the Center for International Business Conference, Dallas, Texas, April 9, 1981.

We learned this at immense cost in the early Carter years when the attempts to pump up the U.S. economy let to the decline of the dollar from 2.6 Deutsche Marks to the dollar to under two Deutsche Marks in two years. After hailing a declining dollar as salutary our economic policymakers woke up to discover that the side effects of domestic monetary and fiscal policy, swamp attempts to stabilize currency exchange rates through exchange market intervention and that the depreciation of the exchange rate abroad brings more inflation at home.

We learned that lesson the hard way. Take the two conscious devaluations of the dollar in the 1970s. There were few U.S. economists or economic policy makers who believed at the time that these would be an independent engine of inflation. Attention was focussed on what those devaluations were supposed to do for our exports. The poverty of that line of thinking was demonstrated by the explosion of inflation in the 1972-1975 period and again in the Carter inflation of the last few years.

In the last ten years the dollar's depreciation vis-a-vis the currencies of the fourteen other industrialized countries amounted to 17 percent. Vis-a-vis the Deutsche Mark the depreciation was a full 50 percent and vis-a-vis Japan's Yen it was 37 percent. This drastic devaluation failed to make American products more competitive in world markets and our trade deficit increased alarmingly. Indeed, the decline in the dollar boomeranged to generate an inflation which burdened our competitiveness. OPEC justified raising petroleum prices substantially, largely to recoup their losses of "real" income from being paid in devalued dollars for their export of oil.

What is most disturbing is that vis-a-vis West Germany and Japan the competitiveness of our technology-intensive industries keeps on deteriorating despite the depreciating dollar.

One of the most important industries in the group of our technology-intensive industries is aerospace. Since at least World War II this industry unquestionably has been technologically the most sophisticated, most competitive vis-a-vis all other countries, and the greatest contributor to the U.S. balance of payments. In 1979, its export surplus amounted to about $10 billion. Industry specialists estimate that in the mid-1960s our aerospace industry commanded as much as 90 percent of the free world's market for large transport jets. Since then, however, foreign competitors have chipped away this share and it is now about 80 percent. Moreover, we – meaning the industry and the government –

are doing many a thing that greatly accelerates this process. Military and civil-shared production programs reach ever-higher levels that continue to increase the foreign content of U.S. aerospace shipments.

In terms of technological sophistication, our semi-conductor industry is unexcelled. Moreover, unlike most other industries, the basic technology on which this industry was built was almost entirely U.S.-made. Of the fourteen *pivotal* innovations, thirteen were developed in the United States and one in West Germany. This industry's products have been critical to the development of computers, telecommunications, most sophisticated military equipment, and innumerable other products. In the future it is also expected to become the key to progress in automotive technology, industrial process control (including robotics), office automation and the like. Practically since its beginning, however, the industry has been subject to intense foreign competition, mostly from Japan. By now, although the Japanese semiconductor industry has captured only 5 to 6 percent of the total U.S. market, in the technologically newest product areas – 16K and 64K RAM – their penetration is 40 to 50 percent of the U.S. market – a much larger share than they have captured of our automobile market. In some semiconductor lines the Japanese manufacturers are clearly striving to become world leaders – and to accomplish this leadership largely on the basis of technology they obtain from U.S. companies.

Probably the third most technologically sophisticated industry is the metalcutting machine tool industry. For over a century it has provided technological improvements not only to the huge domestic metalworking industry, but also worldwide. But now it, too, seems to be in trouble – the United States has become a net importer of metalcutting machine tools (about $500 million worth in 1979 and $600 million in 1980). We are also host to subsidiaries of German and Japanese companies.

Finally, there is a huge problem facing our automobile industry. In its almost century-long existence, this industry managed not only to implant the automobile-orientation in our entire economy, but also did the same for many other countries. The current challenge it faces from the 22-year-old Japanese industry is deadly serious – the Japanese have not only conquered about one-fourth of the U.S. automobile market, but also have a cost advantage of at least 20 percent over U.S. producers, and they have a product-mix that is at least six years ahead of U.S. industry's. The economic and financial dynamics also work in favor of Japanese industry; for example: relative productivity growth, relative wage rates, and relative price changes.

All this has very serious consequences for our prosperity, for our ability to pay our way in the world, for the value of our currency, for our ability to mobilize the capital we need. It also has serious implications in undermining the industrial base which underlies our national security. Our leadership in electronics is critical to the technological edge we have in the weaponry and the transport which is basic to military strength.

How do we address this slippage? Well, the first thing we need to do in both our governmental policies and our managerial strategy and tactics is to recognize that we face worldwide competition in a global market.

We need to ask ourselves tough questions about where our economy is headed. For example, what will the increasing globalization of the automobile industry do to the industrial base on which we must depend for national defense? As the auto industry becomes globalized our need to keep the sea lanes open will become more critical.

Let us look for a moment at the way we misapply the antitrust policy on the false concept that the market is America and not the world. We are told that four U.S. auto firms have upwards of 90 to 95 percent of the market. Yet when one looks out the window one sees that one-quarter, perhaps even more, of the new cars on the street are produced by firms outside these four. Nearly all of these additional cars are, of course, imported. If imports account for one-quarter of domestic consumption, we tend to say that four firms have 75 percent of the market — still a rather high figure.

This way of looking at the automobile market is surely wrongheaded. There are not four American firms and some faceless imports in the market. On the contrary, there are eight or ten important firms in the market and they include such powerful and vital firms as Volkswagen, Toyota, Nissan, Renault, and Peugeot-Citroen. The reason Chrysler seems so out of place in a list of dominant firms is precisely that it is unable to compete effectively in this world market and in fact has been withdrawing from it, a step at a time, by selling off foreign plants. It is now retreating even in the United States much like a formerly dominant military power reduced to a house-by-house defense of its capital city. In a world perspective, American Motors too begins to look even less imposing than concentration statistics imply. Whereas in 1959 it was fifth in the world, it had dropped below fifteenth by 1978. Indeed, its recent arrangements with Renault make it look more like a Renault affiliate than a jointly dominant firm.

The market in automobiles has clearly become the world. In that market GM had only 28 percent in 1978 and probably less today. Ford had only 19 percent. Volkswagen and Daimler-Benz together had 12 percent. Toyota and Nissan together had another 10 percent, and probably even more today. Renault and Peugeot-Citroen together had still another 10 percent. Although GM and Ford are large, they hardly dominate the real market, as opposed to the antitrust construct of a market. The top four have less than 50 percent of the world market in autos and less than 15 percent in steel.

In this larger world market the position of U.S. firms is slipping badly. In chemicals, for example, DuPont dropped from first in 1959 to fourth in 1979, with Union Carbide falling from second to seventh. In 1959, the United States accounted for seven of the top ten firms, in 1979, for only three.

In electronics and appliances, six of the top eight firms in 1959 were American. In 1979, only three were still in that group.

In metal manufacturing, in 1959 the United States accounted for nine of the ten top companies, in 1979, for only two.

In pharmaceuticals, in 1959 seven of the ten top companies were American, in 1979 only five.

Many reasons can be advanced for the slippage of U.S. firms in world markets. Surely the general productivity problem is one. So too the inexorable workings of the principle of comparative advantage play a role. The United States now has a comparative advantage in agriculture, services, and, though the advantage is slipping, in specialized manufactures such as wide-bodied aircraft and computers. We know that Japan is taking dead aim, through government-subsidized research and government-influenced consolidations to create more powerful competitors to take on IBM in the world market. At the same time our antitrust policy, ignoring the reality of a world market, seeks to break up IBM and many antitrust rules make it difficult for U.S. companies to rearrange their affairs in a way that reduces costs and increases productivity, in order to permit them to compete both here and abroad on equal terms with their foreign competitors.

In this world market we face government-subsidized and government financed competition. In industry after industry, in country after country, there is no need for the competitors of U.S. firms to diversify or to merge to acquire a stable source of capital because those competitors are owned by their governments and thus have a direct claim on the public treasury. In this open world the conglomerate merger has become an important means of competition against state-owned and state-subsidized companies.

Not enough American firms adapt their pricing and other managerial policies to the fact of a world marketplace. Our Japanese competitors set their marketing and pricing policies in terms of a global market. The domestic market is the base which permits them to price to get established and maximize their share of the larger world market. Too many American firms plan and price in terms of the domestic market and view the foreign market as an add-on to be picked up later. By that time they are likely to find Japanese firms well established in the world market, competing vigorously in the American market from a worldwide base.

As we lose market position in basic industry, it becomes more vital to stay ahead in the technological sweepstakes. U.S. industry still puts a greater share of its production into research and development than Japanese and German industry. But we lag in recognizing the world marketplace in technology, and exploiting foreign technology imported in "naked form" of patents, licenses, and know-how.

The use of advanced foreign technology in "naked" form immensely speeds up the importing industry's technological progress and usually at only a fraction of the cost of developing similar indigenous technology. The more voluminous an industry's imports of such technology, the faster will be its growth of international competitiveness. Conversely, the greater a manufacturing industry's sales of advanced technology in naked form, the less competitive it is likely to become once the transferred technology is put to use abroad. Based on receipts and payments of royalties and license fees it appears that throughout the 1960s and 1970s our industry sold from seven to ten times as much advanced technology in naked form as it bought. In 1977, the latest year for which there are comprehensive statistics, our industry received about $2.9 billion for sales of such technology and made purchases amounting to $282 million. Most of our industry's sales are voluntary, but at least 100 or so major companies are under court decrees to sell their technology to foreigners mandatorily – as a result of our antitrust laws and regulations.

Both German and Japanese industry policies with respect to sales and purchases of advanced technology in naked form have been just about the reverse of our industry's policy. Throughout the 1960s the German industry's purchases (imports) of such technology were about 2.4 times as great as sales, and in the 1970s about 2.6 times as great. In 1977 German industry paid out for such technology about $1.1 billion and received $392 million.

In the 1960s Japan, in turn, was importing some fifteen times as much of such technology as it was selling, and in the 1970s about six times as much. In 1977 Japanese industry's outlays for such technology amounted to $1.3 billion and receipts of $204 million.

Neither Germany nor Japan (nor any other foreign country I know of) has a policy of requiring its firms to license their technology to foreigners mandatorily.

So much for the need to get more deeply involved and relate more realistically to the global marketplace. Let's spend a few minutes assessing the risks and opportunities we can see over the horizon out there. It's a rapidly changing world.

Change is nothing new. When our first ancestors were driven out of paradise, Adam is believed to have remarked to Eve: "My dear, we live in an age of transition." We are always transiting from one age to another. What is new is the accelerated rate of change. Today we live in a world of increasing nationalism, increasing terrorism, and vanishing resources. It is these three realities I'd like to discuss briefly today.

First, the tide of nationalism is running strong in the less-developed countries of the world. There is hostility and negativism toward free enterprise. There are potential dangers there for American, European, and even Japanese multinational corporations. Local politicians cannot always manage this distrust of foreigners. Free enterprise from abroad suddenly appears as foreign domination or neo-colonialism. It is difficult to predict when and where this hostility will break out.

Nationalism is not new. Its manifestations range from restrictive policies to outright expropriation. What is new today is that it is accompanied by global economic distress. This is caused by the explosive growth in energy costs – in both the industrialized countries and the less-developed ones.

The enormous cost of fueling economic activity is forcing the less-developed countries into austerity and no-growth policies. They are running out of credit. They cannot meet the very high interest rates required. All this intensifies instability.

On the plus side, there is in the less developed world a growing awareness of the importance of foreign capital, know-how, and technology. The leaders in these countries now see more clearly the importance of foreign investment and access to foreign markets as a way out of their economic dilemmas.

One form of instability that I'm afraid we'll see more of around the world is terrorism – hijacking, hostage-taking, kidnapping, assassination, bombing, armed attack, sniping, and coercive threats – mindless acts of violence designed to create a political effect regardless of the innocence of the victims.

We have been keeping statistics on this subject since 1968. During that period, some 6,000 terrorist incidents have been recorded. Violence has been increasing and the last three years have been the worst.

Terrorists can come from either the left or the right extremes of the spectrum. Recently we have seen a sharp increase in right-wing terrorist activity in Europe.

Last year also marked the first time that a large number of deadly attacks were carried out by individual nations. This is a dangerous development. It is one thing for a demented individual or a private group of fanatics to resort to terror. For a nation to resort to it with all the resources it can command is another – and much more serious – matter.

What or who are the primary targets of international terrorism? Americans are. Two out of every five incidents involve U.S. citizens or property. The U.S. citizens are usually businessmen or diplomats – especially individuals who are symbols of Western power and wealth. Although businessmen have been the most frequently victimized in past years, they were second to diplomats in 1980. Latin America and the Middle East are the main trouble spots, with Western Europe not very far behind.

It is a grim story. What do we do about it? At CIA, international terrorism has been high on the list of intelligence priorities for some time. Defensive tactics are taught to key personnel serving abroad. As for you, I know that corporations have been searching for defensive measures to protect their people. Some have even employed consultants to conduct ransom negotiations and payoffs to terrorist groups. I think this is a mistake. Payoffs are counterproductive in the long run. Successful terrorism encourages more terrorism. Moreover, any money gained is generally used to finance future terrorist operations. What you've got to do is adopt a firm policy and develop a strategy for dealing with terrorism before a crisis situation arises – when the terrorists hold all the cards. You must maintain an awareness of the constant threat of terrorism and learn how to react quickly and decisively. Terrorists must learn that there is little or no payoff where Americans and American firms are involved.

If terrorism is a factor threatening international stability today, of equal importance is our long-term and increasing dependence on fewer critical resources worldwide. Until recently, availability of natural resources has been taken for granted. America's leadership position in the world and our own ample natural resources were sufficient. From this abundance of relatively cheap supplies, we grew rapidly to become a great industrial power.

Roughly a decade ago, we received a jolt. Shifting geopolitical patterns, coupled with rising Third World nationalism, sharply tempered our expectations. These changing circumstances first became visibly embodied in the oil crisis of 1973. Here for the first time, we could actually see and feel the crushing impact of international "non-military warfare" strike us squarely where it hurts the most – in our pocketbooks and in our life-styles.

The crisis haunts us with a new reality. The U.S. can no longer count itself completely as a "free spirit" in the sense of determining its own destiny. Others, well away from our borders, can now place their hands on our economic throttles. International threats are not limited to military ones. There are other power projections far more subtle because they are largely unseen and thus not readily perceived.

This resource dependence applies to more than oil. As critical as oil dependency is to the fate or our economy and to our ability to defend ourselves from outside aggression, a new specter of dependency hovers over us that promises at least an equal level of national woe should we be caught without an adequate "game plan" to deal with it. The experts refer to it as "non-fuel minerals dependency." What they mean is reliance on other nations to supply us such strategic minerals as chromite, cobalt, tantalum, and several other strange names we seldom see in a direct sense. But the reality is there even so, because were we to lose access to these minerals, it would mean massive shocks to our economic system and current life-styles. Without these minerals, we cannot make TV sets or computers or heart-lung machines or produce high-grade stainless steel for a thousand uses. The implications for our defense capabilities are just as grim. No supersonic jets – no jets – no sophisticated submarines.

In the future, we can expect to be in competition with the Soviet Union for both oil and non-fuel minerals. They have both in Siberia, but the technological developments needed and the cost will make it prohibitive for some time to come. In response, the USSR is moving toward a policy of selective and strategic dependency on foreign resources as an alternative to the exceptionally high costs of extended self-sufficiency.

Add to this a growing trend in the Third World in which ownership and control of natural resources are changing from commercial to state dominance. This historic change provides the political environment for Soviet access to Third World natural resources. Soviet support for state ownership and control in the Third World creates a potential for non-market state trading corporations through which the flow of minerals can be organized as barter. This expansion of non-commercial mineral resource control, combined with Soviet power-projection capabilities, are the essential conditions of a Soviet access strategy in the Persian Gulf (oil) and Africa (minerals).

I have talked to you now about nationalism, terrorism, and resource constraints. There are a lot of other problems out there – food, deforestation, decertification, water availability, and so on. But I'll stop with three.

◆ ◆ ◆

TECHNOLOGICAL SWEEPSTAKES

Once again, Casey on the connection between technology and national security. It was his grasp of this connection that led him to order up special studies of Soviet efforts to obtain Western technology. These studies, in turn, led to establishment of the CIA's Technology Transfer Assessment Center. As TTAC pieced together the full range of Soviet efforts to illegally acquire Western technology, it became clear that the illegal acquisition of Western technology was not merely useful to the Soviet Union's weapons programs, but absolutely vital. And with the information TTAC began to provide, Western governments were better able to block illegal technology transfers. These efforts, in which Casey was the driving force, probably did more than any other efforts to slow down the Soviet Union's military programs.

I am pleased to have this opportunity to speak to this distinguished audience associated as teachers, learners, and friends and supporters of Polytechnic. I have long admired the leadership and the faculty at Polytech and the significance of their contribution to so many dimensions of our society. After a few months as Director of Central Intelligence, I am more than ever impressed by the importance of Polytech's work to the future security and prosperity of our country. . . .

In a very real way, technology holds the key to virtually all the public problems that confront us daily in our work, or in the newspapers we read – inflation, jobs, energy, our ability to pay our way in the world.

That's what I propose to talk to you about this evening. Our country's technology-intensive industries are the cutting edge of our economy and the basis from which we draw much of our military capability. They depend on highly trained personnel, substantial investment in R&D and are characterized by a rapidly changing competitive environment. They need sustained nourishment from Polytech and it's counterparts around our land.

The influence of these industries on our economy is enormous. They employ hundreds of thousands of Americans. They are major contributors to our balance of payments. More importantly, these industries

Address to the Polytechnic Institute of New York, New York, New York, June 3, 1981.

offer the greatest hope for fast growth, creation of new jobs and a general enhancement of U.S. economic strength.

We face serious competition from foreign producers in technology-intensive industries. Other industrial countries are way ahead of us in developing policies to increase the international competitiveness of their high-technology industries. Japan, West Germany, and many other countries have national policies designed to shift their industrial bases to knowledge-intensive activities. The sad fact is that the United States is actually losing its leadership position in some of the most important industries – a situation with very real political, military, and economic implications.

Since at least World War II, our aerospace industry has been one of the most sophisticated – an industry in which the U.S. has been highly competitive. It has been one of the greatest contributors to the U.S. balance of payments. In 1979, it's export surplus amounted to ten billion dollars.

However, our leadership in aviation has been steadily declining. While in the mid-1960s we commanded as much as 90 percent of the free world's market for large transport aircraft, we now enjoy only 80 percent. In wide-bodied aircraft alone for 1980, the European Airbus consortium gained 34 percent of a market which we owned only five years earlier. Europe is now on a par technically with the United States in many important areas of aircraft development. In addition, European governments can often arrange far more attractive financing than U.S. firms.

The aircraft industry is also consolidated internationally. The cost of developing new aircraft increases steadily and more and more programs require cooperative efforts by companies located in different countries. As a result of this international cooperation, we no longer see an aircraft of exclusive U.S. origin, but an aircraft with parts from Japan, Italy and elsewhere.

In recent years, our semiconductor industry has been subject to intense foreign competition, mostly from Japan. The Japanese semiconductor industry has captured only 5 to 6 percent of the total U.S. market. But, in some of the newest product areas, such as 16K RAM, they have captured about 40 percent of the U.S. market. And, they claim to have received over 60 percent of the orders last year for the newest memory computer – the 64K RAM. This is a much larger share than they have captured in the U.S. automobile market. In some semi-conductor products, Japanese manufacturers are already showing signs of becoming world leaders – surpassing U.S. capabilities – and largely on the basis of technology originally obtained from the United States.

Another technologically sophisticated field is production technology which includes robots and machine tools. The U.S., once the world leader, has become a net importer of machine tools – about $500 million worth in 1979, and $600 million in 1980. Japanese firms fill orders for machine tools twice as fast as their American counterparts.

Soon we will all be seeing the arrival of robots – and with them automation of the automobile, metal working, and many other basic industries. U.S. inventors were the first to conceive of the industrial robot. Yet today, when major U.S. Corporations like General Motors need thousands of robots, they must order them from Japan or Europe. While U.S. robot manufacturers can only make upwards of a few ten's of robots per month, one Japanese manufacturer is already using robots to make robots!

...The stakes in technological race are enormous. Loss of leadership in key industries like semiconductors and machine tools can also lead to loss of competitiveness in other areas. Our ability to stay competitive in automobiles and aircraft can depend heavily on how strong our semiconductor and machine tool industries are.

There are large political consequences. Losing ground in "cutting edge" technology would have a negative effect on important U.S. relations with other countries.

Technology resources can also give us important leverage in our diplomatic goals. For example, the establishment of cooperative technology programs with other countries can lead to better use of limited resources and closer political ties. U.S. technological assistance to developing countries can help achieve political objectives. Technological assistance also can give us access to energy and scarce materials. Technology can develop substitutes for mineral sources from which we could be cut off. Finally, keeping a strong lead in certain critical technologies can give the West a strong negotiating lever in dealing with the USSR – especially given the technological lag in the Soviet Union.

A loss of technological leadership in the U.S. military can be very serious. If we expect to have the best equipped armed forces, we've got to stay out ahead in technology. In a lot of areas, civil industry is setting the pace for technology developments. . . by contrast, in the past, a lot of important technologies got their start in special military programs. What this means is that the United States military is winding up more and more dependent on civilian technology and if we don't keep up our lead, we may find ourselves dependent on foreign suppliers.

We've heard a lot about the transfer of critical technologies to the Soviet Union, like semiconductors and computers — which have both civilian and military uses. That's a complex and sensitive subject. It's true that we are concerned about the control of certain technologies that could have direct military impact on the East-West balance of power. The Soviets are devoting enormous resources to upgrading their technology capability. But a major element in their technology strategy is the need to get their hands on Western developments — legally or illegally. The Soviets carry on a very large worldwide effort to acquire technology by espionage and smuggling and this can be a matter of life or death in an age when a simple technological breakthrough — lasers, directed energy — can tip the balance of power worldwide.

In light of these serious economic, political, and military consequences, it's distressing to note a number of indicators that suggests that we're in a decline. We've seen shifts in the balance of patents granted to foreign versus U.S. firms. We've seen very little growth in U.S. research and development investments as a percentage of GNP. On the other hand, other countries — like Japan and Western European countries — are scoring impressive gains in the R&D investment. The Soviet Union has showed a consistent rate of 3 percent of GNP invested in research and development since World War II. The U.S. is currently at about 2 percent. Our investment in education is also declining relative to that of other countries. Since 1974, the Japanese have been graduating more electrical engineers than the U.S. On a per-capita basis, the Japanese now have an almost three to one lead. At every level, the Japanese educational system is producing a generation of people which will be prepared to develop and participate in the ongoing technological revolution.

What is most disturbing is the decline in competitiveness in many of our technology-intensive industries vis-a-vis Japan, West Germany, and other industrialized countries. We have already seen dramatic changes in our trade picture for automobiles. Other industries may face a similar future.

Now let's look at the industrial growth rate picture in the United States. It has declined in comparison with foreign industries. Our level of industrial research and development has shown little increase in real terms over the last decade. Right now, Japan is planning increased investments that could result in their surpassing the U.S. in total commercial research and development within a decade.

What else are foreign countries doing to compete more effectively? Other countries, especially Japan, have national strategies to enhance their overall technological and industrial strength. They have programs to stimulate key sectors recognized as important to their economy and to their international trade. For these countries, economic security is equated with national security – in practice as well as in theory.

The technology strategies of other countries involve the coordination of government policies and maintenance of close government-industry relationships – all meant to enhance industrial innovation and competitiveness in a variety of ways. These include incentives for investment in research and development, certain exemptions from antitrust laws, and protection for industries during their infancy.

Don't get me wrong – we're not afraid of competition. Competition speeds up the process of innovation and raises levels of technological capability all over the world. Our job is to show that we can meet those competitive challenges – and not be erecting trade barriers. We've got to make sure that our own governmental laws and regulations do not tie industry's hands but rather encourage it. Then we will do the job that we are capable of doing.

No major U.S. corporation can afford to be complacent. The foreign competition is aggressive and export-oriented. U.S. companies have got to adopt a global, long-range strategy. We ought to be putting less emphasis on short term profits and recognizing the fact that foreign firms – especially in Japan – have different business goals. Foreign firms fight hard for greater market share, for overall company growth, and long range corporate strength. To stay competitive, we've got to have better relationships between industry and government. And industry's got to make greater use of available technical resources – especially in our universities.

We've got to know the impact that all of our government policies have on international industrial competition. We've got to have a complete review of tax policy, patent laws, antitrust enforcement, regulations and other measures – particularly how they all affect U.S. interests in international competition.

A final point. The U.S. government has got to cooperate with all our overseas allies as well as with U.S. industry on technology transfer policy. We've got to protect the technological strength of the West. The Soviets can't be allowed to play us off against our allies. At the same time, we've got to give American industry an equal opportunity to compete with companies in Europe and Japan.

We need to ask ourselves tough questions about where our economy and where our companies are headed, whether we're putting enough in R&D, what we can do to increase capital formation and create incentives for risk and initiatives, and above all, whether we're creating enough engineers and scientists, and entrepreneurs and promoters.

How will the attrition of our computer and semiconductor industry – under the impact of the drive the Japanese have mounted to capture this market – undermine our defense capability? How will it impact our ability to make our way in the world through the manufacture of machinery and equipment which will be increasingly controlled and guided by micro-processors?

If the French, Germans and Japanese, and less developed countries like Korea and Brazil, convert more rapidly than the United States from fossil fuels to nuclear energy, how rapidly will lower power costs in those countries be converted into important competitive advantages in manufacturing costs? How will the instabilities in southern Africa on the one hand and seabed mining on the other affect the structure of our world mineral markets and impact on our manufacturing industries?

Looking at the world more broadly, what do we see as we look around the world?

- ◆ We see a Soviet Union rapidly building its military strength as ours has been permitted to decline.

- ◆ We see the U.S. falling behind in economic competitiveness as the Japanese and Germans give, invest and innovate more, and Koreans, Singaporans, Taiwanese, Brazilians, and Mexicans increase their share of the world market as ours diminishes.

- ◆ We see political and economic instability in the Middle East, Africa, and Latin America where we get the fuel and minerals to keep our economy going.

Yet, there is reason to take heart. Here in the U.S., Congress has taken action to revitalize and make our economy competitive again and restore our military strength, which will restore confidence.

◆ ◆ ◆

AWAKENING TO CHANGE

Casey was among those who believed that change itself is among the dominant forces in world affairs. In this short speech, he traces some key changes since World War II.

It is a great and happy privilege for me to be with so many distinguished graduates of SOE and SAS and their friends on this sparkling occasion and to extend to you the greetings of the veterans of OSS. Today OSS stands for Old Soldiers Society but we carry on, and at our last annual dinner had the honor of presenting the William J. Donovan Award to Margaret Thatcher. On that occasion I remarked how pleased and how proud Bill Donovan would be to have the lady, who sits today where Winston Churchill sat, receive the Donovan Award.

This is not the first time I have crossed the Atlantic to bask in the warmth and companionship of the friends and colleagues who gather for this occasion from both sides of the English Channel. I recall that Al Haig was commanding NATO last time I was here. I recall that after the votes were in last November, Jimmy Carter telephoned Ronald Reagan in California to extend his congratulations. Then he said, "Ronnie is there anything I can do for you?" Reagan thought for a minute and then said, "Yes, run again in 1984."

While I have been at your dinners before, this is the first time I have been permitted to say anything, and I have pondered nightly on how such a great opportunity should be used. I can not fully resist the temptation to indulge in a little nostalgia for what were many of us the most challenging and rewarding days of our lives.

I remember as though it were yesterday flying out of New York, landing in Prestwick, and arriving by train in London.

Address to the Special Forces Club, London, England, October 23, 1981.

It was my first visit to London and I surely contributed to the impression which moved Malcolm Muggeridge to say: "Ah those first OSS arrivals in London. How well I remember them, arriving like young girls in flower straight from a finishing school, all fresh and innocent, to start work in our frowzy old intelligence brothel." I was full of admiration and awe for the spirit and will that I felt on this island which had stood alone against the brutal dictatorship which held all of Europe in its grasp. For almost four years you had waged subversive war against this oppressive and totalitarian power.

Yet in 1943, when we arrived here, despite the array of talent Bill Donovan had collected, we were amateurs. We were the new boys on the street, and very sensibly, you preferred to take us into new ventures and avoid the risk that, in our innocence, we might foul up or slow down operations you had built up over four years and already had under way. Yet you found time to share your experience with us, and we well remember that OSS. Coming into the European war three years late, we would not have been able to do very much at all if our British friends had not taken us in as junior partners and so generously taught us all they knew.

This partnership — including the great and courageous resistance of France and Belgium, of Holland and Luxembourg, of Norway and Denmark — flourished until victory was achieved. Then, when another threat was perceived in the East, there developed a broader partnership, which we call NATO. Today we can say that we have kept the peace in Europe, the Atlantic, and the North American continent for 36 years.

Yet, today there are new and broader and increasingly severe challenges, and to meet them it will take the full power of our partnership, the full range of skill we created in World War II and have elaborated on over the years, and quite possibly the Churchillean will you displayed in those darkest hours.

We live today in a different world, and as the need to maintain the European-American partnership intensifies, it comes under sharper challenge.

The broad Atlantic is no longer the impassable barrier to any serious aggression against the United States. Cities in the western part of the United States are as vulnerable today to the heavy Soviet missiles as are Birmingham and Frankfurt. Indisputably heavy Soviet buildup in conventional and strategic military power has been taking place over the last fifteen years, to a point which demands the serious thought and attention of the North Atlantic Treaty Alliance.

Because of the desire of the USSR to extend its hegemony over all of Europe, we can continue to expect a constant effort from the Soviet Union to foster a divided Europe, sharply separated from the United States. . . .

To the extent that the Soviet Union is faced with a convincing European-U.S. determination and capacity to meet any attack, or any threatened attack, the chances of it ever occurring greatly diminishes. This joint will, in itself, suitably demonstrated, would be worth many missiles and many tanks. I believe the Soviet leaders would never be so foolish as to attack, or attempt to blackmail, either Western Europe or the U.S. once they were convinced of the solid unity and determination of the alliance to protect itself. Only if there existed any likelihood of a division within the alliance would there be a real temptation for the USSR to confront us head on.

As we face the need to turn back a concerted effort to divide us in the defense of Europe, it is no longer possible for us to confine our perceptions, whether from Europe or the United States, to the NATO area. And as the world becomes more diverse and our perceptions vary, new strains, and quite possibly serious differences, will develop as we face our respective problems. We shall need to apply our best combined statesmanship to resolve them. This is the stage at which I sense we now find ourselves.

For a quarter of a century, our primary worry has been the missiles that can destroy us in half an hour, and the preponderance of tanks and planes and troops that can be thrown against NATO. It has only recently dawned upon us that it is coups and subversion and wars of national liberation and economic aggression which have damaged us most severely over the last decade. Even as we worry about having fallen behind the Soviet Union in both missiles and conventional arms, we need to face up to a growing vulnerability of Third World Countries to subversion, to wars of national liberation, to disinformation and propaganda, and to the provision of arms and advisors to gain influence.

While we spend seven billion dollars a year to provide economic assistance to these countries, the Soviets and its proxies spend twice that to exploit these vulnerabilities in a way that could tip the world's geographical balance against us.

I believe that the Soviets grasped that as a result of the expulsion of the United States from Vietnam, it would be some time before the American public would support any kind of significant intervention in a Third World insurgency. It was, thus, "not by accident" that Soviet support for the Cubans in Angola followed in 1975. There and in Ethiopia we witnessed a remarkable display of power projection as Soviet arms were quickly transported over huge distances to meet up with Cuban troops brought across the Atlantic. Since then we have seen the Soviets and their proxies preposition large stockpiles of heavy arms in Libya, Yemen, Syria, and Cuba — and that process seems to be under way in Central America and in southern Africa.

We have seen two countries with tiny populations — Libya and Cuba — spread terror and spawn insurgencies on the continents. Libya has entered into a pact with Ethiopia and South Yemen for joint action to overthrow adjoining governments in the Horn of Africa and on the fringes of Arabia. A superpower of a Central American scale is building up a tiny Nicaragua, which with Soviet tanks and planes and Cuban organization and troops and with a population of a little more than two million will soon be able to militarily dominate its neighbors with a population eight times as great.

Managua, the capital of Nicaragua, has become an international center where Russians, East Germans, Bulgarians, Vietnamese, North Koreans, and PLO advisors join Libyan money and Cuban soldiers to provide very sophisticated training and direction to insurgencies in El Salvador and Guatemala. Today, the Sandinistas have a military force seven times as large as the one they overthrew two years ago. Its Cuban advisors train and organize it down to company level. Its airfields are extended to take Soviet planes to be flown by aviators being trained in Bulgaria and Cuba.

Over the six years or so that these latent threats to our oil, mineral sources, shipping, and our entire geopolitical position have been developing, we have hardly noticed. Yet over this same period, in an oddly disjointed and disconnected way, the kind of intangible assets which worked for us in World War II have quietly manifested themselves. We stirred ourselves to help the Portuguese people overthrow the communist forces that had almost closed in on them. The Special Air Service has demonstrated from Malaysia to Oman that externally supported insurgencies can be defeated. Afghan freedom fighters have made it as dangerous for a Russian solider to be out at night or for a Soviet convoy to stray off a main road as it was for the Germans in France in 1944. The prospect of a Polish population aroused to economic sabotage and organized resistance and of Western allies united in political and economic retaliation has kept the Soviets from the kind of brutal repression similar liberalization caused them to inflict on Hungary and Czechoslovakia. Let us hope that these expressions of the human will to freedom, together with the commitment of British, French and American troops to a peace-keeping force in the Sinai, are signs that the West is awakening to manifest the will and the statesmanship which can keep the peace around the world as we have in Europe for these 36 years.

◆ ◆ ◆

SCOUTING THE FUTURE

This speech is central to any serious evaluation of William J. Casey's tenure as Director of Central Intelligence. For it is in this speech —from which is drawn the title of this book — that Casey defines his perception of the role of U.S. intelligence.

Casey believed that U.S. intelligence has a responsibility on behalf of the entire government for "Scouting the Future" —for looking "across the broad spectrum of international political, economic, military, sociological, and demographic developments. . . and to distill from them careful assessments of problems we will face now and past the year 2000."

With this perception Casey in effect doubled the intelligence community's mission. Under his tenure not only would the community fulfill its "primary purpose," which he defined as "averting war by alerting our leaders to any military dangers to our national security." Now, there was to be a "second role," which he defined as "helping the President and his top advisers frame sound policies needed to retain American strength against a myriad of political, economic, and even technological threats to this country."

Address to the Harry J. Sievers Lecture Series, Fordham University, New
York City, Feburary 25, 1986.

It was the effort to play this second role that led the intelligence community to produce a steady stream of long-range analyses and projections of a sort that had never been attempted before by intelligence, or perhaps even by any other branch of government. Casey took special pride in these products. "These aren't the kinds of reports we wake up the President in the middle of the night to tell him about," Casey used to say. "But these are important in a different way. These are the ones that help see ahead." Producing these long-range analyses was a frustrating, time-consuming, often discouraging business. Casey was always there to keep flagging spirits up. "We're learning while we do these things," he used to tell analysts. "Don't worry if what we come up with is a little thin. This is our first shot. Next time we take a look at this subject we'll do better. Just keep going."

Unfortunately nearly all these long-range products are classified, and therefore can't be listed here. But future historians of U.S. intelligence, and of the Casey years, will find an enormous cache of reports and analyses that provided policymakers with a glimpse of the future such as their predecessors had never been given.

In this speech Casey also offers his perception of the KGB's role. The contrast to the U.S. intelligence community's role is striking, and well worth noting.

I am most pleased to be here again at Fordham. I spent here what I count among my happiest and most valuable years. The theme of this series of Harry J. Sievers Lectures is U.S. foreign policy. I will undertake to give you a view of the range of our foreign policy concerns as seen by American intelligence.

Back when Lyndon Johnson was President, one of my predecessors, Dick Helms, asked me and a few others out to CIA Headquarters at Langley, Virginia. He wanted us to put together a scholarship fund to help keep experienced people who had joined CIA at its inception twenty years earlier and who were now tempted to move to the private sector to make enough money to send their kids to college.

I recall saying, "Dick, what keeps you here?" He said, "When you sit here every day and see all these messages coming through, and realize how beleaguered this United States is in the world, you just have to stick with it."

122   Scouting the Future

Now, at that time, we dominated the world economically and militarily. Russia was largely confined to the European landmass. And the only other worry was a war brewing in Vietnam.

How different the world is today!

Today, the Soviets possess a powerful arsenal of nuclear offensive missiles that is capable of taking out our land-based deterrent force. In the past twenty years, the Soviets have built up a huge weapons industry capable of turning out an amazing profusion of new, highly-sophisticated conventional and nuclear weapons.

Consider for a moment that the Soviets have developed a new missile like our *Midgetman* and another similar to our MX, both of which are road- or rail-mobile. And the steady buildup in conventional weapons opposite NATO goes on and on. Today, the Soviets have twice as many troops and planes, three times as many tanks, and four times as many guns as we do on the NATO central front in Germany.

Perhaps most alarming, the Soviets have invested between fifteen and twenty years of research on their strategic defenses – something we have ignored to our peril. As you know, they have completed a ballistic missile defense system around Moscow. We have no comparable system. Despite this feverish effort to build their own strategic defenses, the Soviets loudly beat the propaganda drum in an effort to scuttle the President's effort to build a credible strategic defense of our own.

The Five-Year Plan which Secretary Mikhail Gorbachev is even now proposing to the 27th Party Congress will call for ambitious growth and modernization of critical high technology industries that support the Soviet armed forces.

Even at a time of economic difficulty and a reordering of domestic priorities, Soviet defense programs have been protected. Indeed, the current high level of miliary spending will continue over the past five years; the United States has only recently begun to catch up with Soviet weapons acquisition programs.

Now, this huge military force may never be used against the United States or its NATO allies – although the Soviets clearly are quite prepared to use it if they believe their homeland to be threatened. The larger threat may lie elsewhere. The Soviets' massive nuclear and conventional forces may be only a shield for Mother Russia, making it easier and less risky for the Soviets to intimidate weaker governments and to gobble up pieces of territory around the globe. We've seen this happen over the last two decades – and we really shouldn't be surprised at what we've seen. Indeed, three generations of Soviet leaders have told us what they were going to do.

Back in 1961 – fully a quarter of a century ago – Nikita Khrushchev, then Premier of the Soviet Union, said that communism would win not by nuclear war or conventional war, but by "wars of national liberation." Since then, the Soviets have established beachheads throughout the Third World. Today they have client states in Cuba, Vietnam, Kampuchea, Angola, Ethiopia, South Yemen, Mozambique, Nicaragua, and Afghanistan. Many of these countries are located either near strategic choke points or in areas of almost certain regional conflict. Slowly, but surely, the Soviets are linking these geostrategic positions around the world by a growing logistic network.

Let me illustrate by describing the Soviet complex in the Caribbean, where with the Cubans and Nicaraguans they are working to build the first communist base on the American mainland.

The Soviets have, over the past twenty years, created in Cuba the second strongest military power in the Western Hemisphere. Only the U.S. has a larger military establishment. Especially over the last few years, the Soviets have given Cuba massive amounts of sophisticated weaponry. Much of this weaponry – plus Cuban manpower – serves Soviet ends in Africa. Yet another extension of this Cuban base is Nicaragua. The Cubans are building in Nicaragua one of Latin America's largest airports. When completed, this airfield will be able to handle the large Soviet bombers and reconnaissance aircraft which fly regularly from the Kokla Peninsula in the Soviet Arctic down past our east coast to Cuban airfields and eventually on to Angola. The Nicaraguan base will enable these same aircraft to fly along our west coast and into Pacific regions.

During the Brezhnev era, the Soviets announced the so-called Brezhnev Doctrine which says, in effect, "once communist, always communist." There is every indication that – despite his smiles and smooth manner – Gorbachev will apply that doctrine with renewed vigor. He will do this by shipping more weapons to Cuba for use against Jonas Savimbi in Angola and Arturo Cruz and his Contras in Nicaragua. He will supply Vietnam more weapons for suppression of resistance in Kampuchea. And there is every indication that he will redouble Soviet efforts to crush the valiant *mujahideen* who have resisted communist aggression in Afghanistan for more than six years.

We recently witnessed a sudden and dramatic display of Gorbachev's application of the Brezhnev Doctrine in its South Yemen satrapy. As you may be aware, the Soviets succeeded in establishing a Marxist-Leninist regime in South Yemen in the early 1970s. They soon established a naval base and communications center there to support their operations in the Indian Ocean. Recently, Ali Nasser, President of South Yemen, began to draw away a little from the Soviets and seek some help elsewhere. Less than a month ago, hardline pro-Soviet elements in his government initiated a coup against him. The coup soon escalated into a bloody civil war between military and tribal elements loyal to President Ali Nasser and those of the hardline pro-Soviet camp.

Now the hardline Yemeni Vice President happened to be in Moscow "for consultations." The Soviets sat and watched the blood flow for a few days, while evacuating Soviet dependents from the country. Neighboring countries, North Yemen and Ethiopia, sought to help the South Yemen government. A few days later, it appeared that the pro-Soviet rebels were gaining the upper hand. Moscow thereupon warned both North Yemen and Ethiopia not to help the government forces. Moreover, Moscow ordered Soviet fliers, using MiG-21s given to the South Yemen government, to pound beleaguered government forces. And Soviet transport planes started bringing in additional weapons for the hardliners. To tie things up, the South Yemen Politburo then met — perhaps at Moscow's suggestion — and declared the Vice President, then sitting in Moscow, to be the country's new President.

Now this is not new. The Soviets removed two puppets in Afghanistan in 1979, and probably were behind the murder of Maurice Bishop of Grenada in 1983. The message in all these cases is clear: leaders of governments installed by Moscow who seek improved relations with the West do so at their peril.

Yet another worrisome problem for the U.S. government is the spread of small wars, many of which are waged by proxy. There are presently 42 conflicts raging that involve some four million people in wars, rebellions, or uprisings. Few of these conflicts have been formally declared. This ambiguity about hostilities places a special premium on effective intelligence.

The massive lethal power possessed by the great nations — and especially by the United States and the Soviet Union — has had a still inadequately understood effect upon warfare. Smaller nations are infinitely more free to undertake belligerent action than are the two muscle-bound giants. This does not mean that we and the Soviets are equally paralyzed, or that the propensities of smaller nations all too often involve the interest of the superpowers and, somewhat less often, the participation by a superpower by means short of war. How, where and why such indirect intervention occurs is a crucial difference between the Eastern bloc and the West. So, too, is the freedom or eagerness with which such indirect action occurs.

The Soviet Union has pressed to the hilt its use of proxy nations to carry out its wars abroad. It is perfectly content to rely on our fear of wider — especially nuclear — war to keep us largely paralyzed.

During the 1970s, the Soviets used this process of destabilization, subversion, and support of insurgencies to gain control of Vietnam, Angola, South Yemen, Ethiopia, Cambodia, Afghanistan, and Nicaragua. From these bases they threaten other nations in Central America, Asia, Africa, and a communist-led insurgence has gained control of a large portion of the Philippines.

Now, people around the world are no longer joining communist insurgencies. Rather, close to half a million people have taken up arms against oppressive regimes in Afghanistan, Cambodia, Angola, Ethiopia, Laos, and Nicaragua.

More importantly, over the last few years democracy has taken hold or made great progress in El Salvador, Honduras, Guatemala, Argentina, Brazil, Pakistan, and other countries.

Just in the past three weeks, one-man rule in Haiti and the Philippines has been replaced by governments committed to a democratic future. We can particularly rejoice in this weeks's development in the Philippines where the whole nation took part in an election — quite free, though marred by fraud — in which large numbers of people used non-violent popular expression to free themselves of two decades of martial law. Now we must help Haiti resist Cuban subversion, and the Aquino government deal with a sagging economy and communist insurgency in the Philippines.

In recent years we have seen the growth of a new form of war — terrorism — supported, if not spawned by, national states to provide the

Soviets their foreign policy. The Soviets and their friends have discovered in terrorism a low-cost, low-risk means of attacking democratic
governments in Europe, the Middle East, and Latin America. Unfortunately, some victim nations have been noticeably reluctant to punish
those who unleash terror on them.

One of the most difficult tasks for the intelligence in the years ahead
will be to penetrate the small, fanatical groups which carry out the
criminal acts of murder, robbery, bombing, and kidnapping. These
groups are utterly without moral restraint, and hold even innocent people
in complete contempt.

Terrorism today is more lethal and more widespread than it was ten
or even five years ago. This is so because many groups now are state-
supported, sponsored, and even directed in some cases. A "radical entente" consisting of Iran, Libya, North Korea, Cuba, and to some extent
Syria, is making a great effort to undermine the influence of the United
States and its allies in many parts of the globe. Some tin pot despots like
Muammar Qadhafi of Libya see in terrorism a new gospel of violence
that will result in fundamental political change in the Middle East and
elsewhere.

The Soviet Union is not far in the background. The Soviets' well-
documented role in international terrorism is to provide money and training, arms and explosives, passports and other documents, infiltration
and escape routes, and are aided in this effort by their East European allies, notably East Germany, Czechoslovakia, and Bulgaria.

Yet another challenge to the West, and one that is not well recognized
for its true importance, is the threat to our national economy from rapidly growing world indebtedness. It is here that the interdependence between industrial and less-developed countries is most apparent.

A decision was made a few years ago by a handful of men which led
to a reduction in the price of oil — a price reduction by more than a third
in less than a month. The life and death of nations and their economies
now rests on how low that price falls. Some nations will benefit. Others
will face social and economic chaos.

Only wise, and swift, government policies can provide the possibility
of moderating these consequences. And policy formation, if not based
on sound intelligence, will be partially blind.

A number of less-developed countries (LDCs) are now indebted to
banks, governments, and international lending institutions by some $850

billion. Now, it is less the debts themselves than it is the consequences which flow from their possible non-payment that holds the world economy in thrall.

It is unfortunate that many countries that now have enormous debts are those which only recently adopted democratic governmental forms. Political and social unrest in those countries can swiftly snuff out the gains made, and return those countries to authoritarian rule.

Indeed, the situation resembles that of the Weimar Republic in Germany which was saddled with enormous war reparations that it could not pay. Even when these huge debts were stretched out under various repayment schemes, Germany's debt continued to burgeon and led to unemployment and political extremism. The result was the collapse of democracy in Germany and the rise to power of a totalitarian regime. Today, the situation is equally dangerous — perhaps more so — because the economy is global, and banking and credit sources are closely interlinked.

Even as we speak, the total Third World debt stands at more than $850 billion. Despite efforts at belt-tightening, rescheduling, and economic restructuring, the debt burden has significantly worsened since 1982. To be precise, the total LDC debt has increased by 43 percent in just over three years, and in the case of some smaller countries like Panama, the increase has been as much as 82 percent.

As the debts continue to mount up, the economies of debtor countries weaken, and result in lower living standards. This creates conditions ideal for serious political and social upheaval and the growth or spread of radical movements.

Political pressures on leaders of debt-ridden countries are growing daily. Mexican leaders are facing growing pressures to take unilateral action that could lead to debt repudiation within the next few weeks. If Mexico goes this route, Argentina and Peru might be tempted to follow. And, outside Latin America, many African and some Asian countries, like the Philippines, could follow suit.

Given these pressures, the debtor countries may be drawing closer to the point where they face the choice between debt repudiation and upheaval. Obviously, neither option is good for us.

To stop this potential landslide, new initiatives need to be considered.

The truth is that the debtor countries are ripe for something like a reorganization under Chapter 11 of the Bankruptcy Law to private corporations overburdened by debt. Such an action usually works out into a three-way split on handling the excessive load of debt. Applying this to world debt, the industrial countries would approve the write-off of some existing loans to troubled LDC debtors. International financial institutions – the IMF, the World Bank, and regional development banks – would assume responsibility for a second segment. The debtor countries themselves would continue to be responsible for the remainder. Moreover, enough cushion would have to be created in the global financial system to follow a resumption of economic growth in debtor countries.

The advantage of this option over current discussions on interest rates is that it deals with cause – large and growing principal – rather that the symptoms – interest payments. More importantly, it puts the initiative in our hands rather than the debtors'. If the debt situation is going to unravel in any case, the United States should be in the driver's seat.

So what does all this have to do with American intelligence?

The primary purpose of American intelligence is to avert war by alerting our leaders to any military dangers to our national security. The second role is to help the President and his top advisors frame sound policies needed to retain American strength against a myriad of political, economic, and even technological threats to this country.

We live in a world in which our interdependence increases faster than our understanding of the significance of that interdependence. We are increasingly dependent, for example, even for our vital sources of military strength on capabilities and resources which are diminishing here and increasing elsewhere. That interdependence involves manufacturing and trade, commodities and credit, communications and ideas, and vital resources. Sometimes, that interdependence has the effect of stimulating tensions between nations or increasing instability within them.

Intelligence is an indispensable tool that enables us to understand the consequences of this rapid movement to a profoundly changed and interdependent world. It enables us to devise policies which enhance our ability to shape our destiny.

Increasingly, there is a broad recognition that the intelligence community has a responsibility on behalf of the entire government for "scouting the future." Nowhere else in government is there the information, expertise, or resources to look across the broad spectrum of international political, economic, military, sociological, and demographic developments taking place, and to distill from them careful assessments of problems we will face now and past the year 2000.

There is a fundamental difference in the mission of intelligence in the Western democracies, and as it is practiced in the Soviet Union and other Marxist-Leninist states. In the West, intelligence is intended to understand broad trends so as to ensure international stability and to make change as orderly as possible. It is true that, upon occasion, its errors and biases tend toward the maintenance of the status quo.

Now in the Soviet Union, the KGB's role is almost the exact opposite. Its function at home is to suppress dissent and to root out dissenters. Indeed, its primary function is to ensure the continued rule of the Communist Party of the Soviet Union. Secondarily, its function is to generate and exploit turbulence beyond Soviet borders. "The worse, the better" is an old Russian Nihilist maxim which aptly describes the thrust of Leninist intelligence activities in other countries. The Soviet intelligence apparatus is, by its very nature, the merchant of disorder, the provocateur, the magnifier of social, economic or political weakness or distress. It is the ultimate force for enhancing the possibility of external upheaval – and is careful only that the flames ignited do not singe the hands that throw them.

Ladies and gentlemen, in closing my address to you this evening, I wish to assure you that American intelligence will protect not only our nation's freedom, security, and stability, but enhance the security and stability of all democratic nations. This mission will increase in importance with each passing year.

◆ ◆ ◆

NEW WORLDS TO CONQUER

Once again, Casey outlining the challenges of a new era. Here, he exhorts young people to reach for excellence. "Lofty goals, hard work, and enthusiasm still matter. . . . With perseverance and devo-

---

Commencement Address, Bryant College, Providence, Rhode Island, May 19, 1984.

tion to duty, you too will pass on the baton so that the opportunities
and freedom you enjoy will be enjoyed by those who follow. "

I feel more at home here than you might imagine. I came here from
the collegiate setting of the Virginia campus of the Central Intelligence
Agency where we are separated from Washington by the broad Potomac.
Contrary to what you may have read in spy novels or seen in James Bond
movies, most of our people spend their time not in bars or seedy hotels
but in interviewing and consulting, sitting at computers or working in
libraries to gather, evaluate, and analyze information. We have scholars
and scientists in every discipline of the social and physical sciences –
as well as engineers, computer specialists and communications experts
– in a profusion unmatched by any university. We have developed a
variety of technical marvels and sophisticated techniques to gather and
interpret facts and relationships from every corner of the earth and
beyond.

Graduating is a time of joy and celebration. You have worked hard to
earn the degrees you will be awarded today, and you and your families
are properly proud of that achievement.

Indeed, whether or not your future careers bring you into the foreign
affairs field, each one of you will, I trust, continue after graduation to
increase your understanding of the complex, interrelated world in which
we now live.

We can no longer divide our work, our interests, into neatly labeled
boxes. We cannot easily separate the private from the public sector, or
domestic from international affairs. Our most important problems over-
lap. World events will affect you, no matter what path you decide to pursue; none of you will be insulated from foreign shocks and crises. It is
more important now than ever before that each graduate participate in
an informed way in the dialogue about how this country should protect
its ideals and values. We should also consider how each of us can contribute to igniting the interest of less fortunate nations, within an
economy based on incentives and the benefits and obligations of freely
elected representative government. Let me now share with you a look at
the world you are entering and which you will help to shape.

The world has fused into one global economic system. Our economy
is much more sensitive to the international market and financial trends.
About 25 percent of goods produced in the world are traded across na-

tional borders. Governments have become economic powers in their own right. American businesses must compete in the world marketplace or our economy, and eventually our national security, will wither. The expert who is well-versed in the latest information processing techniques but cannot relate his or her expertise to the surrounding world environment will simply not function at full capacity and will not be able to understand the range of planning and decision-making that will create opportunities and affect our lives.

What then are the major international trends which could change and shape the environment in which you will live? The Soviet Union still dominates any broad discussion of international affairs, and with good reason. For all its weaknesses, especially its sluggish economy, the Soviet Union alone possesses the armed might that has the potential for destroying the United States. But perhaps more worrisome is the continuing Soviet effort to expand the power, influence and control of communism around the world.

I believe that the Soviet Union is perhaps the last genuine empire. The men in the Kremlin — whether Andropov or Chernenko — are unrelenting in their quest to expand Soviet power and domination. Moscow's geographic expansion of power to all the continents of the world in a mere decade is unprecedented.

In 1961, Nikita Khrushchev said that communism would win, not through nuclear war which could destroy the world, or conventional war which could quickly lead to nuclear war, but through wars of national liberation in Africa, Asia, and Latin America. We were reluctant to believe him then, just as we were reluctant to believe Hitler in the 1930s when he said he would take over Europe.

During the mid to late 1970s, the Soviet Union unfurled a new strategy to expand its power and influence in the Third World. And the strategy has worked. Soviet power has been established:

◆ In Vietnam along China's southern border and astride the sea lanes which bring Japan's oil from the Persian Gulf.

◆ In Afghanistan, 500 miles closer to the warm water ports of the Indian Ocean and to the Straits of Hormuz through which comes the oil essential to Western Europe.

◆ In Southern Africa, rich in minerals, which the industrial nations must have.

◆ And in the Caribbean and Central America on the very doorstep of the United States.

The Soviets have accomplished this astonishing expansion by using proxies and surrogates, in peace and in war. The role of these Soviet surrogates is as much political as military. East Germans in Africa, Cubans in Latin America, Vietnamese in Asia all have helped carry the Soviet banner.

If history has taught us anything it is that military strength deters aggression. This means that we cannot slacken in our commitment to a strong national defense despite its burdens. The alternative is slow economic strangulation and political isolation.

Those of you who will seek careers in private industry will have a key responsibility in ensuring that our national defense remains strong. Technological innovation, entrepreneurial drive, and willingness to meet the competition head-on have traditionally been the hallmark of the American business spirit. And if we live up to this tradition, we need not worry about our ability to stand up to our adversaries. But we have to realize that the Soviets have been quick to take advantage of our technology.

In fact, the Soviet Union is able to sustain its enormous military machine in part because American business, and American know-how provide the technological research and development that helps fuel the Soviet military buildup. They trained thousands of spies and hundreds of dummy corporations to steal our technology. The Soviet military had our plans for the C-5A *Galaxy* plane before it flew. The precise gyros and bearings in their latest generation of ICBMs were designed by us. Their space shuttle is a virtual copy of our first design. And the list goes on and on.

They comb through our open literature, religiously attend our scientific and technological conferences, and send students over here to study.

The West must organize to protect itself; and this will take the combined efforts of both business and government. The businesses in which you will work will be our first line of defense. Industrial security measures need to be strengthened to protect our nation's most valuable commodity — our own innovations and brainpower — from being used against us.

Whether you seek a career in the private sector, or as I hope, some of you decide to join us in government, you must be aware that the world today is far from benign. As one writer has put it, there is an "anarchic reality" to international relations, and it affects all of us. Perhaps the most insidious manifestation of this sort of anarchy is international terrorism. As practiced today, terrorism obliterates the distinction between peace and war. We count over fifty major terrorist organizations and a great many more "mom and pop shops" which can be hired by Iran, Syria, Libya, and other radical governments. The U.S. government and the intelligence community are taking strong measures to deal with terrorism but it is something we all will have to live with and must defend against because U.S. citizens are often the targets of terrorist groups.

Over the longer term, however, the challenge to America may well lie in the rapid pace at which technological change is taking place in various parts of the world. American business is being challenged by newly industrializing countries such as Singapore, South Korea, Taiwan, and Brazil. Such countries are aggressively reshaping their industries from producing simple, labor-intensive goods to new, high-growth, technology products such as telecommunications equipment, small computers, and machine tools. Lower labor costs and government subsidization of manufacturing will make them tough market competitors.

Irregular rates of growth in technology will contribute to economic strains with key U.S. allies, and may actually slow economic growth in some Third World countries. The spread of technology will make it easier for more countries to produce sophisticated weapons, but can also reduce the real value of some commodity products and reduce the value of the currencies and savings in countries that lag behind. Thus, your success and skill and efficiency in the future can mean a lot to the nation and all its people.

We face tough competition around the world. Japan Inc. is, of course, already a formidable business competitor and will become even more so in the computer and robotics field. Leading Japanese firms are developing and will soon market large-scale, scientific computer systems —the "supercomputers."

The Japanese have also put us on notice that they are intent on capturing a share of the U.S. personal computer market, while the increasing number of cooperative agreements between Japanese and U.S. companies is altering dramatically the structure of the world computer industry.

Japanese firms are also installing industrial robots four to five times faster than their U.S. counterparts and plan to export a growing share of their production. There is more at stake than the sale of robots since robots are often sold as part of complete manufacturing systems. These complete systems can be worth ten to twenty times the value of the robots alone.

I outlined these challenges not to give you a feeling of despair, but rather to show you something about the worlds that are out there for you to conquer – and there are some good reasons to be optimistic. Remember that this country and its people have many strengths. The United States enjoys enormous respect and envy around the world, even from our adversaries.

During the 1960s, the early 1970s, and indeed even today, there are those who say that the United States has lost its way in the world – that we no longer can influence or control important forces that will affect our future. Do not heed these voices. True, we need to use our military power and our economic and political influence judiciously and some events are outside our control. But our natural resources, our size, the creativity of our people, and particularly our values give us enormous influence around the world and control over our national destiny. In that you may take great pride.

Despite what appears to be a string of successes, over the longer term our major adversary has a few things to worry about. Within its own borders, the Soviets have some serious economic problems, and must face the growth of ethnic minorities that want to retain their heritage and traditions. And the export of the Soviet system has not been without some drawbacks. Without exception, the economic record of the countries which have come under Soviet domination has ranged from poor to very poor. Economic progress has been far greater in the free areas of Asia, Latin America, and Africa, than in those that have been subject to the Soviet or Cuban style of socialism.

I believe American business is one of our greatest international assets. And we must find a way to mobilize and use this great advantage particularly in the Third World where the Soviet challenge is immediate and threatening. All that is needed for Soviet expansionism to succeed is for the U.S. to do nothing – to simply acquiesce through inaction.

We cannot back away from the Soviet challenge in the Third World, but neither we nor the Soviets can offer unlimited or even large-scale economic assistance to the less-developed countries. Investment is the key to success in the Third World and we, our NATO allies, and Japan have superior ability to promote investment and support it with know-how.

Another vital strength we possess is our heritage of political values – our democratic traditions, our freedoms. Human beings, in incredible numbers, are risking their lives every day in desperate attempts to escape dictatorship. Over two million Vietnamese risked their lives for a chance to come here or to other democracies – 150,000 perished in the attempt. Almost four million Afghans have fled their country; at least 150,000 have been killed or wounded; and remember the Haitians, Ethiopians, Cubans, and more recently, in Central America, the 10,000 to 15,000 Miskito Indians who have had to flee into Honduras. Their flight is testimony to the emptiness of dictatorship and the continuing allure of freedom. Thus, we must foster in the Third World the infrastructure of democracy, the system of free press, unions, political parties, and universities, which allow a people to choose its own way, to develop its own culture, and to reconcile its own differences through peaceful means.

It is your challenge, as this country's future leaders in business and government, in education and the professions, to know and understand world affairs and history, not just for your personal benefit or your company's, but also for the benefit of this nation as a whole. You are embarking on an exciting – though not always an easy – future. Dealing with the world realistically does not mean you cannot or should not have high hopes. As Thomas Wolfe wrote in his novel, *Of Time and the River*: "It's a fabulous country – the only fabulous country. The one where miracles not only happen but they happen all the time."

Lofty goals, hard work, and enthusiasm still matter. Remember your political heritage and the values imparted to you by your families and this college. With perseverance and devotion to duty, you too will pass on the baton so that the opportunities and freedoms you enjoy will be enjoyed by those who follow.

* * *

Chapter 5

Understanding the Soviet Threat

WHAT WE FACE

Although Casey worked hard writing all his speeches, there is no question that he worked longest and hardest on this one. After all, it was a singular honor to be invited to the podium at Westminster College, where in 1946 Churchill stood and delivered his immortal "Iron Curtain" speech. Casey wanted to make his own Westminster speech memorable, and he devoted hours to writing one draft after another until he was satisfied.

In this speech Casey provides not only the purest distillation of his own worldview, but of the worldview he shared with so many others who fought on in the public arena and never gave in, because they knew what they were fighting for. In a nutshell: "The thought that I would leave you with is that the struggle with what the Soviet Union represents is not confined to Churchill's generation, or to my generation, or the generation of your faculty and parents, or your generation. This is a conflict deeply rooted in ideas. This conflict is as old as recorded history. The threat posed by the Soviet Union is the lineal descendent of the same threat Western civilization has faced for better than two thousand years: it is the threat posed by despotism against the more or less steadily developing concept that the highest goal of the State is to protect and to foster the creative capabilities

Address to Westminister College, Fulton, Missouri, October 29, 1983.

and the liberties of the individual. It is a contest between two elemental and historically opposed ideas of the relationship between the individual and the State. The chief threat posed by the Soviet Union, therefore, is not necessarily the vastness of its military forces — though vast they are — but in the relentlessness of its assault on our values. "

President Saunders, Ambassador Luce, honored guests, teachers, parents, and students of Westminster College. I thank you my dear friend Clare Luce for the generosity of that eloquent introduction. I am honored and grateful at becoming an honorary alumnus of Westminster, and by the warmth of your welcome and at the honor of being asked to speak here at Westminster in the Green Lecture Series, on which Winston Churchill and those who followed him have conferred such distinction.

I feel more at home here than you might imagine. I came here from the CIA campus in Virginia, across the Potomac from Washington. Contrary to the spy novels and movies, most of our people in intelligence spend their time sitting at computers or in libraries evaluating and analyzing information. Today's James Bonds have graduate degrees and are more conversant in economics, science, engineering, demography and history than with gambling casinos, fast cars, smokey bars, or rundown hotels around the world. They develop and use technical marvels and apply the finest scholarship to gather, analyze, and interpret facts and relationships from every corner of the earth and beyond.

The most difficult task in intelligence is forecasting developments a few months or years ahead. Winston Churchill had an uncanny, perhaps unique, capacity to look into the hearts and minds of civilization's adversaries and accurately foretell their intentions years and even decades ahead. He was a prophet alone in the early 1930s and, more significantly, he was still a prophet nearly alone in his vision of Russia here at Westminster College in 1946.

On that occasion, he defined a challenge with which my generation has struggled for a third of a century and which the generation now at Westminster must also face. Listen to his words:

> From Stettin in the Baltic to Trieste in the Adriatic,
> an Iron Curtain has descended across the con-
> tinent....The Communist Parties which were very
> small in all three Eastern states of Europe, have been

raised to pre-eminence and power far beyond their
numbers and are seeking everywhere to obtain
totalitarian control.

He went on to say:

In a great number of countries, far from the Russian
frontiers and throughout the world, communist fifth
columns are established and work in complete unity
and absolute obedience to the directions they receive
from the communist center.

Speaking of the American atomic bomb and the peril that would exist
if a communist state had that capability, he said:

The fear of them alone might easily have been used
to enforce totalitarian systems upon the free
democratic world, with consequences appalling to
human imagination.

All this, less than a year after he had won the long struggle against
Hitler with Russia by our side, was new and startling to the American
people. Churchill allowed himself a cry of anguish that again his warning would go unheeded:

The last time I saw it all coming, and cried aloud to
my own fellow countrymen and to the world
but....No one would listen and one by one we were
all sucked into the awful whirlpool.

How much more alarmed would Churchill be if he looked around the
world today and saw how the Soviets have grown in strength and how
far they have extended their power and influence beyond the Iron Curtain he so aptly labeled. He would see Soviet power:

 ◆ In Vietnam along China's southern border and astride the sea lanes
    which bring Japan's oil from the Persian Gulf.

 ◆ In Afghanistan, 500 miles closer to the warm water ports of the
    Indian Ocean and to the Straits of Hormuz through which comes
    the oil essential to Western Europe.

 ◆ On the Horn of Africa overlooking the passageway of Suez, which
    connects the Mediterranean Sea and the Indian Ocean.

♦ In Southern Africa, rich in minerals, which the industrial nations must have.

♦ And in the Caribbean and Central America on the very doorstep of the United States.

And what would Churchill think of the cataclysmic events in Lebanon and Grenada during the last seven days. For reasons which you will understand, I am not in a position to go into in any detail beyond what you have learned from the media, and like any good reporter I'm prepared to go to jail to protect my sources. But I will hazard an attempt to relate the events to what Churchill called the sinews of peace when he spoke here.

The disaster in Lebanon would have reminded him of the awful price that can be levied to maintain peace. The response of both our Marines in Lebanon and the flood of new recruits here would have reminded him of the courage and spirit his countrymen demonstrated when they stood alone against the forces of darkness in Europe.

He would have been gratified to see in Grenada a free nation act to check the potential communist aggression which he warned against here, as he had failed to get his own country to act against fascism of the thirties. He would rejoice that for the first time the West has restored to a colony of the Soviet empire the freedom which had been stolen from it.

Today, we are as a nation challenged on many levels. The most potentially devastating threat comes from the nuclear missiles which are aimed at us. The second threat comes from the land, air, and sea forces of the Warsaw Pact nations in Europe which continue to gain on NATO forces in quantity and quality. The third threat is the growing ability of the Soviets to project power over long distances, an ability vividly demonstrated by their use of air and sea transport to link up advanced Soviet weapons with Cuban troops thousands of miles from their borders. We saw them do this first in Angola and again in Ethiopia.

The fourth level of threat is something we might call creeping imperialism. The Kremlin uses a variety of techniques to exploit economic, racial, and religious divisions around the world and to destabilize and subvert other countries by fostering internal insurgency. The Soviet Union then supplies weapons, training, and advisors to bring in radical governments which will extend Soviet power and further Soviet interests.

It is to the strategic nuclear threat and that of conventional forces in Europe that we devote most of our concern and commit most of our defense resources. Yet, the appalling devastation which would result from the use of these weapons is such that this threat is less likely to materialize than that of aggressive protection of power and intrusion into other countries.

All of these threats are interrelated, and the measures needed to deal with them are closely interconnected. We must maintain a strategic posture that convinces the Soviets that the risk of any attack on the U.S. or its allies far outweighs any possible benefits. But more than that is necessary. The growth in overall Soviet military power, unmatched by the West over the last fifteen to twenty years, has encouraged them to try intimidation to split our allies away from us and undermine our credibility. If the adverse shift in the strategic balance of recent years is permitted to go far enough, it will become easier for the Soviets to exploit soft spots around the world. It will seem to have become less risky for the Soviets to involve themselves in smaller conflicts, especially in less-developed parts of the world.

To face these threats effectively we have to deal with the Soviet Union not as we would like it but as it is. We live on the same planet, we have to go on sharing it. We must therefore stand ready to talk to the Soviet leadership. The character of modern weapons, not only nuclear but conventional, makes this dialogue indispensable. But we must resolve not to hand an advantage to the other side, to do nothing that would either risk credibility of the Western alliance or unsettle the military balance on which peace itself depends.

We must recognize, too, that the Soviets will exploit arms control talks and agreements to slow down improvements in Western military capabilities while they continue to build up and modernize their own forces. Thus far they have succeeded in this objective. They have negotiated ceilings which permit their continued military buildup or they have avoided restrictions on new weapons they intend to build. The Soviet Union has been unwilling to forego any of its major military programs in order to induce us to drop our own programs.

Nevertheless, we should persist in arms negotiations in order to contain this competition. We must continue to hope that at some point there will be a change in Soviet perceptions and behavior.

Here at Westminster, Churchill wondered:

> Nobody knows what Soviet Russia and its com-
> munist international organization intends to do in
> the immediate future, or what are the limits, if any,
> to their expansive and proselytizing tendencies.

A month after Churchill made his speech here at Westminster College, his question was echoed in Moscow. The new U.S. Ambassador
to Russia, General Walter Bedel Smith, met with Stalin in the Kremlin
to ask, "What does the Soviet Union want and how far is Russia going
to go?" Stalin accused the U.S. of trying to thwart Russia and declared
that Churchill's speech here at Fulton was an unfriendly act. Asked
again, "How far is Russia going to go?" Stalin coolly replied, "We're
not going much further."

We know today that Russia has gone a lot further. It is essential that
we understand how this was accomplished. During the mid to late 1970s,
the Soviets unfurled a new strategy on a new front – the Third World.
And their strategy has worked.

The most effective technique employed in this strategy has been the
use of proxies. This is not exactly new in history. The Romans used men
from conquered countries to fight their enemies. Later, Swiss and German mercenaries were available to the highest bidder all over Europe.
The British army had its Ghurkas and the French had their Foreign
Legion. But the Soviets use the Cubans, East Germans, Libyans, and
Vietnamese in a quite different role.

These proxies act in peace as well as war. Their role is as much political as military. East Germans in Africa, Cubans in Latin America, and
Vietnamese in Asia have a certain legitimacy and freedom from imperialist taint that Soviet troops would not enjoy. Different proxies have
specialized functions. Of the more than 40,000 Cubans in Africa, 80 percent of the soldiers are on active duty. Vietnam, with the fourth largest
army in the world, keeps China and Thailand worried as it solidifies its
position in Kampuchea. Most of the thousands of East German experts
in Africa or Latin America are active in administration, education, industry, health, and, above all, the security forces which protect the
regimes from the people.

Libya, Cuba, South Yemen, East Germany, and Bulgaria operate
camps for training terrorists and insurgents who are then sent around the
world. The Libyans have helped promote Soviet foreign policy goals

through their invasion of Chad and through their assistance to rebels in the Philippines, Morocco, and Central America. Let us also not forget their coups, plots, and assassination attempts against the leaders of pro-Western countries, nor their financial help to so-called "liberation" groups and terrorist organizations in the Middle East and at least ten countries in Latin America.

Grenada provides a vivid illustration of how the Soviets practice creeping imperialism by proxy. Early reports indicate that, in addition to the Cubans on the island, there were on the island Soviets, North Koreans, Libyans, East Germans, and Bulgarians working together to establish a military base in the Eastern Caribbean. This should come as no surprise. It is a microcosm of Nicaragua. For more than two years Managua has been an international city with Cubans, Soviets, East Germans, Vietnamese, North Koreans, Bulgarians, Libyans, and PLO elements working together to fasten a totalitarian grip on Nicaragua, to make Nicaragua militarily dominant over its neighbors and to project revolutionary violence into El Salvador, Honduras, Costa Rica, and Guatemala.

With the exception of the Allende government in Chile, committed pro-Soviet governments have never come to power through peaceful means, but always through violence, coups, and civil wars. The Soviets recognize that in most Third World countries power rests with the military. They have focused, therefore, on either winning over the officer corps or helping to overthrow and replace them with others more likely to do their bidding. Having for decades denounced the "merchants of death," the Soviets have become the world's leading supplier of arms. Over recent years, their arms shipments to the Third World have been four times greater than their economic assistance. This has made Third World arms recipients dependent on the Soviets for thousands of advisors, for spare parts, and for continued logistical support.

Yet the Soviet Union is crippled. It is crippled in having only a military dimension. It has not been able to deliver economic, political, or cultural benefits at home or abroad. Without exception, the economic record of the countries which have come under Soviet influence has ranged from poor to very poor. Economic progress has been far greater in the free areas of East and Southeast Asia, in Central America until disruption by Soviet and Cuban-backed insurgency and in the Ivory Coast and other non-socialistic countries in Africa.

Military support can establish a relationship between a superpower and a small country. But in the long run it is economic, financial, scientific, technical, and cultural exchanges that deliver benefits and maintain close relationships with Third World countries. The Soviet Union cannot compete in these areas. This forces the Soviets to rely on subversion and disruption of stable political and economic relationships to weaken Western relationships and create a condition of chaos in which their surrogates and internal allies can seize power.

In this strategy of disruption, the areas most heavily targeted are clearly the Middle East and Central America. By fanning the flame of conflict between Arab and Israeli, Sunni and Shia, radical and moderate Arab, by playing both sides against the middle in the Iran-Iraq War, and by nailing down a military position in Syria and Afghanistan, the Soviets hope to keep the Middle East in turmoil and the oil resources on which the Western world depends under constant threat. The other sensitive target is the Caribbean and Central America. Soviet power is already solidly established in Cuba and Nicaragua. This threatens the Panama Canal and the sea lanes of the Caribbean. Insurgencies and revolutionary violence have been unleashed to topple governments in El Salvador, Honduras, and Guatemala.

Since World War II, we have seen that countries falling under communist control promptly produce a heavy flow of refugees – people voting with their feet to go elsewhere. Millions of refugees have left Eastern Europe and Cuba since the communists took over. Hundreds of thousands of people have put their lives at stake to escape from Indochina in leaking ships. More than one-fourth of the population of Afghanistan has fled to Pakistan and Iran. The flow of refugees from Central America is already under way.

A Cubanization of Central America would quickly create new refugees by the millions. The Soviets can calculate that a greatly increased military threat on our southern flank, and the internal disruption that would result if millions of Latin Americans walked north, would distract the U.S. from dealing with what could be more lethal threats elsewhere in the world. At the same time, American influence in Central America will be damaged if the West is unable to sensitively and constructively assist the people of Central America and Mexico in defending themselves as well as solving their social and economic problems on their own terms.

The U.S. needs a realistic counter-strategy. Many components of that strategy are familiar, but they must be approached and linked in new ways. The measures needed to address the Soviet challenge in the Third World have the additional appeal that they also represent a sensible American approach to the Third World whether or not the USSR is involved:

◆ **We have too often neglected our friends and neutrals in Africa, the Middle East, Latin America, and Asia until they became a problem or were threatened by developments hostile to our interests.** These countries now buy 40 percent of our exports; that alone is reason enough to pay greater attention to their problems before our attention is commanded by coups, insurgencies, or instability. The priority of less-developed countries in our overall foreign policy needs to be raised and sustained.

◆ **We must be prepared to demand firmly, but tactfully and privately, that our friends observe certain standards of behavior with regard to basic human rights.** This is required by our own principles, and essential to political support in the U.S. Moreover, we have to be willing to talk straight to those we would help about issues they must address to block foreign exploitation of their problems – issues such as land reform, corruption, and the like. We need to show how the Soviets have exploited such vulnerabilities elsewhere to make clear that we aren't preaching out of cultural arrogance but are making recommendations based on experience.

◆ **We need to be ready to help our friends defend themselves.** We can train them in counterinsurgency tactics and upgrade their communications, mobility, police, and intelligence capabilities. We need changes in our foreign military sales laws to permit the U.S. to provide arms for self-defense more quickly. We also need to change our military procurement policies so as to have stocks of certain basic kinds of weapons more readily available.

◆ **We must find a way to mobilize and use our greatest asset in the Third World: private business.** Few in the Third World wish to adopt the Soviet economic system. Neither we nor the Soviets can offer unlimited or even large-scale economic assistance to the less-developed countries. Investment is the key to economic suc-

cess in the Third World and we, our NATO allies, and Japan need
to develop a common strategy to promote investment and support
it with know-how in the Third World. The Soviets are helpless to
compete with private capital in these countries.

Without a sustained, constant policy applied over a number of years,
we cannot counter the relentless pressure of the USSR in the Third
World. It is past time for the American government – executive branch
and Congress – to take the Soviet challenge in the Third World seriously and to develop a broad, integrated strategy for countering it. The less-
developed nations of the world will be the principal U.S.-Soviet battleground for many years to come.

There is also a political weapon we can deploy around the world which
is more powerful than the Soviets' military arsenal and subversive bag
of tricks. All the people of the world on both sides of the Iron Curtain
remain united as they were in Churchill's day on one issue: their abhor-
rence of dictatorship in all its forms, most particularly totalitarianism
and the terrible inhumanities it has caused in our time – the Great Purge,
Auschwitz and Dachau, the Gulag, and Cambodia. They have certainly
noted it was not the democracies that invaded Afghanistan, or suppressed
Polish Solidarity, or used chemical and toxic warfare in Afghanistan and
Southeast Asia.

Around the world today, the democratic revolution is gathering new
strength, in Asia, in Africa, in our own hemisphere. In Latin America,
18 of 34 countries have freely-elected governments and six are working
toward democratization – altogether representing 70 percent of the
people of that continent. In the United Nations, eight of the ten developing nations which have joined that body in the past five years are
democracies. We must foster the infrastructure of democracy, the system of a free press, unions, political parties, and universities which allows a people to choose its own way, to develop its own culture and to
reconcile its own differences through peaceful means. Finally, if we are
to win the struggle for the world's freedom and liberty, we need to rees-
tablish what Sir John Plumb described so eloquently as the true dominion
of history when he spoke on this campus at last May's Kemper Lecture.

It is in the true study of our history and our values that we can establish the same historical confidence in our society that Winston Churchill
had in his, and which enabled him to speak so eloquently to his people
and they to respond so wholeheartedly. It is your challenge, as our fu-

ture leaders, to bring a proper sense of our destiny to our affairs, and that can only come through a knowledge of our past and a feeling for the heritage which is ours to preserve and pass on. And I can imagine no setting and no atmosphere more conducive to kindling and developing that learning and that sentiment than the one which blesses you in these surroundings.

President Kennedy some twenty years ago observed that we were involved in a long twilight struggle. Winston Churchill's speech here at Westminster College marked the initial recognition by the West that the struggle had begun. Churchill also observed that, "What we have to consider here today while time remains, is the permanent prevention of war and the establishment of conditions of freedom and democracy as rapidly as possible in all countries."

It is now nearing forty years since Winston Churchill spoke here. The thought that I would leave with you is that the struggle with what the Soviet Union represents is not confined to Churchill's generation, or to my generation, or the generation of your faculty and parents, or your generation. This is a conflict deeply rooted in ideas. This conflict is as old as recorded history. The threat posed by the Soviet Union is the lineal descendent of the same threat Western civilizations have faced for better than two thousand years: it is the threat posed by despotism against the more or less steadily developing concept that the highest goal of the state is to protect and to foster the creative capabilities and the liberties of the individual. It is a contest between two elemental and historically opposed ideas of the relationship between the individual and the state. The chief threat posed by the Soviet Union, therefore, is not necessarily in the vastness of its military forces — though vast they are — but in the relentlessness of its assault on our values.

Three days after his speech here in Fulton, Mr. Churchill addressed the Virginia State Assembly, the oldest legislative body in the Western Hemisphere. In that speech he stated:

> It is in the years of peace that war is prevented and those foundations laid upon which the noble structures of the future can be built. That peace will not be preserved without the virtues which make victory possible in war. Peace will not be preserved by pious sentiments expressed in terms of platitudes, or by official grimaces and diplomatic correctitude, or

by casting aside in dangerous times our panoply of
war-like strength. There must be earnest thought.
There must be faithful perseverance and foresight.
Greatheart must have his sword and armor to guard
the pilgrims on their way.

I am confident that Sir Winston would agree that despite our fondest
hopes to fulfill Isaiah's prophecy, all of human history, and especially
all of Russian history, points to our need and the need of our children
for swords as well as plowshares. I see, therefore, the same future Churchill saw here so long ago. Not an easy future – but, with perseverance
and devotion to our duty, a free one in which our values and opportunities are preserved.

A HISTORICAL POSTSCRIPT

While at Westminster, I read Martin Gilbert's lecture on "The Origins
of the Iron Curtain Speech," the first in a series endowed by the Cros-
by Kemper Foundation. Mr. Gilbert, Churchill's official biographer,
disclosed a letter which Churchill wrote, two days after speaking here
at Westminster, to his successor Prime Minister Atlee. Churchill con-
fided that, in his journey from Washington to Fulton, President Truman
informed him that the United States would send the body of the Turkish
Ambassador, who died in Washington a few days earlier, back to Turkey
on the American battleship *Missouri*. This ship, on which the Japanese
surrender had been signed, was at that time probably the largest battleship afloat. It would be accompanied by a strong task force which
would remain in the Sea of Marmara around Turkey for an unspecified
period. Churchill told Atlee that he viewed this as a very important act
of state calculated to make Russia understand that she must come to
reasonable terms of discussion with the Western democracies. It would
reassure Turkey and Greece and send a signal against cutting the British
life-line to the Mediterranean by establishing a Russian naval base at
Tripoli, as well as a signal against ongoing treaty breaches in Persia,
encroachments in Manchuria and Korea, and pressure for Russian expansion at the expense of Turkey. Churchill emphasized that some show
of strength and resistance power was necessary to a good settlement with
Russia.

The *Missouri*, carrying the remains of the Turkish ambassador,
departed New York on March 22nd, anchored in the Bosphorus off Is-

tanbul on April 5th, and rendered full honors, including a 19-gun salute, during both the transfer of the remains of the late ambassador and the funeral. The *Missouri* departed Istanbul on April 9th, sailed to Piraeus, and stayed in Greek waters until April 21st.

All this was in response to Soviet misbehavior in Iran, Turkey, and Greece. During the war the British and Russians had occupied Iran to restrain a government suspected of pro-German sympathies and to secure a supply line vital to supporting the Soviets' fight against the Germans. After the war the Soviets stated that no time limit had been set for the Soviet military presence in Iran and, in other ways, showed great reluctance to withdraw. Matters reached a point where, on January 19, 1946, Iran complained about Soviet behavior to the United Nations Security Council. Three days before Churchill spoke here, the Soviets announced that they would withdraw only a portion of their troops; the rest would remain "pending examination of the situation." Earlier the Soviet government had denounced the Turkish treaty of friendship and neutrality, and demanded the secession of parts of Turkey, joint Russo-Turkish control of the Straits, and a new alliance of friendship along the lines of those signed with the East European countries.

Churchill noted this in his speech here saying: "Turkey and Persia are both very profoundly alarmed and disturbed at the claims which are being made upon them and at the pressure exerted by the Moscow government."

While the *Missouri* was on the high seas, agreement was reached between Moscow and Teheran, and on May 22nd, discussions in the United Nations were concluded and Gromyko confirmed the evacuation of all Soviet troops from Iran.

The *Missouri* arrived at a time when, in addition to great Soviet pressure on Iran, there were ominous Russian overtures and activities in the entire Balkan area. Greece had become the scene of a communist-inspired civil war, as Russia attempted to extend Soviet influence throughout the Mediterranean region. Demands were made on the Turkish government to grant the Soviets a naval base in the Dodecanese Islands and joint control of the Turkish Straits leading from the Black Sea into the Mediterranean.

The *Missouri*'s voyage was seen as a symbol of U.S. interest in preserving Greek and Turkish liberty, and to convey that the U.S. was ready to use her naval sea and air power to stand firm against a clearly threatening tide of Soviet subversion against nations along its southern borders and seaways.

President Reagan has recently made a similar response to ominous Russian and Cuban overtures and activities on our Caribbean approaches. Addressing a joint session of Congress on April 27, 1983, President Reagan quoted from President Truman's promulgation of the Truman Doctrine before a joint session of Congress in 1947, to wit: "I believe that it must be the policy of the United States to support free people who are resisting attempted subjugation by armed minorities or by outside pressures." On that occasion President Reagan asked the question: "Will our response — economic, social, and military — be as appropriate and successful as Mr. Truman's bold solutions to the problems of postwar Europe?"

◆ ◆ ◆

THE SOVIET ARSENAL

Under Casey's leadership the intelligence community broadened its study of the Soviet threat far beyond military issues. In this speech he talks about establishment of the CIA's Center for the Study of Insurgency and Instability and the Technology Transfer Center. Casey viewed the establishment of these Centers as an especially important part of his achievements. And he devoted an enormous part of his time to shaping these Centers' research programs and then to working with the analysts themselves on various projects.

Through speeches like this one, Casey sent strong signals to Moscow that he was onto their game — and out to stop them. The Soviets were quick to recognize that Casey was a serious threat to their plans, and in their print and broadcast propaganda they singled out Casey for special treatment. The CIA unit that monitored Soviet remarks about U.S. officials regularly brought such reports to Casey, and he read them with relish. He was especially fond of one TASS commentary that described him as a "Queens (New York) gangster."

Address to the 64th Annual Convention of the American Legion, Chicago, Illinois, August 24, 1982.

Today, it has become widely recognized that we have in the Soviet Union a powerful and determined adversary which is carrying on a huge military buildup to which it devotes over twice as much of its national effort as we and our allies are able to devote to our defense.

But what is not so widely recognized is the ability and the will that the Soviets have demonstrated in recent years to project their power over great distances. We have seen them bring planes and sophisticated weapons as far as Angola or Ethiopia to meet troops brought in from Cuba. We see Soviet chemical warfare weapons employed on the Arabian Peninsula and in Indochina. We've seen Soviet planes and troops come across the mountains into Afghanistan.

Still less widely recognized is the Soviet ability and will to project its power worldwide through subversion and insurgency and the adept use of proxy forces, arms sales, and thousands of military advisers scattered around the world.

Recently I had our cartographers prepare a map to show the Soviet presence in its various degrees of influence. They colored in red on a map of the world the nations under a significant degree of Soviet influence. When this map was finished, 50 nations were in red. Ten years go, in a similar map I had prepared, only half as many of the nations of the world were colored in red. In those ten years, between 1972 and 1982, four nations have extricated themselves from Soviet grasp, and 25 nations either fell under an increased degree of Soviet influence or faced an insurgency backed by the Soviets or their proxies. Each of the eleven nations now faced with insurgencies throughout the world today, supported by Cuba, Libya, the Soviet Union or South Yemen, happens to be close to the natural resources or to the sea lanes on which the United States and its allies must depend to fuel and supply their economic life.

It's not hard to understand how all this has come about. Time and again, we've watched agents of the Soviet Union, the communist apparatus, move in to exploit underlying social and economic discontents, which are plentiful around the world. This became the basis for their expansion with training and massive weapons. With this help, local insurgents attack economic targets and drive out investment. This further heightens the political and economic discontent on which this kind of thing feeds. As this discontent grows, more people go over to the insurgents, which makes them bolder, stronger and more difficult to deal with.

Now there are still more subtle and less widely understood threats. One is the monster known as international terrorism. The Soviet Union has provided funding and support for terrorist operations via Eastern Europe and its client nations like Libya and Cuba. With at least tacit Soviet approval, many terrorist groups have trained together in Cuba, Libya, Iraq, South Yemen, Lebanon, and the countries of Eastern Europe. . . .

Another threat is the ability of the Soviet Union, largely through its intelligence arm, the KGB, to insidiously insert its policy views into the political dialogue in the United States and other foreign countries. The KGB is adept at doing this in a way that hides the Soviet hand as the instigator.

We see Soviet-authored or -inspired articles surreptitiously placed in the press around the world, forged documents distributed; manipulation of indigenous foreign communist parties; international and local communist-front organizations, and clandestine radio operations; all employed aggressively to erode trust in the United States as the leader of the free world.

Late last year, for example, delegations attending an important security conference in Madrid received copies of a forged letter allegedly sent by President Reagan to King Juan Carlos of Spain. This letter cited "Highly Secret Information" advising the King that several of his staff were opposed to Spain's joining NATO and urging that the King move against them. Obviously, this forgery was intended to disrupt Spanish-U.S. relations and to provoke internal opposition to Spain's joining NATO.

This type of thing has been repeated again and again in examples that cannot be discussed in an open forum, but which have been laid out in closed sessions of congressional committees.

Still another low-key but highly damaging threat can only be called a hemorrhage. Only recently have we established the degree to which the accuracy, precision, and power of Soviet weapons — which we are required now to counter with budget-busting appropriations, are based on Western technology to a far greater extent than we ever dreamed. The Soviet political and military intelligence organizations, the KGB and the GRU, have for years been training young scientists to target and roam the world to acquire technology for their military arsenal from the United States, Western Europe, Japan, anywhere they can get it. They have acquired in this way technology worth many billions, some of it by purchase, legal or illegal, or by theft, espionage, bribery, scientific exchanges, and by exploiting our open literature and our Freedom of Information Act. The damage to our national security becomes all too obvious as we face the need to spend billions of dollars to defend ourselves against new Soviet weapons – weapons in which a great deal of time and effort has been saved by leap-frogging development stages and in which new power and accuracy has been achieved through use of our guidance and radar systems, our bomb and weapon designs, and our production methods.

Now I've outlined for you a horrifying and really alarming range of challenges. How do we deal with this far-flung and aggressively pursued range of threats? We have lost a lot of time. Fortunately, if we understand and speak clearly to our own purposes and the nature of the threat I have outlined, we can enlist the help of friends and sympathizers across the world, as well as the support of the American people which is critical.

President Reagan has taken four critical first steps. He has made an unambiguous commitment to: first, strengthening our overall military strength; second, to working for mutual reductions in nuclear arms and weapons of mass destruction; third, to enhancing our ability and activity in speaking openly to the people of the world; and fourth, to rebuilding our intelligence capabilities.

Let me give you a brief report on the health of the American intelligence community and its role in meeting this range of threats I have outlined for you. . . .

My highest responsibility as Director of Central Intelligence is to produce sound national intelligence estimates on issues relevant to our national security. We've taken steps to assure standards of integrity and objectivity, relevance and timeliness, accuracy and independence in these intelligence assessments.

The chiefs of all our intelligence components (the National Security Agency, the Defense Intelligence Agency, the State Department's Intelligence and Research component, the intelligence services of the armed forces – Army, Navy, Air Force, Marines – Treasury, FBI, and Energy) now meet as a Board of Estimates to assure that all available information and all the different, substantiated views are fully reflected to provide our decision-makers with a range of real and specific expectations as to what may be ahead.

We've established a Center for the Study of Insurgency and Instability to provide advance warning of potentials for destabilization around the world, this to protect against the kind of surprise we experienced with the fall of the Shah in Iran. The small and weak countries in which an insurgency could be developed to overthrow governments do not need and cannot handle expensive and sophisticated weapons which they all seek. What they need is light arms to defend themselves against externally trained and supported guerrillas, good intelligence, good police methods, good communications, training in small arms and their use in small unit actions, and the mobility to keep up with the hit-and-run tactics used by insurgents and guerrillas around the world. We can introduce an element of stability into the Third World by helping small countries develop those skills and capabilities, and we can do this for a fraction of our foreign aid budget. After all, governments facing civil war cannot achieve the economic and social objectives of our foreign aid until they're able to control and combat internal disruption. Social progress does not come in the middle of civil war. . . .

To counter the terrorists, with operational headquarters in Beirut, Tripoli in Libya, Aden in South Yemen, and other centers across international borders and into five continents, we work with the intelligence services of friendly nations. Together we are developing a network to track terrorist organizations and activities and train local quick reaction forces to carry the fight against terrorism around the world.

To combat the loss of critical technology to our adversaries, we've established a Technology Transfer Center to provide ammunition to other government agencies plus ways to sensitize our scientists, engineers, and sales forces to the possibility of technology pickpockets — the dummy customers and the forged papers used to funnel sensitive technology and equipment behind the Iron Curtain. We helped develop and enforce restrictions limiting the flow of sensitive technology in trade and other normal business transactions.

To combat false propaganda, our intelligence can identify the forgeries and distortions. But to expose and rebut them, the private sector of the free world will have to tackle much of the load. This is a challenge for everyone who believes in the value of a free, open society. And nobody meets this challenge more effectively and more vigorously than the American Legion in its publications and its organized activity around this country. So I urge you and other organizations, we need a great deal more of this activity.

In the final analysis, all these threats boil down to a struggle for the hearts and minds of men. The courage of the Afghan freedom fighters, supported by arms and training provided by many other nations, escalates the price and deters armed aggression and insurrection everywhere. The world has seen the communist system fail in Poland. There the once-proud call of Lenin, "Workers of the world unite," makes those in Warsaw and the Kremlin tremble.

One concluding thought. As a nation, we have a propensity for shooting ourselves in the foot. One of these self-inflicted wounds close to my heart leaves the United States the only country in the world which gives foreign intelligence agencies, and anyone else, a legal license to poke into our files. I question very seriously whether a secret intelligence agency and a Freedom of Information Act can co-exist for very long. The willingness of foreign intelligence agencies and their services to share their information and to rely on us fully, and of individuals to risk their lives and reputations to help us, will continue to dwindle unless we get rid of the Freedom of Information Act.

Secrecy is essential to any intelligence organization. Ironically, secrecy is accepted without protest in many areas of our society. Physicians, lawyers, clergymen, grand juries, journalists, income tax returns, and crop futures all have confidential aspects protected by law. Why should national security information be entitled to any less protection?

In conclusion, I would only echo the sentiments so eloquently expressed by your National Commander that we have nothing to fear in any of these challenges if we deal with them directly, with calm and with faith.

◆ ◆ ◆

THE SOVIET ASSAULT ON WESTERN VALUES

Casey's speeches were always packed with information and analysis; he didn't know how to write any other kind of speech. As a result, his speeches often contained bits of journalistic dynamite — the stuff of headlines. Casey was often disappointed, but not surprised, when journalists ignored the facts he provided to them and instead published only those "secrets" they had managed to ferret out.

Arnaud, Clare, members of *The Washington Times* Advisory Board and Editorial Board. Thanks for dinner tonight. I have enjoyed the stimulating conversation thus far and look forward to some more before we adjourn. I know the main purpose of this occasion is to provide an opportunity for you to fire away at me with questions. But before the fun begins, let me set the stage by touching briefly on a few recent events and challenges confronting the U.S. and its intelligence capabilities.

First on the Daniloff matter. Unlike Zhakharov, Nick Daniloff is not a spy and has never had a relationship with CIA. His only crime was to be an enterprising journalist with a nose for news. He used his familiarity with Russian culture and history to mingle widely in Soviet society and explore such stories as the use of chemical and biological agents in Afghanistan — the yellow rain issue that the Soviet government has good reason to hide. Of course, we don't know for sure, but I suspect that the Soviets sincerely believe they have a real case against Daniloff. This simply means that in the Soviet Union a Western journalist who is practicing his profession is considered to be a spy and guilty of espionage. In accusing Nick Daniloff, the Soviet government has only indicted itself.

This leads now to a more philosophic point. I believe our national attention, all too often, is fixed on the surface questions and manifestations of our competition with the Soviets and far too little on why we are engaged in this confrontation in the first place, the real nature of that contest, and its historical context. It's important that our nation understand that we are involved in the lineal descendant of the conflict Western civilization has struggled with for millennia — state despotism versus

Address to the *Washington Times* Advisory Board and Editorial Board, Washington, D.C., September 25, 1986.

the notion that the highest goal of the state is to protect individual freedom and creativity.

The fact that the Soviets are incapable of making a distinction between journalism and espionage, but perfectly capable of indulging in the most blatant form of hostage-taking, tells me that we are dealing with a fundamentally alien and totally unpalatable value system that threatens our own cherished institutions. We should *not* get bogged down, for example, in the question of whether or not the Soviet Air Defense Command knew for a fact that it was shooting down a Korean Airlines 747. All we need to know is that the Soviet system was perfectly capable of shooting down a large unidentified aircraft on the *mere suspicion* that it *might* have been engaged in espionage.

We know that many in the West decry the cost and question the wisdom of our competition with the Soviets, simply because they don't understand its nature. There are those who should measure the effectiveness of our efforts to manage the Soviet relationship simply by whether or not a summit meeting can be held. This kind of perspective on the U.S.-Soviet contest is short-sighted, over-sighted, and tragically underestimates what we are against.

There is another manifestation of this problem that weighs heavily on my mind. How can we fully sensitize and alert public opinion throughout the land to the threat posed by Soviet and Soviet surrogate subversion in the Third World? You are magnificent in laying out the creeping Soviet imperialism that threatens the oil fields of the Middle East and the Isthmus between Central and South America – the imperialism that has added five new client states to its fold since the Vietnam War and that threatens at least twelve other Third World regimes at present.

Some of you have heard me on this general subject before and I am sure all of you know where I am coming from. You know I believe the stakes in Central America are particularly huge and historic. I could talk all night about what is going on in Nicaragua and will happen to our interests if the Sandinistas are allowed to consolidate their position. But on a more general note let me say that I believe the pendulum of history is beginning to swing away from Soviet Marxism as a model for Third World development and toward democracy and free market economics. After a particularly aggressive and successful surge during the ten years following the Vietnam War, Moscow now finds itself on the defensive supporting high-cost, long-term efforts to maintain in power unpopular repressive regimes that they have installed or co-opted all over the world, including the one in Managua. Even while we are enjoying this lovely dinner tonight, more than 300,000 freedom fighters are risking their lives in Afghanistan, Cambodia, Angola, Ethiopia, Nicaragua, Mozambique and Yemen.

This could be a golden opportunity to check Third World Marxist-Leninist regimes that are stamping out democratic liberties and threatening our own national security. We could be on the verge of an historic turning point in this century. But it will only work out this way if the U.S. together with its allies can understand the problem and muster the resolve to stay the course.

Unfortunately, I have very little doubt about Moscow's resolve to stay in this game and to do what it can to keep the pressure on. Let me give you a particularly graphic example of what we are up against. In the last several years, we have begun to see a trickle of Vietnamese-supplied arms cropping up in trouble spots around the world. The Soviets and their surrogates apparently have decided to start using the tremendous stockpile of U.S. weaponry seized by the communists in 1975. It's showing up in various places in Asia and Latin America, including Honduras, El Salvador, Jamaica, Pakistan, and Colombia, with Cuba almost certainly doing the delivering. . . .

The transfer of only a tiny fraction of this booty to, say, the communist insurgents in the Philippines, could quickly transform a bad security situation into a catastrophe, and once the Philippine Communist Party drops its ideological objection to receiving such foreign assistance — probably only a matter of time — I see little to stand in the way of such a transfer. U.S. policy has to deal with the reality of a Soviet and Soviet-surrogate network of international subversion. It cannot be wished away.

Now I don't want to leave you with the impression that we see the world through an anti-Soviet prism. We know better than that. The U.S. and the Soviet Union are no longer the only two players that matter. The number of players has proliferated, issues have become bewilderingly complex, the pace of change and technological advance almost overwhelming, and the world smaller and independent. Today we face threats to our longer-term interests from all directions and from a variety of sources.

Right now, for example, we are becoming increasingly concerned about the Iran-Iraq War. This week marks the 6th anniversary of what has become the bloodiest conflict since World War II. It has resulted in more than one million casualties, including 500,000 deaths. Despite some seesawing back and forth, the war has essentially been a charnel-house draw. Now, however, signs are beginning to accumulate that Khomeini is preparing for a final push to knock Iraq out of the war and topple his hated arch rival, Sadam Hussein. Should the Iranians break through to victory, the result could be a devastating setback for U.S. and Western interests – comparable in impact to the Iranian revolution itself. Iraq would likely end up a Shiite-dominated vassal state. While the responsibility for the war itself cannot be laid at Moscow's doorstep, the instability and uncertainty that would result from its conclusion on Iranian terms would open new opportunities for Soviet meddling and create more problems for the U.S., not to mention Israel. And can anyone in this room doubt that Moscow would be eager to test such waters?

The Iran-Iraq War, despite its particularly disturbing potential consequences, is for the most part a relatively old-fashioned intelligence problem – a regional conflict characterized by World War I infantry tactics. Today's intelligence agenda, however, is increasingly dominated by a totally different set of problems. I am talking about the type of transnational issues that are posing an increasing challenge to our society and world position. The list is long and getting longer – international finance and debt, industrial competitiveness, narcotics, the proliferation of chemical, nuclear, and biological weapons, rapid population growth and urbanization, just to mention a few.

And, of course, the issue at the top of this new agenda is international terrorism. There are two things I can say with utmost confidence about this problem: One, a credible threat of force must be one element of a successful terrorism policy. And two, international terrorism is going to be with us for a long time.

Our military raid on Libya had some very therapeutic effects. Terrorist organizations and their state sponsors must now factor into their equation the certainty of swift and painful retaliation. This already has had in inhibiting effect on international terrorism and a galvanizing effect on the resolve of our friends, and on their willingness to act in concert with us.

But, I also have to tell you that the longer-term trend line is not particularly encouraging. During the first half of 1986, the number of terrorist incidents — 450 — was up some 25 percent, and the number of casualties up some 30 percent over the comparable period last year. Middle Eastern terrorism remains, of course, our greatest concern. The Karachi hijacking and the spate of bombings that have left eight dead and hundreds wounded is a testimony to terrorists' willingness to maim and kill indiscriminately.

So I think we have to be better prepared for matters to get worse before they get better. But I do think we are on the right track. Again, the trick is for the West to remain willing to stay the course. And here there is some reason for optimism. In France, for example, public and political resolve against terrorism — never a strong suit in the French deck — has been stiffened by the recent terrorist outrages in Paris to a point that should make it easier for Chirac to take a firm stand.

Incidentally, I read with interest your two stories this morning about British plans to talk to the Soviets about countering terrorism. I have my own doubts, which I will pass on to Sir Geoffrey. There may be some who are not yet fully persuaded about Moscow's own links to terrorism, but not me. We continue to obtain solid evidence that Moscow is supporting terrorism where its interests are served. We also know that Palestinian terrorist groups are permitted to use Eastern Europe for illicit commercial operations, arms deals, and staging attacks in the West. We know that the leaders of well-known Middle East and European terrorist groups continue to travel and deal with East European communist states. These East European regimes act in some cases as Soviet surrogates in making arrangements with these groups. This is just some of what we know. And aside from the utter cynicism that would surround such an exchange with the British, someone needs to worry about Moscow's ability to use such a forum to elicit information about the West's counterterrorism methods and capabilities.

I didn't really come here tonight to try to depress you. As we move into the last two years of this administration, I feel a great sense of accomplishment over how, thanks to the support of the President and Congress, we have rebuilt this nation's intelligence capabilities. Our intelligence system today is more robust than at any time in our history and in far better shape than six or seven years ago.

In our business we cannot afford to stand still. It takes constant effort and continual investment to monitor and project the capabilities and characteristics of Soviet strategic and conventional military forces — for example, the new mobile missiles and missile-carrying aircraft and submarines Moscow is now deploying in amazing profusion.

It takes a major collection and analysis effort to keep up with the huge Soviet missile defense program, one that dwarfs our own in terms of both investment and continuity. Moscow has undertaken an ambitious program to provide leadership protection in times of nuclear war, including deep underground headquarters facilities with extensive communications and control capabilities. The overall magnitude of the steps Moscow is taking to put itself in position to fight, survive, and win a nuclear war is the best and most urgent argument for our own Strategic Defense Initiative program.

It takes a lot of people, training, and commitment to keep up with the KGB and its allied intelligence services and front organizations. They constitute a worldwide apparatus that is working to steal our technology, damage our reputation, divide us from our friends, and destabilize, subvert, and overthrow governments friendly to us. Their rumors, agents of influence, and forgeries, spreading poison around the world, have to be spotted and countered. CIA is the only organization in the West with the resources and capabilities necessary to deal effectively with this challenge. We are in action every day tracking and countering drug-runners and gun-smugglers, the violent revolutionary organizations, and terrorist training camps around the world.

I'm proud of the way we are doing the job. What really hurts is when we shoot ourselves in the foot by not being able to keep control of our own leadership. Of course, I am talking about leaking of classified information and its replaying in the media – a chronic problem that is becoming more and more intolerable. Last night, I addressed this issue in some detail before the Washington Chapter of Professional Journalists. Some of you no doubt were there and, don't worry, you won't have to hear it again tonight. Let me just say that our country has invested time, effort and talent, not to mention billions of dollars, to collect the information needed to address the problems I have alluded to tonight. Good intelligence sources are critical to our national security and our hopes of effective arms control. Secrecy and confidentiality as to how and through whom we collect information is essential to our effectiveness.

The time has come for this nation to regain control of its national secrets. We must tighten discipline and enforce laws Congress has enacted to protect classified information, and we must develop better cooperation between the media and the government as how to handle stories which put intelligence sources and methods at risk.

Some in the media cite the First Amendment of the Constitution and the "public's right to know" to make the point that there should be no restraint on what the media can reprint or broadcast and that they should be the sole judges of what should, or should not, be made public. I think that most of us know better. Most of us know that the First Amendment states only that Congress shall make no law abridging freedom of the press and, as the late Justice Potter said "Nowhere in the Constitution can anyone find anything about the public's right to know."

Our legal system has clearly recognized that without the secrecy needed to maintain our national sovereignty, we may not have freedom of speech or the other freedoms we all enjoy. The Court wrote in 1963 in *Kennedy v. Mendoza-Martinez* that "While the Constitution protects against invasion of individual rights, it is not a suicide pact." We can have both a free press and national security, but without national security we will lose our freedom.

◆ ◆ ◆

CREEPING IMPERIALISM: SOVIET STRATEGY IN THE MIDDLE EAST

A very sound tour d'horizon *outlining Soviet strategies in the Middle East and around the globe.*

I plan to talk to you about the Middle East in the context of some new dimensions which we see in the strategic balance between the Soviet bloc and the free democracies. In this context I want to look at the present dangers and how we can meet them in the Middle East.

I do it this way because I believe that today we are witnessing particularly intensive efforts to tilt the overall strategic balance against the West and because we Americans have failed, thus far, to see the interrelationship between what is happening in Central America and the Mid-

Address to the American Israel Public Affairs Committee Policy Conference, Washington, D.C., April 6, 1986.

dle East, the Mediterranean and the Persian Gulf, and the South Atlantic and the South China Sea. Increasingly, what we are trying to do in the Middle East and elsewhere must be geared to an ever more aggressive Soviet involvement and the growing danger from radical and violent groups operating in the Middle East. And while we confront this threat, we must continue to protect our overall strategic posture from similar and complementary pressures elsewhere.

We all know roughly the history of the strategic balance and how essential it is to protect the free world. From the beginning, the Soviets had the dominance in land warfare. This was countered by America superiority in strategic weapons. By 1980, the Soviet strategic offensive forces had caught up and, in many areas, surpassed ours. The Soviets are now protecting their land-base missile force by making it mobile, whereas the U.S. mobile missiles will not be deployed until sometime in the 1990s.

They have for well over a decade conducted a vigorous missile defense program. They are completing a missile defense system around Moscow. We have no comparable system. Facing this combination of offensive and defensive missile forces capable of a first strike against our nuclear deterrent, our SDI research is examining whether effective defenses, which threaten no one, can provide a more stable deterrent to all our interests.

While we negotiate to scale down the huge nuclear arsenal with which the two superpowers confront each other, a more insidious threat may be developing. This massive nuclear and conventional force which the Soviets have may be only a shield to make it easier and less risky to intimidate and subvert weaker governments and to gobble up pieces of territory around the globe. They have acquired bridgeheads in Cuba and Vietnam, in South Yemen and Ethiopia and Angola, and in Nicaragua, Cambodia, Afghanistan, and elsewhere. These bridgeheads are being linked in a growing logistical and support network supported by expanding Soviet naval and air power.

In the Caribbean, the Soviets have created in Cuba the strongest military force in the Western Hemisphere, with the exception only of our own. Over the last few years, they have given Cuba massive infusions of military hardware.

Today, we have an extension of this Cuban base on the American mainland in Nicaragua. Similar links and components of this network have been established all around the globe. From Angola, for example, Soviet naval and air forces now routinely operate astride Western shipping lanes in the Atlantic. Similarly, this network threatens Western sea lanes in the Red Sea, the Arabian Sea, and the Indian Ocean from bases in Ethiopia and South Yemen. And Soviet naval and air forces operating out of our former bases at Cam Ranh Bay and Da Nang in Vietnam command the vital sea lanes linking Japan, Taiwan, and South Korea with Middle East oil supplies and their Southeast Asian allies.

It is the Mediterranean segment of this Soviet global network which here concerns us most. It is anchored in Libya and Syria, which are gaining influence and control in Lebanon and Sudan to further squeeze Israel and the moderate Arab states of the Middle East.

These bridgeheads are very real and they are not static. They have a purpose. The Soviets are locating their strategic choke points in the world's sea lanes or in areas of high tension or potential conflict. They are being used to spread subversion and terror and to spawn new bridgeheads in neighboring countries. From Cuba and Nicaragua, terrorism and subversion are being exported throughout Central America and into Chile, Colombia, and elsewhere in Latin America. From Libya there is the invasion of Chad, attempts at destabilizing governments in Egypt, Tunisia, Zaire, and Sudan, and subversion throughout West Africa. From Angola, there are intrusions into Zaire. From Soviet-occupied Afghanistan there are continuing incursions into Pakistan.

And we have a new Soviet leader, Mr. Gorbachev, and already a hallmark of his regime is an intensified effort to nail down and cement these bridgeheads and make them permanent. Having piled close to two billion dollars worth of arms into Angola, Soviet advisors and Cuban troops are feverishly preparing a campaign, likely to be launched this month, designed to wipe out the forces resisting the Marxist government of Angola.

Starting two months ago with half-a-billion dollars worth of sophisticated weapons recently acquired, the Sandinista army, with Cuban helicopter pilots and combat direction, has been going all out to destroy the Contras down there before the Congress acts to renew assistance to them. Last week some 1,500 Sandinista troops crossed the Honduran border for this purpose, and this week we have seen thousands of Miskito Indians of the eastern part of Nicaragua driven across the border into Honduras.

The Soviets are also moving hard to nail down their bridgeheads in the Middle East. In South Yemen we have recently seen the application of the so-called Brezhnev Doctrine which says: "Once communist, always communist."

The government of South Yemen had begun to open up to the West. But hardline pro-Soviet exiles returned from Moscow and initiated a coup against the South Yemen President. This coup soon escalated into a bloody civil war between military and tribal elements loyal to the president and those of the hardline Soviet camp there. And after the Soviets watched the blood flow for a few days, planes flown by Soviet pilots pounded pro-government forces and Soviet weapons began to flow into the country to rebel forces.

We have seen this message before. In Afghanistan in 1979 and in Grenada in 1982. It has told us that leaders of governments installed by Moscow who seek improved relations with the West do so at their peril. The Soviets are not ready to brook any challenge in any part of their empire.

Now until recently in all this, the Soviet hand was more carefully screened and more subtly used in the Middle East. Today the Soviet investment in Syria and Libya is at all-time high, with some 6,000 Soviet bloc military advisors and a massive arsenal there of Soviet planes, tanks, and rockets. These two countries, along with Iran, have discovered in terrorism a new low-cost, low-risk method of attacking democratic governments in Europe, the Middle East, and Latin America. Terrorism is today an integral part of the foreign policy and defense apparatus of these states. Tiny Libya reaches south into the heart of Africa and east to press, together with Ethiopia, on Sudan. And we see Syria pushing hard to complete its domination of Lebanon and bring sophisticated Soviet weapons south, closer to the Israel border.

The only thing that the Soviets have to sell in the Middle East is weapons and munitions. They will expend major effort to preserve the traditionally Soviet-dominated arms markets in Iraq, Algeria, and North Yemen against Western competition. They will work to expand the Soviets' share of traditionally Western-dominated markets, particularly in Jordan and Kuwait, and to win back a share of the market in Egypt and Sudan. We can expect to see enhanced Soviet or Soviet-controlled reconnaissance and firepower all along the coast of the eastern and southern Mediterranean. We can expect them to step up their efforts to reunify the PLO and convince Syria to end its dispute with its Arab rivals.

It is also possible that to sabotage U.S.-sponsored peace negotiations, Moscow might back an aggressive Syrian military posture toward Israel, abandon Africa, throw full support behind the leftist and Syrian-backed factions of the PLO, and provide greater backing for the subversive elements of Libya and other radical leftist groups. Thus, from the north: Syria; from the west: Libya; from the south: South Yemen; and from the east: Iran and perhaps Iraq – all threaten the stability of the Middle East and have the potential to surround Israel and the oil fields of the region. The United States and Israel have a shared vital interest in arresting this pattern of Soviet and radical expansionism. . . .

What do we do about this? To thwart the threat of Soviet expansionism and radicalism in the Middle East, we have used in this government and will expand upon, together with our friends and allies, three inter-related strategies: improved strategic cooperation, the pursuit of peace, and economic development.

In the last few years, the United States has strengthened and invigorated its strategic partnership with Israel. As Secretary Shultz said here last year "strategic cooperation between the United States and Israel has become a formal, institutional process." And he repeated that in his talks this week with Prime Minister Peres. I can add that this institutionalization has included enhanced cooperation on the part our intelligence community, particularly in the fields of terrorism and counterterrorism. At the same time, we have also expanded our cooperative relationship with friendly Arab states, who also see a Soviet and radical danger.

Together we must fight terrorism, a threat which faces all our friends in the Middle East and elsewhere. Middle East radicals dedicated to weakening the West and Israel are also dedicated to the destruction of moderate and pro-Western regimes in the Arab world. They are determined that a peaceful settlement never be reached, determined to polarize the Arab world so that no accommodation can ever be reached, so that Arab states pursuing a pragmatic course collapse in front of Marxist or fundamentalist assaults. The Soviet Union, while it cannot always control these movements, profits from them as they weaken or eliminate areas of Western influence in the region.

We remain deeply committed to pursuing a political process to end the Arab-Israeli dispute. The reinvigoration of the peace process is, in my view, of overriding geopolitical importance in order to assist the parties directly concerned to negotiate face to face a solution to their difference. We reaffirmed this determination to the Israeli Prime Minister last week.

Finally, we are convinced that economic development is critical to building barriers to radicalism and Soviet imperialism. Prime Minister Peres has proposed joint economic cooperation among Israel, Egypt, and Jordan under a new "Marshall Plan" style program. Already the United States provides more economic aid to these states than any others. We are determined to stand by this commitment. We hope that other states with an interest in the region – including the Europeans and Japan – will enlist in regional economic help.

So, strategic cooperation, diplomacy, and economic development are the keys to maintaining the momentum built in these last years to haltering Soviet advances in the Middle East. We have vital interests there and shared values with Israel. Working together we must maintain those values in the Middle East, and the Mediterranean, and elsewhere.

* * *

Chapter 6

The Battle for Third World Freedom

COLLAPSE OF THE MARXIST MODEL: AMERICA'S NEW CALLING

Casey held a complex, coherent view of Third World development. He viewed the U.S. role as vital. He believed that President Reagan's speech on this subject at Cancun, Mexico – in which the President outlined an approach to helping the Third World – was among the most important the President had ever given. Casey cited that speech often, and would give out copies to visitors and even other members of the Administration. As time went by, Casey became increasingly frustrated by the U.S. government's inability to follow up on the President's Cancun initiative, by organizing the programs that would provide Third World countries with the economic wherewithal to develop, and the security shield to protect them from Soviet-sponsored insurgencies while they did.

A serious and long-time student of economic development, Casey read everything on this subject that he could get his hands on. During one of many conversations in his office about development he asked if I had ever read anything by P.T. Bauer, the great British economist who was elevated to a peerage for his work on Third World issues. "On this subject," Casey added, "Bauer is my rabbi." What was amazing was not so much Casey's choice of "rabbi" (that is, instructor) but rather that a U.S. intelligence chief had thought deeply enough about development issues to have any "rabbi" at all. I made it a point to pass along Casey's

Address to the Union League Club, New York, New York, January 9, 1985.

*comment, with the happy result that analysts throughout the intelligence
community began reading Bauer's books to the extent that the CIA's excellent library began a frantic effort to locate and buy as many copies
as they could.*

*It was a widely-held assumption in Washington that the job of Direc-
tor of Central intelligence was Bill Casey's last hurrah, and that when
he stepped down from this office he would retire, and perhaps resume
his writing and research projects. As with most widely-held assumptions
in Washington, this one was wrong. Late one afternoon in the Spring of
1985, in the midst of yet another conversation with him about the Third
World, Casey suddenly lunged forward in his blue leather chair. "You
know, there's one more thing I want to do after this. I want to form some
kind of structure — not exactly a think tank, not exactly a bank — but
something that will do the kinds of things no one in this town is doing.
I'm thinking about it, but I haven't quite figured out how to structure the
thing. When I do figure it out, I'm going to bail out of here and do it."*

*Of course, that plan never came to fruition. But during his tenure
Casey used every public speaking opportunity he could to educate his
listeners about Third World problems and the importance of Third
World economic development to U.S. national interests.*

It is a special pleasure for me to speak at this important forum cover-
ing public policy for almost a century and a quarter and I'm here as a
member of this club. I hope my dues are up to date. The club seems to
be doing alright with or without my dues. I see Abraham Lincoln looking down on me and I think he'll understand if I speak about human
rights. We are challenged today by flagrant abuses of human rights in
Africa, Asia, and Latin America which are massive and laden with a horror unequaled since the Nazi holocaust of forty years ago. The horror
of the wars and brutal repression inflicted by Marxist-Leninist regimes
is compounded by the failure and devastation wrought by the bankruptcy
of Marxist-Leninist economic and political policies wherever they
prevail. All this, with its enormous implications for our national
security, and in the challenge and opportunity it presents to the free
world, is largely ignored to a degree which we can only find appalling
if we appreciate the true nature and dimension of what is happening,
from Ethiopia to Afghanistan to Cambodia, and to our own hemisphere.
That's what I want to lay out for you today.

Where should one start on so sweeping a phenomenon? In the aftermath of the Geneva talks and the hope that they have laid the groundwork for a gradual scaling down of the nuclear monster, I would go back twenty years to a warning Nikita Khrushchev gave the world. He proclaimed that communism would win not by nuclear war which might destroy the world, nor by conventional war which might lead to nuclear war, but by wars of liberation. In those twenty years, the Soviet Union was transformed from a continental power to global power, acquiring bases and surrogates in Cuba, Vietnam, Ethiopia, Angola, South Yemen, Mozambique, Nicaragua, and Afghanistan. Their navy has secured the use of harbors, airports, communications stations, or port of call rights in some fourteen nations. In a mere ten years, the number of Warsaw Pact and Cuban troops, military advisors, and technicians stationed in Third World countries increased an incredible 500 percent. They have expanded their reach to a number of countries near the strategic choke points of the West – the Panama Canal, the Straits of Gibraltar, the Suez Canal, the Strait of Hormuz, the entrance to the Red Sea, and from Can Rahn Bay in Vietnam to the sea lanes of East Asia.

Elsewhere, Marxist-Leninist policies and tactics have unleashed the Four Horsemen of the Apocalypse: famine, pestilence, war, and death. Throughout the Third World we see famine in Africa, pestilence through chemical and biological agents in Afghanistan and Indo-China, war on three continents, and death everywhere.

The horror of what has been happening calls for a closer look. Apart from a few islands of vitality – mostly in East Asia, less impressive in Latin America and Africa – we see countries like Afghanistan, Angola, and Cambodia kept under control by more than 300,000 Soviet, Cuban, and Vietnamese troops. We see half a dozen other countries – Ethiopia, Nicaragua, South Yemen, Cuba, and Vietnam – controlled by committed Marxist-Leninist governments with military and population-control assistance from the East bloc. Most of the other countries in the Third World are suffering some degree of stagnation, impoverishment or famine.

What do we see in the occupied countries – Afghanistan, Cambodia, Ethiopia, Angola, Nicaragua – in which Marxist regimes have been either imposed or maintained by external forces? In the aggregate there has occurred a holocaust comparable to that which Nazi Germany inflicted in Europe some forty years ago. Over four million Afghans, more than one-quarter of the population, have had to flee their country into Pakistan and Iran. The *Helsinki Watch* tells us that they have fled because "the crimes of indiscriminate warfare are combined with the worst excesses of unbridled state-sanctioned violence against civilians." It cites evidence of

> civilians burned alive, dynamited, beheaded; crushed by Soviet tanks; grenades thrown into rooms where women and children have been told to wait. . . From throughout the country comes tales of death on every scale of horror, from thousands of civilians buried in the rubble left by fleets of bombers to a young boy's throat being dispassionately slit by occupying soldiers.

Tens of thousands of children have been taken from their parents and sent outside of the country for reeducation.

In Cambodia, two to three million people, something like one-quarter of the pre-war population, have been killed in the most violent and brutal manner by both internal and external Marxist forces. The invasion of the country by the Vietnamese army in 1978 and the scorched earth policy adopted then created a famine. When international relief agencies, including the Red Cross and the International Rescue Committee, tried to feed the starving population by a "land bridge" coming in from Thailand, the Vietnamese government blocked them. We estimate that some 350,000 civilians died in that year.

In Nicaragua, our Department of State has reported – and intelligence sources confirm – widespread violations of basic human rights. The International League for Human Rights has stated that the Sandinistas have forcibly relocated up to 14,500 Indians and completely destroyed entire villages. In late 1983, some 200 members of one of the largest non-Marxist political parties, the Democratic Conservative Party, were in jail for political activities. Censorship is extensive, opposition leaders have been prevented from traveling abroad, people in the cities are organized block-by-block and kept under the scrutiny and control of a system of neighbor informers based on the Cuban system.

Angola is an economic basket case as a Marxist government is kept in power by the presence of 30,000 Cuban troops. In all these countries the indigenous army formed by the Marxist government suffers large and continuing desertions to the resistance and is almost entirely ineffective.

In Ethiopia, a Marxist military government is supported with extensive support from Moscow and thousands of Cuban troops as it spends itself into bankruptcy trying unsuccessfully to extinguish opposition in its northern provinces. By collectivizing agriculture, creating state farms and collectives, and keeping food prices low in order to maintain urban support, it has exacerbated a famine which threatens the lives of millions of its citizens. It has blocked emergency food deliveries to the hungry remote areas, particularly those in provinces where insurgencies are active. It has exploited the famine by using food as a weapon. In urban areas, for example, food rations are distributed through party cells. In government-controlled emergency feeding stations, incoming victims must be registered and certified by party authorities. The government is using the drought and famine as an excuse to forcibly relocate tens of thousands of victims from northern provinces hundreds of miles to the south, without any evident efforts to receive them in the new camps.

Cuba, Vietnam, Ethiopia, Angola, and Nicaragua, all economic basket cases, receive in the aggregate five to six billion dollars in military and economic aid from the Soviet Union. This enables Vietnam to maintain the fourth largest army in the world; Ethiopia the largest army in Africa; Cuba the second most powerful military apparatus in the Western Hemisphere; and Nicaragua a military force larger than all its Central American neighbors put together. There are over 100,000 Soviet troops in Afghanistan, 170,000 Vietnamese troops in Cambodia, and 40,000 Cuban troops in Africa. This is worldwide military aggression directly and by proxy. That and the horror of it is the bad news.

The good news is that the tide has changed. Today in Afghanistan, Angola, Cambodia, Ethiopia, and Nicaragua, to mention only the most prominent arenas, hundreds of thousands of ordinary people are volunteers in irregular wars against the Soviet Army or Soviet-supported regimes. Whereas in the 1960s and 1970s anti-Western causes attracted recruits throughout the Third World, the 1980s have emerged as the decade of freedom fighters resisting communist regimes. In many places, freedom has become as exciting and revolutionary as it was here in America over 200 years ago.

Despite this reversal of momentum, the communists continue to come on strong to consolidate the positions they have established. They are spending close to $8 billion a year to snuff out freedom in these countries.

It is not necessary to match this in money, manpower or military weapons. Oppressed people want freedom and are fighting for it. They need only modest support and strength of purpose from nations that want to see freedom prevail and which will find their own security impaired if it doesn't.

The communists have this strength of purpose but not the means to consolidate the far off positions they have established if the local resistance can count on durable support. In Afghanistan, communist strategy is to keep at bay and grind down the resistance, to isolate it from the mass of the population or drive larger numbers out of the country, and to slowly build up a communist civil-military infrastructure through training, indoctrination, and cooption — counting on a perception there and abroad of inevitable victory. In Nicaragua, they are piling in weapons to extinguish the armed resistance, cracking down on the political opposition and pushing negotiations to cut off outside support and influence in order to buy time to consolidate their first base on the American mainland.

Now let me turn to what's happening in the unoccupied Third World countries. There, too, the Marxist economic model has failed. Third World leaders have become disillusioned with Marxist-style economics. They have discovered that communist countries supply only meager amounts of economic aid and are unable to offer significant markets for Third World goods. Last year, Moscow's commercial trade with the Third World was less than that of South Korea!

The communist model of tight, centralized control is the major cause of the economic stagnation in many countries. The state-owned industries became highly inefficient, while collectivization of agriculture lowered the incentive to produce food and increased migration to already over-burdened cities. Many Third World countries have found themselves increasingly dependent on imported grain. In fact, like Russia itself, some Third World countries that once were grain exporters now find themselves buying grain abroad.

The contrast between North and South Korea as well as the experience of newly industrialized economics such as Singapore, Hong Kong,

Taiwan, and Brazil have not been lost on Third World leaders. Both North and South Korea share a common cultural heritage, indeed both share a small peninsula. Yet from 1976 to 1983, South Korea's Gross National Product grew some 7 percent a year while North Korea's growth was a paltry 1.7 percent. Export-led growth in the newly industrialized countries have raised their per capita GNP to $2,400 – more than three times the average of the rest of the Third World.

The experience of the Third World in the last 30 years indicates that while elements of economic progress cannot be easily pinpointed, the private sector is the crucial link. Only private initiative can marshal the entrepreneurial resources necessary for sustained growth. Third World countries need an economic environment that rewards individuals for their hard work and their creativity.

They need to give the same fair treatment to foreign and domestic investment. Foreign investment brings more to a developing nation than just money. It brings technology, training, management skills, and marketing links. Foreign assistance should be used to supplement domestic savings. We have seen that too much reliance on foreign assistance breeds dependency. Trade must also must be developed. Third World countries need exchange rates that favor exporters rather than importers.

There are signs that many Third World countries are beginning to reassess their economic polices. Investment barriers in some places are beginning to be eased. A growing number of countries are making innovative use of export processing zones and joint ventures.

Public perceptions toward government regulatory practices and public employment are also changing. State-owned enterprises have been turned over to private firms in Pakistan, Somalia, Sudan, Zaire, the Philippines, Jamaica, and Chile. Free markets have sprung up in China and Algeria. Farmers in China now sign contracts with the state on what they will produce and market their surplus freely. This has been a economic boon to the countryside where for the past three years production has jumped over 30 percent and rural income has climbed rapidly. State farms have been dismantled in Mozambique, Mali, and Zambia. Bangladesh is turning from government to private channels to distribute fertilizer.

"Second economies" are springing up and beginning to be recognized as helpful to economic development and also as a cushion during hard times. In Peru, where it takes scores of permits to do business, a second, "freer" economy has grown to the point that it is nearly 50 percent larger than the legal economy.

This changing climate presents significant economic opportunities for the United States. We can help by promoting small-scale enterprises for the Third World. Third World countries have often ignored the beneficial impact of small businesses and even cottage industries. Yet these businesses help achieve government goals through industrial decentralization, employment generation, and income redistribution in rural areas. Small-scale, domestically-oriented entrepreneurs help create a critical mass in terms of economic progress. Entrepreneurs flourished in many West African countries until government policies dampened their efforts. Likewise, Central America, especially El Salvador, was fertile ground for beginning entrepreneurs until their gains were set back by political turmoil.

In order to make the most of his increasingly important evolutionary and grass roots development process, we need to reorder economic aid programs so that more assistance reaches the small-scale entrepreneur and the flow of private capital, technology, and skill to less-developed countries is stimulated.

We can use foreign capital to help state enterprises become more efficient and find ways to relinquish some functions to the private sector; we can strengthen our trade, finance and investment links to less developed countries based upon a growing mutuality of economic interest.

The forces at play here have security implications as well. They can strengthen the West's position relative to that of the communist bloc in the Third Word. Soviet domestic economic and foreign financial constraints over the next ten years will make Moscow even less able to compete in nonmilitary sectors. At the same time, Western security interests will often coincide with opportunities for economic support, and security assistance can reinforce the willingness and ability of less-developed countries to bring in and develop capital, technology, and needed skills.

I don't want to leave you with the impression that all the problems and threats we find around the world stem from Moscow or even from Marxist-Leninist doctrines. In Africa, not only Marxist Ethiopia but all across Sub-Saharan Africa, at least 14 million people, possibly more, face permanent disability and even death from famine during this year.

The whole civilized world faces a scourge of international terrorism. These perils are so imminent and severe that they cry out for coherent international action.

We have launched the "African Hunger Relief Initiative" to relieve famine in several African countries. Our country does not have the food resources to meet African aid requirements fully but with other Western countries enough food can be pulled together. However, African ports and poor ground transportation can't distribute all the food that is required. It will take Western equipment, technical assistance, and air transport to meet the needs of millions of people living in rural and remote locations. It can be done but it will take leadership and a degree of cohesion and cooperation which Western nations with their legislative and budget limitations find difficult to achieve. But the need cries for all-out action to work through the necessary procedural steps as early this year as possible.

The continent-wide African food crisis will continue into 1986 and beyond. Large populations will continue at risk because of declining agricultural production, continuing civil wars, and continuing failure to achieve agricultural reform and development. We have the knowledge and technical ability to restore African food productivity. Western nations generally agree on the urgency of improvements in agricultural pricing, and restructuring economic priorities in favor of food producers instead of urban populations.

The several threads of our current policy, such as pressing for meaningful reforms from recipient governments, offering new forms and amounts of assistance, and moving quickly, could all be brought together in a major, coordinated rescue effort. We have here an opportunity not only to save many lives but to generate a new wave of progress which would demonstrate for all peoples the fundamental superiority of free market policies and practices over statist models. A dramatic and effective response to the food crisis could serve to galvanize our efforts to generally reorient Western foreign assistance programs toward the free enterprise development approaches President Reagan outlined at Cancun in 1982.

Similarly, international terrorism calls for concerted action. We face here a new weapons system which is dissolving the boundary between war and peace. We've seen it move from plastic charges to assassinations, to hijacking, to car bombs; and we worry about nuclear and biological terrorism. This terrorism has a home in North Korea, Iran, Libya, and Bulgaria. It is increasingly used as a foreign policy instrument of sovereign states. This weapons system, this foreign policy instrument must not be allowed to work. The implications are too ominous.

American citizens and installations abroad are the primary targets. Qadhafi recently assigned his most radical advisors to increase Libya's capabilities for terrorist operations in Latin America, to strengthen leftist militants, and to promote anti-U.S. actions there. He clearly intends to launch a more aggressive effort to undermine U.S. interests in this hemisphere.

Today there is no more urgent task for statesmanship than to develop and effective way to check rampant terrorism through improved security, intelligence gathering, retaliation and preemption against specific targets, and by imposing political isolation and economic squeeze on states sponsoring terrorism. To be effective the response to terrorism must be a concerted one on the part of all civilized and peace-loving states. We got together to develop defenses against airplane hijacking in the seventies. We are already late in achieving international cooperation against today's more widespread and virulent international terrorism.

There's no time left for me to deal with the enormous burden of debt, or rapidly growing population straining resources. But I would conclude by re-emphasizing that none of these problems can be handled unless more advanced countries step up to counter politically motivated violence and to re-energize constructive economic forces in what promise in the years ahead to be the major battleground between those who want to see freedom prevail and those who want to extinguish it.

◆ ◆ ◆

SOVIET SURROGATES IN THE THIRD WORLD

During the Reagan years, the Soviet Union vastly increased its efforts in Third World countries including Ethiopia, South Yemen, Mozambique, and Nicaragua. More than any other senior Reagan official, Casey focused on countering the Soviets in the Third World. Indeed, Casey was a serious student of economic development. He read widely on the issue, met often with scholars, foreign aid administrators, and Third World business executives to understand the problems of development and the nature of the Soviet Union's efforts. He visited Third World countries often, and his purpose invariably was to better understand what those countries' development plans were and what were the threats to their stability.

Casey recognized that victory in these countries by Soviet-sponsored forces would profoundly – and adversely – affect U.S. interests. He believed passionately that a combination of U.S. economic and entrepreneurial strength – and military assistance – should be deployed to block the Soviets and enable Third World countries to set development courses that would succeed.

I am grateful to Earl Smith and The Society of the Four Arts for this opportunity to discuss American intelligence with you today. It is a large and wide-ranging subject with many dimensions. I think I should at the onset apprise you of the limitations of my freedom to discuss some aspects of this subject publicly. I cannot discuss or disclose anything which might jeopardize the sources of our intelligence. Decisions as to what action is indicated by the information we collect and the analysis we do are the responsibility of the President and the Congress and I am careful about treading on their territory. . . .

Beginning in 1971 and 1975, the Soviet Union undertook a new, much more aggressive strategy in the Third World. They found destabilization, subversion, and the backing of insurgents in other countries around the world attractive and relatively risk free. Exploiting the availability first of Cuba and subsequently of other countries to serve as Soviet sur-

---

Address to the Society of the Four Arts, Palm Beach, Florida, Feburary 23, 1982.

rogates or proxies, they have been able to limit the political, economic, and miliary cost of intervention.

In the aftermath of Vietnam, the Soviet Union soon began to test whether the U.S. would resist foreign-provoked and supported, instability and insurgence elsewhere in the Third World. Fully aware of the political climate in this country, in the 1980s they developed an aggressive strategy in the Third World. It avoided direct confrontation and instead exploited local and regional circumstances to take maximum advantage of third-country forces (or surrogates) to attain Soviet objectives. This enables Moscow to deny involvement, to label such conflicts as internal, and to warn self-righteously against "outside interference." There is little disagreement among analysts that Soviet and proxy successes in the mid- to late-1970s in Angola, Ethiopia, Cambodia, Nicaragua and elsewhere have encouraged the Soviets to rely on the Cubans, Vietnamese and, recently, the Libyans ever more aggressively.

Over the last several years, the Soviets and their allies have supported directly or indirectly, radical regimes or insurgencies in more than a dozen countries in every part of the Third World. The United States and its friends have had difficulty countering these insurgencies. It is much easier and much less expensive to support an insurgency than it is for us and our friends to resist one. It takes relatively few people and little support to disrupt the internal peace and economic stability of a small country.

It's truly remarkable the way the combination of money and manpower from two tiny countries – Cuba and Libya, with skills and arms provided by the Soviet Union and it's satellites like Vietnam, North Korea, and East Germany – has terrorized four continents over the last ten years.

Subversion and terrorism destabilize existing governments. Insurgency is organized and supplied with weapons and experienced guerrilla leaders. Manpower is brought for training to Cuba, Lebanon, South Yemen, Bulgaria, or Libya, where more than 25 terrorist training camps seem to make up the second largest industry next to oil.

Qadhafi and Libya got into the terrorist business by default. The death of Nasser in 1970, just a year after his own assumption of power, left Qadhafi looking for a kindred spirit. He found this in the PLO. It was revolutionary, Muslim, anti-imperialist, and fighting Israel. He opened his doors and treasury to the Palestinians.

Terrorism, the sophisticated terrorism of today, is big business and requires big money. Safehouses in safe areas, modern secure weapons, travel documents, transportation, etc., are very expensive. Terrorists need more than money. They require safe training sites, use of diplomatic bags, safe embassies, multiple travel documents, and they need a country to back them. Qadhafi decided to pick up the tab. Although he can call on them at will, it is not certain he knows the size of the tiger he has by the tail. Does he fully realize their ties to the Soviets and East Germans, that their training camps produce "Marxist" revolutionaries and that he really doesn't own them, only rents them? In any event, the degree of his knowledge and control is not important — he uses them and houses them.

Qadhafi uses terrorists or mercenaries for two general purposes – to terrorize those who would oppose him or prevent him from achieving his goals and to train "revolutionaries". Lenin put it succinctly: The purpose of terror is to terrorize. Qadhafi has sent hit teams to seek out his Libyan opponents in Egypt, Italy, France, the U.K., and the U.S. He wants to send a very clear message – my arm is long and it has a gun in its hand.

Qadhafi has attempted – by act or by *just leaks* of an act – to strike at senior American officials at home and abroad. In so doing he has caused disruption of our normal way of life on the official level, the expenditure of millions, and some degree of skepticism among our allies about our intelligence and subsequent actions. All this at very little cost and a great deal of "revolutionary" publicity for him. He also, at one time or another, has tried to assassinate Nimeriri and Sadat, his neighbors in Sudan and Egypt.

Then there is the weapon of military hardware and advisors. The Soviets and their proxies actively pump arms, money, and other forms of assistance (such as training) into many Third World areas which are already seething with domestic discontent. The increasing availability of money, training, and weapons directly endangers U.S. diplomats and businessmen and indirectly undercuts the viability of many moderate governments which the U.S. supports. Opposition groups in less-developed countries are turning to violence more frequently. The number of sovereign governments willing and able to support armed opposition against others as a foreign policy tool is rising. The U.S. must now concern itself with the support of externally-directed political violence provided by Iran, Iraq, Syria, South Yemen, Nicaragua, and Ethiopia, in addition to the Soviet Union, Cuba, Libya, and the satellites of Eastern Europe.

Since the Camp David accords in September 1978, Libya has sharply increased miliary assistance to Third World clients. In the three years ending December 1981, he has provided more than $500 million worth of weapons and funds to buy arms. Qadhafi now provides aid to more than 60 insurgent and dissident groups, as well as supporting selected governments. An increasingly important facet of his program is training, including more than 10,000 insurgents and dissidents. Thousands of troops have also been sent to Libya, and Qadhafi gives certain clients more advanced, specialized training, giving all the assistance free of charge.

Cuba is the other worldwide troublemaker. For a nation of ten million people, Cuba has displayed a remarkable reach on a worldwide scale. It has 70,000 military and civilian advisors abroad in almost thirty countries. Of these, more than half are military. Over 40,000 are in Africa, and some 7,000 in the Middle East. There are 12,000 Cuban technical trainees working in Czechoslovakia and East Germany, and 5,000 to 6,000 studying in the Soviet Union.

How did this phenomenon develop? Part of it springs from the demographics; the same source — a combination of overpopulation and youth unemployment — which gave us 150,000 Cuban refugees in the Mariel boat lift. Since 1980, there has been a 50 percent surge in the 15 to 19-year-old age group. Castro has admitted that tens of thousands of youths are out of work. He said in a recent speech that he would like to send 10,000 Cuban youths to Siberia to cut timber for Cuban construction projects. Cuba has lots of young men to train and send into other countries — and that's the way to get preferment in government employment in Castro's Cuba.

The other source of Cuba's aggression is Soviet influence and support. The Soviets sell their weapons. Arms sales earn about 20 percent of their hard currency. Last year they gave 66,000 tons of weapons, four times the previous ten-year annual average of 15,000 tons.

In addition to free military equipment, the Soviet Union gives Cuba $8 million a day, or $3 billion a year, to keep its economy going. The Russians buy sugar at a premium and sell oil at a discount. There is no way that Cuba could play the role it does in Latin America, Africa, and the Middle East without this cash and military support from the Soviet Union. Moscow doesn't give away $4 billion a year unless it has a purpose.

Today Cuba sits astride the Caribbean with a modernized army of 150,000 troops, reserves of 100,000, and 200 Soviet MiGs. It now has the largest military establishment in the Western Hemisphere, save those of the U.S. and Brazil.

Cuba's recent combat experience in Angola and Ethiopia, together with its overwhelming qualitative and numerical superiority in weapons, provides it with a particularly ominous intervention capability in the Caribbean and in Central America. This is clearly not the sole source of violence and instability in the Caribbean Basin, but it magnifies and internationalizes what would otherwise be local conflicts.

Cuba's most immediate goals are to exploit and control the revolution in Nicaragua and to induce the overthrow of the governments of El Salvador and Guatemala. At the same time, the Cuban government is providing advice, safehaven, communications, training, and some financial support to several violent South American organizations. Training in Cuban camps has been provided in the last two years to groups from Uruguay, Chile, Haiti, Jamaica, the Dominican Republic, Grenada, Colombia, Honduras, Costa Rica, and Guatemala, in addition to the more publicized training for combatants from Nicaragua and El Salvador.

There is every indication that Nicaragua is being built up to a superpower on a Central American scale. With a population of about 2.5 million, its army and militia is twice as large as that of El Salvador, a country with twice its population. Soviet tanks and the expected arrival of MiG aircraft will give Nicaragua military domination over neighboring Honduras, El Salvador, Guatemala and Costa Rica with a combined population seven times theirs. The insurgency in El Salvador is being directed, trained, and supplied with the help of 1,800 Cuban military and security advisors, 75 Soviets, and smaller numbers of East Germans, Bulgarians, Vietnamese, North Koreans, and radical Arabs gathered in Managua. Under Cuban and East German guidance, the Sandinista junta is imposing a totalitarian control with a neighborhood block system of population control on the Cuban model: repression of newspapers, opposition politicians, labor unions, and other private sector leaders.

Insurgents in El Salvador are being supplied with arms by air, by sea, and by land through Honduras from Nicaragua. They are being directed from Managua by Cubans and Nicaraguans experienced in waging guerrilla war with a sophisticated communications network located in Nicaragua. The conflict has been stalemated for over a year. Government forces can make large sweeps, and after they return to their bases the guerrillas regain control of many roads, villages, and large segments of the countryside. They are now attacking provincial towns and economic targets to intimidate voters from going to the polls in the March election, and to depress the economy.

The insurgency has spread to Guatemala where trained leaders and arms coming from Cuba and Nicaragua have put the Guatemalan government under heavy pressure.

There is a growing concern about all this on the part of other Latin American countries. Fifteen of them spoke out against the declaration of support for the El Salvador insurgency promulgated by Mexico and France. The Organization of American States, by a vote of 22 to 3, supported the elections in El Salvador with only Nicaragua, Mexico, and Grenada voting against. This last month Costa Rica, Honduras, and El Salvador joined in requesting protection from the United States, Venezuela, and Colombia against the threat they perceived from the growing militarization of Nicaragua.

Other major recipients of Soviet assistance also have been especially active in the past year in fomenting trouble in their regions. Last August, for example, Ethiopia, Libya, and South Yemen signed a military alliance ostensibly aimed at "imperialist" forces in the Near East and Horn of Africa region. Their aim is to overthrow the governments of North Yemen, on the border of Saudi Arabia, Somalia and Sudan, controlling the Red Sea and the shores of the Indian Ocean, develop close relations with Moscow, and oppose miliary interest in the Persian Gulf region.

Vietnam continues to create major regional tensions not only by occupying Kampuchea, which alarms its ASEAN neighbors, but also by prompting a vast migration of refugees. Since the spring of 1975, more than two million persons have fled Indochina. This exodus has constituted by far the greatest refugee problem in East Asia, has created a major threat to regional stability, and has involved the rest of the world in costly lifesaving and resettlement efforts.

◆ ◆ ◆

NICARAGUA: THE CLASSIC COMMUNIST BLUEPRINT

As events in Central America moved to center stage, Casey pushed the intelligence community to produce more and more analyses of what the Sandinista regime in Nicaragua was up to and how the Contras were faring. Of course, there were the usual analyses of military developments and political prospects. These sorts of products were vital, albeit prosaic. But under Casey's prodding, the intelligence community began to produce wholly new kinds of analyses. The idea for developing a "blueprint" to illustrate taking over a government and consolidating a totalitarian regime – outlined in this speech – was Casey's. Not only did the "blueprint" developed by the analysts show how far the Sandinistas had come toward consolidating their power, but it provided the U.S. government with a clear picture of just what this sort of process really looks like. Thus future policymakers and intelligence officers would be able to spot it earlier in other places.

Today, I would like to tell you about the subversive war which the Soviet Union and its partners have been waging against the United States and its interests around the world for a quarter of a century or more. This campaign of aggressive subversion has nibbled away at friendly governments and our vital interests until today our national security is impaired in our immediate neighborhood as well as in Europe, Asia, Africa, and Latin America.

This is not an undeclared war. In 1961, Khrushchev, then leader of the Soviet Union, told us that Communism would win not through nuclear war which could destroy the world or conventional war which could quickly lead to nuclear war, but through "wars of national liberation" in Africa, Asia, and Latin America. We were reluctant to believe him then, just as in the 1930s we were reluctant to take Hitler seriously when he spelled out, in his book *Mein Kampf*, how he would take over Europe.

Over the last ten years, Soviet power has been established:

Address to the Metropolitan Club of New York City, New York, New York, May 1, 1985.

♦ In Vietnam, along China's southern border and astride the sea lanes which bring Persian Gulf oil to Japan.

♦ In Afghanistan, 500 miles closer to the warm-water ports of the Indian Ocean and to the Strait of Hormuz, through which comes the oil essential to Western Europe.

♦ In the Horn of Africa, dominating the southern approaches to the Red Sea and the southern tip of the Arabian Peninsula.

♦ In southern Africa, holding the sources of minerals which we and the other industrial nations must have.

♦ And in the Caribbean and Central America, on the very doorstep of the United States.

Capabilities to threaten the Panama Canal in the short term and Mexico in a somewhat longer term are being developed in Nicaragua where the Sandinista revolution is the first successful Castroite seizure of power on the American mainland. They have worked quietly and steadily toward their objectives of building the power of the state security apparatus, building the strongest armed forces in Central America, and becoming a center for exporting subversion to Nicaragua's neighbors.

The American intelligence community over recent months unanimously concurred in four National Estimates on the military buildup, the consolidation and the strategic objectives of the Soviets, the Cubans, and the Sandinistas in Nicaragua. If I were to boil the key judgments of those estimates down to a single sentence it would be this. The Soviet Union and Cuba have established and are consolidating a beachhead on the American continent, are putting hundreds of millions of dollars worth of military equipment into it, and have begun to use it as a launching pad to carry their style of aggressive subversion into the rest of Central America and elsewhere in Latin America.

Let me review quickly what has already happened in Nicaragua. The Sandinistas have developed the best equipped military in the region. They have an active strength of some 65,000 and a fully mobilized strength including militia and reserves of nearly 120,000. These forces are equipped with Soviet tanks, armored vehicles, state of the art helicopters, patrol boats, and an increasingly comprehensive air defense system. This gives the Sandinistas a military capability far beyond that of any other Central American nation put together.

In addition to this military hardware so threatening to neighboring countries, there are now in Nicaragua an estimated 6,000 to 7,500 Cuban advisors; and other communists and radical Arabs total several hundred in assisting the regime in its military buildup and its consolidation of power. Under Cuban direction and guidance the Sandinista security forces control the media, create and spread propaganda and disinformation, and expel or neutralize those who oppose Sandinista totalitarianism.

Today, we see Managua becoming to Central and Latin America what Beirut has been to the Middle East for almost fifteen years, since 1970 when the PLO was expelled from Jordan, and Lebanon became the focal point for international and regional terrorists. Managua's support for training of Central American subversives is well documented – they support Salvadoran communists, Guatemalan communists, radical leftists in Costa Rica, and are attempting to increase the number of radical leftist terrorists in Honduras. More recent evidence indicates Nicaraguan support for some South American terrorist groups, and growing contacts with other international terrorist groups.

Yet, just last week the American Congress refused to approve $14 million for the people resisting communist domination of Nicaragua, on the very day that a Soviet ship unloaded about $10 million worth of helicopters, trucks, and other military cargo at Corinto, the principal port in Nicaragua. On the very next day, Ortega, the Nicaraguan communist dictator, traveled to Moscow to ask the Soviet Union to make $200 million available to him to consolidate a Leninist communist dictatorship across a stretch of land which separates South America from North America.

This development in our immediate neighborhood should not be viewed in isolation but as part of a worldwide process which has already worked in Europe, Africa, Asia, and Latin America.

Let me now give you an insight on how all this happens. In early 1981, I had a talk with Bob Ames, our CIA Middle East expert, who died at the hands of a terrorist attack in Beirut in 1983. Stationed in Aden, South Yemen, in 1967, he met and befriended the young revolutionary Abd'al Fatah Ismail, who became President of South Yemen and is now back in Aden after being exiled briefly to the USSR. Abd'al Fatah told Bob of his experience in the higher Komsomol school which the Soviets maintain for training young revolutionaries from non-communist countries. He explained that he had been taught in Moscow that he would need twenty years, a generation, to consolidate his revolution. He would have to control the education of the youth. He would have to uproot and ultimately change the traditional elements of society. This meant undermining the influence of religion and taking the young away from their parents for education by the state. He was taught that to control the people he would have to establish neighborhood block committees and a powerful secret police. Finally, Abd'al Fatah spoke in impassioned terms of a need to export revolution to carry out his mission as a dedicated Marxist-Leninist and to ensure that attention was focused on neighboring countries, thus diverting attention from his own country and allowing it to consolidate its revolution.

Bob Ames said that as he looked back, Abd'al Fatah – with Soviet bloc help – had done as he said he would. He captured and subverted a legitimate war of liberation. He killed or drove into exile those members of the movement who believed in democracy and then went about the work of consolidating a communist regime and began armed subversion against Oman and North Yemen.

In Ethiopia, Angola, Afghanistan, Nicaragua, and Grenada, dedicated Marxist-Leninist revolutionaries followed this Soviet blueprint with only slight modifications.

Our analysts have studied this blueprint for taking over a government and consolidating a totalitarian regime as it has been exemplified in seven totalitarian regimes: six Marxist-Leninist regimes in Cuba, South Yemen, Ethiopia, Angola, Grenada, Nicaragua; and the Islamic revolutionary government of Iran. They have identified 46 indicators of the consolidation of power by a Marxist-Leninist regime. These indicators measures:

◆ The movement toward one-party government, control of the military, of the security services, of the media, of education, and of the economy.

◆ The forming or takeover of labor or other mass organizations.

◆ Exerting social and population control.

◆ Curbing religious influence.

◆ Alignment with the Soviet bloc.

Of the 46 indicators, Nicaragua in five and one-half years has accomplished 33. They have established control of the media, taken over radio and TV, censored the broadcasts of Sunday sermons of the Archbishop of Managua, and subjected the only free newspaper, *La Prensa*, to a brutal daily censorship.

They have taken control of the education system. Nicaraguan textbooks now teach Marxism, and attack the tenets of Western democracy. They attack traditional religious teachings and encourage children to maintain revolutionary vigilance by watching for signs of ideological impurities in their neighbors, friends and relatives.

The Sandinistas have taken control of the military. They have taken control of the internal secret police and have established a Directorate of State Security. That directorate, according to our reports, has hundreds of Cuban, Soviet, East German, and Bulgarian advisors. There are Soviet advisors at every level of the secret police. In fact, it is safe to say that it is controlled by the Soviet Union and its surrogates. Block committees have been established to watch and control the people.

The Church has been persecuted. Witness the campaign mounted by the Directorate of State Security to harass and embarrass Pope John Paul II during his 1983 visit to Nicaragua. They have used political mobs (similar to the Red Guards of Soviet and Chinese revolutionary history) to attack democratic politicians, union members and religious leaders.

And finally, just as Abd'al Fatah told Bob Ames what he must do, and following Hitler and Khrushchev, the Sandinistas have told the world, that they would spread the example of Nicaragua beyond El Salvador to Honduras, Guatemala, and the entire region.

An integral part of this blueprint for subversive aggression is deception and disinformation to manipulate and influence public opinion and policies in Western countries. This takes many shapes and forms.

A worldwide propaganda campaign has been mounted and carried out on behalf of the Sandinista regime and Salvadoran guerrillas which would not have been possible without the capabilities, the contacts, and the communications channels provided by the Soviet bloc and Cuba. The Sandinistas themselves have shown remarkable ingenuity and skill in projecting disinformation into the United States itself. Perhaps the best example of this is the systematic campaign to deceive well-intentioned members of the Western media and of Western religious institutions.

There are many examples of Nicaraguan deception. The Sandinista press, radio, and government ministry have put out claims that the U.S. used chemical weapons in Grenada, that the U.S. was supplying

Nicaraguan freedom fighters with drugs, and that the U.S. might give the opposition bacteriological weapons. The debate in the Congress last week disclosed few who think that what is happening in Central America is a desirable state of affairs or that it is compatible with avoiding a possibly permanent impairment of our national security, and a serious deterioration in the American geopolitical position in the world.

There are some who will be content with an agreement that the Nicaraguans will now forego further aggression. Our experience in Korea and Indochina provides some lessons on the value of agreements with communist governments. Korea started to violate the Korean Armistice within days of the truce signing. Under the 1973 Paris Accords, North Vietnam agreed to cease firing in South Vietnam, withdraw its forces from Cambodia and Laos, and refrain from introducing additional troops and war material into South Vietnam except on a one-for-one replacement basis. North Vietnam never observed the cease-fire and troop withdrawal requirements, and within little more than two months after it had signed the peace agreements it had already infiltrated some 30,000 additional troops and over 30,000 tons of military equipment into South Vietnam.

We believe the Sandinistas' main objective in regional negotiations is to buy time to further consolidate the regime. History and the record, and purposes of Marxist-Leninist regimes in general, and the Sandinistas in particular, lead us to believe that unless Nicaragua has implemented a genuine democracy as required by the OAS, such assurances could not be adequately verified and would not be complied with. Cuban officials have urged the Salvadoran communist guerrillas to slow down their attacks against the Duarte government in order to fortify and consolidate the Nicaraguan revolution. We believe that Cuba has assured the Salvadoran communists that it might take as long as five to ten years, but as long as the Sandinista regime in Nicaragua remains, that country will serve as a bases for communist expansion in the area and the Salvadoran insurgency will be renewed once the Sandinistas have been able to eliminate the armed resistance.

What does all this mean for America's future? Should Central America fall under communist control, it could mean a tidal wave of refugees into the U.S.

Every country that has fallen under communist control since World War II has sent refugees streaming over the borders — first Eastern

Europe, then Cuba, and more recently Vietnam and Afghanistan – and the potential influx from Central America is even higher than from any of these. Since 1980, some 200,000 Salvadorans fleeing the communist-initiated violence in their own country have entered the U.S. illegally. Illegal movement from Mexico has increased, with some one million Mexicans illegally entering this country in 1983 alone. In 1984 the Bipartisan Commission on Central America warned that a communist Central America would likely be followed by the destabilization of Mexico and that this could result in many millions of additional Mexicans fleeing into the U.S.

Today, the Cuban and Nicaraguan military forces are together four times the size of those of Mexico and are equipped with vastly superior weapons. Today, with armed forces larger and better equipped than the rest of Central America, Nicaragua could walk through Costa Rica, which has no army, to Panama; and Cuba can threaten our vital sea lanes in the Caribbean.

The insurgency is a major obstacle to Sandinista consolidation in encouraging the erosion of active support for the Sandinistas, creating uncertainties about the future of the regime, challenging its claims of political legitimacy, and giving hope to leaders of the political opposition.

The largest anti-Sandinista insurgent group, the FDN, is still providing strong military resistance despite cutoff of U.S. aid almost a year ago. Popular sympathy for the insurgents is increasing in the countryside, and the FDN continues to receive significant numbers of the new recruits.

That opposition can increase the pressure until the Sandinista support has eroded sufficiently to leave them no option other than modifying their rejection of internal reconciliation. The objective is to allow for the same process of democratization that is taking place in the rest of Central America to occur in Nicaragua.

◆ ◆ ◆

UNDERSTANDING LIBERATION THEOLOGY

Here's Casey setting the stage for another CIA conference on political developments in the Third World.

Good afternoon ladies and gentlemen. We appreciate your participation in the conferences on "Liberation Theology." Let me take this opportunity to thank our guest speakers. Father John Langen of the Society of Jesus and Michael Novak of the American Heritage Institute.

We are here today to examine the problem of "liberation theology." Our concern derives from the contribution "liberation theology" is making to the growth of political instability in the Third World – with its possible political, economic, and military implications.

Today, liberation theology constitutes a rather loose, wide-ranging body of doctrine. It appears to have combined Christian moral determinism with Marxist material determinism to produce a militant form of revolutionary Christianity. In addition, liberation theology's method of analysis and politico-economic lexicon are borrowed from liberalism, social democracy, and Marxist-Leninism. Its concept of the relationship of the state and economy springs directly from the ideals and traditions of Latin Christianity. Finally, it derives its moral principles and concepts of social justice from mainstream Christianity.

Liberation theology – like classic 19th century Marxism – couples an extensive critique of existing society with a shrill call for action. But it lacks a coherent practical plan of action to guide the overthrow of the existing order and the creation of the millennium. Ironically, this is one of its strongest appeals. As was the case with classic Marxism. This characteristic allows room both for radical violent revolution and peaceful social reform to coexist. At the same time, it offers unparalleled opportunity for subversive groups to manipulate the doctrine and its adherents among the reformist clergy – and through them a much wider body of public opinion.

Given the eclectic nature of the doctrine of liberation theology, it is not difficult to understand its broad appeal. Its adherents come from the most diverse political persuasions. Liberation theology provides the in-

---

Address to the Conference on Liberation Theology and Communism, CIA Headquarters, Langley, Virginia, September 19, 1985.

tellectual basis for moderate social reformers and hardcore guerrilla fighters alike. And because of its diverse intellectual foundations it has attained status and acceptance in many theological and intellectual circles.

The doctrine and appeal of liberation theology would be intellectual curiosities of little interest to us but for two facts: First, liberation theology – even in its reformist guise – is openly and intensely anti-American. It pointedly identifies the oppression of the Third World's poor with the U.S. Second, of the 800 million Catholics in the world today, about half live in the poverty-stricken and politically oppressed nations of the Third World – and over 300 million of them are in Latin America and the Philippines.

In many of these countries the Catholic Church is the only organized entity other than the government. Through the medium of liberation theology, radical leftists have mobilized popular support for their cause. In Latin America and the Philippines, leftists have used the so-called popular church to organize political opposition to existing regimes. The *de facto* collaboration of elements of the Roman Catholic Church with Marxist revolutionaries has helped legitimize insurgency movements. While hampering government efforts to contain them. This has also opened doors to American political influence and economic resources for many leftist insurgencies.

In Nicaragua, for example, liberation theology and the popular church have been significant factors in the success of the Sandinistas. They have spawned at least three prominent leaders in the Sandinista movement: Foreign Minister, Father Miguel D'Escoto of the Maryknoll order; the Culture Minister, Father Ernesto Cardenal, a former Trappist monk; and his brother, the Education Minister, Fernando Cardenal, a Jesuit priest. These men have used liberation theology to promote the Marxist Sandinista movement – and to raise politico-religious consciousness through a solidarity campaign with foreign leftist and religious groups – both before and after the overthrow of Somoza.

Liberation theology has provided Fidel Castro with another tool in his ongoing efforts to export the Cuban revolution. He has publicly cited the Nicaraguan model as an example of successful church-state collaboration, and a vehicle for radical change. In addition, such radical religious revolutionaries as Miquel D'Escoto have proven to be useful propagandists and apologists for the Cuban regime.

We have also witnessed the spread of liberation theology to the Philippines, where the steady deterioration of political and economic stability has opened the door to radical revolution. Liberation theology has been the medium through which large numbers of clergymen have entered into active opposition to the Marcos regime. Hundreds of priests and nuns have joined the Communist Party there. Many of them are active in the insurgencies. And a few of these hold key position in the Philippine Catholic Church. Furthermore, Philippine Jesuit adherents of liberation theology organized and still lead the Social Democrats – a terrorist organization with over a thousand members.

Liberation theology promises to be a troublesome phenomenon elsewhere in the Third World as well. It is growing in Asia – specifically South Korea and Sri Lanka. And in Africa liberation theology has increasing appeal to radical churchmen who fear the spread of militant Islam.

Liberation theology is no longer exclusively a Roman Catholic phenomenon, as some more liberal and radical Protestant groups have begun to espouse it. Though in its nascent stages now, over the longer term this could pose serious problems for U.S. interests. Many Third World Protestant organizations are unfettered by the discipline and hierarchical controls of the Roman Catholic Church, and their members can be fiercely independent evangelists.

As intelligence collectors and analysts it is our responsibility to understand the phenomenon of liberation theology. We must accurately grasp the scope of this phenomenon. We must also appreciate the character of its regional variations. And, we must examine carefully the links between adherents of this movement on the one hand and radical leftists and communist organizations on the other, to provide an ongoing assessment of the extent to which clergy and lay elements of the Catholic Church are being unwittingly manipulated.

It was my intent in supporting this conference that these three issues would be addressed here today. I am pleased to note the fine group of speakers who have been assembled to share their knowledge and insights on this topic. I look forward to hearing the results of your work.

* * *

Chapter 7

Terrorism

FIGHTING TERRORISTS:
IDENTIFICATION AND ACTION

Casey had an exceptionally detailed intellectual grasp of the terrorist threat, as this speech makes clear. But unlike most analysts, Casey also knew how to fight in the streets when necessary. Thus, under his leadership the CIA became the U.S. government's lead anti-terrorist agency. Casey built up not only the Agency's analytic capabilities, but the Agency's operational capabilities to respond when trouble came.

On this subject more than any other, the old intelligence maxim applies: everyone knows the mistakes but nobody ever finds out about the triumphs. Note Casey's vague allusion to the threatened hijacking of a foreign commercial airliner, which was aborted thanks to the CIA. In fact, during Casey's tenure – and under his very direct, hands-on management – the CIA helped abort dozens of terrorist incidents.

None of these ever became public, nor should they. But one ought to bear in mind that between 1981 and 1987, quite a few travelers reached their destinations safely thanks to the men and women of the CIA.

International terrorism has become a perpetual war without borders. This evening I will tell you what I can about how American intelligence assesses this dreadful scourge and how I think we should deal with it.

Address to the 14th Annual Conference of the Fletcher School of Law and Diplomacy's national securities studies program, Tufts University, Cambridge, Massachusetts, April 17, 1985.

In just a few years we have witnessed the bombings of our embassies in Beirut and Kuwait; the attack on United States and French forces in Beirut; the vicious attack on the South Korean Cabinet which took place in Rangoon; the assassinations of President Bashir Gemayel and Prime Minister Gandhi; the attempted assassination against Prime Minister Thatcher; and the attempt that was made against Pope John Paul II in St. Peter's Square.

We are engaged in a new form of low intensity conflict against an enemy that is hard to find and harder still to defend against. The number of recorded international terrorist incidents rose from about 500 to more than 700 in 1984. Last year 355 international terrorist bombings occurred, nearly one for every day of the year.

U.S. citizens and property have always been among the most popular targets of international terrorists. Last year a large number of attacks also were directed at the French, the Jordanians, and the Israelis. The Middle East remains a fertile ground for terrorism. And there were ominous developments in West Germany where left-wing terrorist groups combined forces and began attacking NATO targets.

In confronting the challenge of international terrorism, the first step is to call things by their proper names, to see clearly and say plainly who the terrorists are, what goals they seek, and which governments support them.

What the terrorist does is kill, maim, kidnap, and torture. His victims may be children in the schoolroom, innocent travelers on airplanes, businessmen returning home from work, political leaders, diplomats, soldiers, and civilians anywhere. The terrorist's victims may have no particular political identity, or they may be political symbols, like Aldo Moro or even Pope John Paul II. They may be kidnapped and held for ransom, maimed, or simply blown to bits. One defining characteristic of the terrorist is his choice of method: the terrorist chooses violence as the instrument of first resort.

Terrorism has been with us for a long time. But it once manifested itself in fundamentally different forms than those we see today. Earlier in this century we saw forms of terrorism that usually had their roots in ethnic or separatist groups and were confined to a small geographic area and to very selective targets. Even today, remnants of this brand of terrorism still are with us – the Basque separatists in Spain, the Irish nationalists in Northern Ireland, the Moro tribesmen in the Philippines, and other ethnic terrorist groups.

Since the late 1980s, however, we have witnessed the birth and rapid development of a new stripe of terrorism which is primarily urban and for the most part ideological in nature. In Europe, for example, extreme left-wing ideology has spawned such urban terrorist groups as the Red Army Faction in West Germany, the Communist Combatant Cells in Belgium, Direct Action in France, and the Red Brigades in Italy. In the Middle East, we may mention several extremist Palestinian groups, including some factions of the Palestine Liberation Organization.

In South America, which has been relatively peaceful on the terrorist front for the past decade or so, similar groups seem to be maturing in such countries as Chile, Colombia, Ecuador, and Peru.

Today we also have state-supported terrorism used as an instrument of foreign policy. The chief protagonists of this new departure in international murder are Iran and Libya. Probably more blood has been shed by Iranian-sponsored terrorists during the last few years than all other terrorists combined.

Teheran uses terrorism as a major element of its ongoing campaign and to reduce Western influence – especially that of the United States – in the Middle East. In 1983, we identified as many as fifty terrorist attacks with a confirmed or suspected Iranian involvement. Most of these incidents occurred in Lebanon, where radical Shiites, the Hezbollah, operated with *direct Iranian support* from terrorist bases in the Syrian-controlled Bekaa Valley. To protect themselves from direct retribution, these terrorists they try to mask their acts under the *non de guerre* "Islamic Jihad."

Iranian-sponsored terrorism was a major factor elsewhere in the Middle East in 1983. Members of the Islamic Call Party, who received training and direction from Teheran, successfully carried out six bombings on 12 December, including one blast that severely damaged the U.S. Embassy in Kuwait.

Iran also continued its active recruitment and training program for Muslims from the Persian Gulf, Africa, and even Asia. Many of these individuals will be available for subversive or terrorist operations in the future, particularly in the oil-rich Persian Gulf states. Most alarming in 1984 was the accumulating evidence that Iranian-sponsored terrorism was increasing in scope and effectiveness in Western Europe. For example, in July the French arrested three individuals suspected of being Iranian agents, and an Air France flight was hijacked from West Germany to Iran. In August and September Islamic Jihad claimed credit for armed attacks on Saudi and Kuwaiti nationals in Spain. And in November seven pro-Iranian Lebanese students in Italy were arrested after plotting an attack on the U.S. Embassy in Rome. We believe that agents working out of Iranian embassies and Islamic cultural or student centers in several European nations will continue to attempt such operations in the future.

Although Libya's Muammar Qadhafi is not in the Ayatollah Khomeini's league, his reliance on and support for terrorists is well known and must no longer go unchallenged. We identified at least 25 terrorist incidents last year involving Libyan agents or surrogates. The main target of Libyan terrorism is anti-Qadhafi exiles in Western Europe and the Middle East. In March the British arrested a number of Libyan agents following a series of bombings that injured at least thirty people in London and Manchester. Most of the victims were innocent bystanders. In April 1983, a gunman firing from the Libyan People's Bureau killed a British policewoman and wounded eleven anti-Qadhafi demonstrators. Following the siege of the People's Bureau, British police found weapons in the building, documenting once again Libya's practice of stocking weapons and explosives in its embassies – a clear violation of international diplomatic conventions.

Some of the many factions of the Palestine Liberation Organization also practice terrorism. The PLO is actually something of an umbrella organization for eight or nine often-warring factions with varying ideologies and competing sponsors. Even though the PLO's influence is somewhat diminished in recent years – due primarily to its 1982 defeat in Lebanon and heightened internal factionalism – many of its member groups remain a credible threat to Israel and many Western governments. Syria controls or at least influences many of the radical splinter groups of the PLO that are believed to be behind recent terrorist attacks on moderate Palestinians and other Arabs, especially Jordanian officials.

For several years, various European left-wing terrorist groups have called for the establishment of an international united front against "Western imperialism," and particularly against its most powerful symbols: NATO and the American presence in Europe. Since the summer of 1984, at least three of these groups – the West German Red Army

Faction, the French group Direct Action, and the Belgian Communist Combatant Cells – have apparently collaborated in a terrorist offensive against NATO that reached a fever pitch of violence by early February 1985.

The offensive seems to have begun in August with terrorist attacks in Paris on the Atlantic Institute, the West European Union, and the European Space Agency – all targets that a Direct Action communique wrongly asserted were associated with NATO. Then, in October, the Belgian Communist Combatant Cells bombed several multinational firms because of their connection with NATO military activities.

More violence ensued in December. Belgian terrorists bombed the NATO pipeline system at six points. At the same time, the Red Army Faction and its supporters in West Germany began a long-planned offensive – more than 30 imprisoned terrorists began a hunger strike, while dozens of bombing attacks against targets associated with NATO were carried out in solidarity with the hunger strikes.

In late January and early February 1985, the offensive reached its zenith. In Belgium, the Communist Combatant Cells bombed a U.S. military recreational facility and declared its intention to inflict casualties as well as property damage in future attacks. In West Germany, the Red Army Faction continued its bombing campaign and assassinated industrialist Dr. Ernst Zimmerman. In France, Direct Action assassinated a senior official of the Ministry of Defense, General Rene Audran. At the same time, French Direct Action prisoners began a hunger strike in sympathy with their German terrorist colleagues. Following the Audran and Zimmerman killings, the West German and French terrorists ended their hunger strikes, and the wave of anti-NATO terrorist attacks in Northern Europe abruptly stopped – probably only temporarily.

Let me now turn for a moment to the Soviet connection. It may seem shadowy to some, but it seems very close to me. Iran and the Soviet Union are hardly allies, but they both share a fundamental hostility to the West. When Libya and the PLO provide arms and training to the communists in Central America, they are aiding Soviet-supported Cuban efforts to undermine our security in that vital region.

In the Middle East, the Soviets and their East German allies have provided intelligence, weapons, funds, and training at camps in the Soviet Union and elsewhere in Eastern Europe. Those passing through these training camps receive indoctrination in Marxism-Leninism which provides a rationale for terrorism and violence against civilian targets, all in the name of wars of national liberation.

To give the Devil his due, we have only indirect evidence of East bloc involvement in the murders and bombings now carried out by the Europeans themselves. Publicly, the Soviets posture loudly and pietistically that they disapprove of terrorism, and that terrorism is "leftist adventurism" and "simplistic ideology." At the same time, I don't see the Soviets taking any action whatsoever to assist victimized governments in curbing terrorist activities. Moreover, the USSR and its East European allies have allowed West European terrorists to transit those countries en route to the Middle East. Some of the East European countries also have been uncooperative in the extradition of terrorists under international arrest warrants. It is also interesting to note that relatively few Soviet targets worldwide have become the victims of terrorist attacks. Moreover, rarely do we hear of a terrorist attack taking place where there is totalitarian control. Only four terrorist incidents were reported for 1984 for the whole of Soviet-dominated Europe.

The fact is that over recent years the Soviets have changed their operational techniques and have become increasingly sophisticated in their use of "active measures" against the West. The Soviets can now achieve their aims quite well *indirectly* by providing training to selected individuals and very small groups, by providing logistical support to the groups; and upon occasion, by providing weapons and explosives to various groups. They do not have to provide much, if any, money. The terrorists obtain all they need from armed robberies of banks, ransoms from kidnappings, and thefts of materials and weapons from Western European governments and private enterprises.

The Soviets make little attempt to conceal the extent of their financial and military aid for countries like Libya and Syria – countries that have adopted terrorism as part of their state policy. The Soviets are quite willing to sell Libya any weapons it requires. The Syrians also receive considerable quantities of arms from the Soviets. Many of these weapons are passed along to the Palestinian groups for use in Lebanon or Israel. Some of these weapons find their way to radical groups far from the hills of Lebanon.

Even more serious is the continuing willingness of Moscow and its allies to allow radical groups to maintain offices in Eastern Europe and to grant safe passage to operatives traveling to Western Europe or elsewhere to commit terrorist acts. No one can seriously believe that these activities have escaped the notice of the communist authorities.

The chain extends around the globe. Part of the subversive threat we face in Central America is stimulated by outsiders who are well versed in terrorism. For example, Italian Prime Minister Craxi stated in early February that Nicaragua hosts 44 of Italy's most dangerous terrorists — a statement corroborated in part by a former Red Brigades terrorist who stated that at least five of his former comrades now serve as non-commissioned officers in the Sandinista army. Nicaragua played host to Iranian Prime Minister Musavi. Strange how the same names and faces keep turning up whenever the subject is international terrorism.

Let us now turn briefly to the murky area of collusion between the big drug dealers and the terrorists and their supporters. These two groups have radically differing goals. Drug dealers are out for one thing: money, and lots of it. They are, above all, merchants who wish to preserve their trade. Drug dealers see as their interest the corruption and gradual control or manipulation of the established regime, to include the buying of policemen, security agents, judges, members of parliaments, and even premiers. Money is the means and also the object for the narcotics pushers.

Terrorists, on the other hand, are out to *destroy* the existing system. If they had their way, they would not corrupt the policemen and judges — they would kill them. Moreover, money is useful for buying weapons, paying operational expenses, and perhaps for buying intelligence and other information. But the terrorist is above all ideological, not mercenary. He is committed to overthrowing the established system.

This said, there is cooperation between some terrorist and narcotics groups for at least tactical reasons. A symbiotic relationship has grown up between the narcotics dealers along the Caribbean coast and the revolutionary armed forces of Colombia who ordinarily would have little to do with one another. The drug merchant needs a secure transit point for his goods to reach markets in the United States. One such transit point is Cuba. The Cubans funnel arms and money to their guerrilla groups through drug merchant channels. Although Fidel Castro, in interviews with American journalists, roundly denies having dealings with drug merchants, we have caught him red-handed. By helping drug dealers push cocaine and marijuana, Castro gains improved access to the

Cuban community in South Florida, contributes to crime and disorder in the United States, and aids his revolutionary offspring in Colombia.

Similarly, we caught red-handed the Sandinista government in Nicaragua involved in narcotic production and trafficking between Colombia and Miami, apparently looking for money which we have seen deposited in Panama and used to bolster their sagging economy.

Terrorists methods are becoming more sophisticated. Explosives remotely detonated or set off by a fanatical suicidal vehicle driver are examples of both technical and tactical innovation. Dangers from terrorism are greatly enhanced by the involvement of governments in the planning, financing, training, documentation and providing safe haven for terrorists groups. Terrorists are able to use more sophisticated techniques, draw on state-funded training programs and use more violent, more deadly, more difficult to detect weapons. They have better intelligence and planning, and official travel documents and diplomatic cover to mask their true identities, their movements, and their munitions deliveries. They can get safe haven in a sponsoring state after an attack.

Radical states see in terrorism the potential for obtaining concessions that they could never get by traditional diplomatic means. Our ability to endure in our polices is called into question and confused by terrorism. Our decision processes are disrupted. Confidence in the workability of our institutions is eroded. It can impair our international credibility as it did in the Iranian hostage crisis some five years ago. Perhaps worst of all, it has become a tempting instrument to accelerate social, political, and economic collapse.

In some countries in the Third World small numbers of revolutionaries, unable to win popular support through the ballot box, have succeeded in converting a moderate and democratic climate of opinion into one that encourages violence and counterviolence with the resultant breakdown in parliamentary institutions.

Clearly, the Soviet Union and its allies see the potential of terrorist movements for disrupting societies. They see that throughout Asia, Africa, and Latin America there are weak governments with low levels of legitimacy and high levels of instability. They understand that these governments are acutely vulnerable to terrorist disruptions and are good targets for terrorist campaigns.

We must not be confused about the difference between insurgency and terrorism. An insurgency, openly using armed conflict as a means of seeking concessions from a dictatorial or totalitarian government that has denied peaceful forms of redress of grievance or civic change, can readily be distinguished from a group that attacks a democratic society by hostage-taking with suitcases filled with explosives on board airliners full of innocent people.

How do we cope with these small bands of highly trained people, most of them fanatics, many ready to give up life itself to do their evil work; increasingly sophisticated as they move around the world crossing borders with officially and professionally prepared papers; knowing that they will have no trouble obtaining weapons, explosives, and whatever else they need near the site of their intended attack; knowing too that they will be able to find protection and sanctuary pre-arranged for them. We can combat this only with the highest professionalism, dedication, and diligence.

We need to know and understand the various terrorist groups, their style and operating methods, their support structures, the training camps which sprout up around the world. This is a task of continuing collection and analysis of intelligence in which the civilized nations of the world must cooperate. We need to provide security and protection for our people and our facilities. We need to provide the most advanced security and police methods. But against a threat that can move so quickly, widely, and quietly, none of us can do it alone. With increasing tempo and effectiveness, we are developing a worldwide counterterrorist network. It is made up of the intelligence, security, and police organizations of the threatened nations. They exchange intelligence, share data banks, work together operationally, provide training and technical capabilities to the less advanced of their number, undertake surveillance and other intelligence assignments for each other, report their findings, and transmit alerts and warnings.

Terrorist groups are a very tough nut for intelligence to crack. They are small, not easily penetrated. Their operations are closely held and compartmented. They move quickly and place a high premium on secrecy and surprise. Yet prompt reporting and prompt follow-up action does frequently forestall terrorist incidents. The most common example is forewarning to U.S. and foreign embassies, or other institutions, of an actual threat or strong indications of planning for attack on installations or individuals. The usual response is heightened alert, increase in protective measures, or change in plans and schedules. Recently, for example, intelligence on a threatened hijacking of a foreign commercial airliner resulted in a change in travel plans and police work, which prevented the intended hijacking. In other instances in Europe, the Middle East, Africa and Latin America, U.S. officials and businessmen directly targeted by terrorists have been temporarily removed from their posts. On several occasions, our warning and detailed intelligence has directly assisted foreign authorities in capturing terrorists. Through timely intelligence work, two sophisticated suitcase bombs were intercepted and disabled, and warnings on the nature of these types of bombs were provided promptly to intended and potential victims worldwide. This warning led to the discovery of two more such devices by cooperating services.

On the other hand, there are many false alarms. The volume of threat reporting has almost invariably escalated dramatically in the wake of a headline-making terrorist incident. At such a time, some individuals seek to market terrorist events to ferret out any information, even seemingly marginal, concerning possible planning for attacks that could threaten U.S. lives and property. The flip side of that is that when such threat reporting rises, more reports of dubious credibility tend to make it through the system that normally would filter them out. This can also produce false confirmations. We have made very good progress in developing a system of very rapid communications to gather assessments, have reports tested by intelligence experts throughout our government and others, and pass conclusions quickly to the point of threat.

What is our policy in dealing with terrorism? We resist it by all legal means. Whenever we obtain evidence that an act of terrorism is about to be mounted, we take measures to warn and protect our citizens, property and interests, and our friends and allies as well. We will work intensively with other countries to eliminate this threat to free and open societies.

We are spending and working to improve the physical security of our diplomatic missions and overseas facilities. Training programs are sensitizing our diplomatic and military personnel to the nature of the terrorist threat. We work closely with other governments to improve the quality and quantity of security provided to our personnel and to our facilities abroad. Here, we are working to provide additional protection to foreign diplomats and dignitaries and visitors in our own country.

The United States does not use force indiscriminately. But we are ready to consider an armed strike against terrorists and those who support them where other means of defense or deterrence are not sufficient. We face very difficult and sensitive problems in choosing appropriate instruments of response in each case. Yet, we cannot allow this to freeze us into paralysis.

If we do not use force where its use is clearly justified, we lose both the direct benefits of action and the deterrent value of having the capability to retaliate. We need that deterrent. We cannot permit terrorist groups or their sponsors to feel they can use free and unopposed violence against us. We must demonstrate our will to meet a terrorist challenge with measured force applied quickly when the evidence warrants. We cannot permit terrorists and their sponsoring states to feel that we are inhibited from responding or that our response is going to be so bogged down in interminable consultations or debate that we, in fact, do not have a deterrent.

We need not insist on absolute evidence. Nor do we need to prove beyond all reasonable doubt that a particular element or individual in state-supporting terrorism is responsible for specific terrorist acts. There is today, for example, sufficient evidence that radical Shia terrorists are responsive to Iranian guidance, for us to hold Teheran responsible for their attacks against United States' citizens, property, and interests.

The legitimacy of using force against terrorism depends also on making strong efforts to deal with this challenge by means short of force. Physical security, training, diplomatic resources and knowledge of other countries, the force of law — all these measures must also be applied in an integrated fashion as rigorously as possible. We must continue to prove our ability to wield all of the elements of national power — political, economic, diplomatic, military, informational, and covert — against the scourge of terrorism.

Western nations have on the whole been weak, in my view, in applying economic, political, and diplomatic measures to check state terrorism.

Sanctions, when exercised in concert with other nations, can help to isolate, weaken, or punish states that sponsor terrorism against us. Too often, countries are inhibited by fear of losing commercial opportunities from provoking further terrorism. Economic sanctions and other forms of countervailing pressure impose costs and risks on the nations that apply them, but some sacrifices will be necessary if we are not to suffer even greater costs down the road.

Examples of how the international community can move in concert are the 1973 Convention for the Suppression of Unlawful Acts against the Safety of Civil Aviation (the Montreal Convention) popularly known as the Anti-Hijacking Convention, and the 1979 International Convention against the Taking of Hostages. The international community should put teeth in existing agreements of this sort by severely punishing violators.

Today, there are additional initiatives that must be taken bilaterally and multilaterally if we are to deal with this problem effectively. For example:

♦ We should review international treaties and agreements that define diplomatic privilege to identify standards of diplomatic practice and behavior which could be more vigorously enforced. We may need new international measures to counter misuse of diplomatic privileges by states sponsoring terrorist activities.

♦ Although the issue of extradition is dealt with bilaterally under normal circumstances, terrorism violates all civilized norms. We should think about developing international treaties whereby: Persons who commit terrorist acts against citizens of signatory states could be routinely extradited; and individuals who use false passports and other documentation, and who cross international boundaries can be detained to permit investigation of the purpose of such travel. It would be an important signal for those nations signatory to existing counterterrorism conventions and agreements to proceed to ratify those agreements. Five European nations, for example, have yet to ratify the Strasbourg Convention (the European Convention on the Suppression of Terrorism).

A strong beginning has been made. Parliaments have begun to authorize funds, and governments to establish effective counterterrorist units. Intelligence and security services are developing new capabilities and improving their methods and performances. A conference such as this goes far to air the tough issues in dealing with terrorism, and directs attention to this vital subject.

♦ ♦ ♦

COMBATTING TERRORISM AT ITS ROOTS

Casey's views on the terrorist threat often put him at odds with other senior Administration officials. Note his reference in the last paragraph of this speech to the lack of a national will to fight terrorism at its roots. This lack of will, in turn, leaves no choice but to cope with terrorism's effects. " And that," Casey warns, "will not be enough."

Here he sets the stage for yet another conference – this one not under CIA sponsorship.

In this conference we have undertaken examination of one of the critical issues of our day. For perhaps no other topic poses as much of a threat to the orderly functioning of democratic societies as does international terrorism. The grim reality is that terrorism is on the rise worldwide, and we can expect only more violence and death during the closing years of this century.

In the next few minutes I plan to tell you something about how the American intelligence community assesses this dreadful scourge, and how I think we should deal with it.

Whatever his specific political program, the terrorist always pursues one general goal – to fix in the public's consciousness a sense of the terrorist's omnipotence and the public's helplessness. The terrorist, in short, has declared war on the mind. It is the impression of being everywhere and nowhere, of striking with impunity at whomever and whatever he will, that gives the terrorist his real power. To do this, the terrorist takes advantage of the very civilization he seeks to destroy.

The terrorist depends upon two factors for success in conducting his war on the mind. Both of these factors, ironically, are found only in the urban centers of open societies like ours and those of our friends around the world. The first, and most important of these, is coverage by the media. In this decade more people can be addressed by newspaper, television, radio, and magazines than ever before in history. What is more, the media are so effective that millions of people may learn of a terrorist attack that has taken place half a world away in a matter of minutes or at most, hours. It is no accident that the vast bulk of the most

Address to the Symposium on "Terrorism and Industry: Threat and Responses," sponsored by the Stanford Research Institute and the Center for Strategic and International Studies, Washington, D.C., October 14, 1985.

heinous terrorist murders, bombings, and hijackings take place not in isolated villages in Africa or among remote Asian tribesmen but in cities that possess excellent communication links with the rest of the world.

The terrorist hopes that his deeds will be bannered on the six o'clock news throughout most of the developed world, will be commented on at length in world's leading newspapers, and perhaps become the subject of everyday conversation. People will ask: When will the next attack occur? Who will be the victim? Such uncertainty has a numbing effect on millions of people who expect to stand by helplessly to witness the next outrage. Or, perhaps, they expect to be killed or maimed in the next savage terrorist attack.

Even if an attack fails, as in the case of the assassination attempt on Prime Minister Margaret Thatcher, the terrorists will nonetheless gain the maximum psychological impact of his deed by a bold public threat. As many of you may recall, the Irish Republican Army in a public notice told Mrs. Thatcher that, "This time you were lucky. But you have to be lucky all the time. We only have to be lucky once." Clearly, the threat and the uncertainty is a powerful weapon. In the case of the failed assassination attempt against Prime Minister Thatcher, the terrorist nonetheless succeeded because their objective was the creation of an atmosphere of fear and uncertainty.

The second factor that aids terrorists in their campaign is the nature of modern urban society. The concentration of population offers anonymity to the terrorist. Weapons and money can be obtained through an infinite number of channels, thus preserving the terrorist's operational security. The variety and efficiency of transportation enhances the terrorist's mobility. Moreover, industrialized societies have more vulnerable high-value targets — such as computer centers, airlines, factories, shopping arcades, and even apartment complexes.

It is also no secret that democratic societies provide more opportunities for a terrorist, and certainly more room for maneuver. Unlike the Soviet bloc, or other closed societies that require internal passports and have frequent police checks on visitors and travelers, Western societies have only the lightest checks on movement. The ability to live where one pleases and to associate with whomever one chooses aids the terrorist in his operations. Thus, Western democracies by their very nature are particularly vulnerable to terrorist attacks.

Moreover, for the first time, terrorist attacks directed at American private businesses and businessmen overseas outnumbered terrorist attacks against U.S. military and diplomatic facilities. I speculate that this shift may be due in part to the greatly improved physical security measures taken by the State and Defense Departments. Terrorist groups may have concluded that American-owned businesses present "softer targets" that nonetheless yield very high-visibility headlines when hit.

In my view, the Congress acted very wisely when it voted $360 million to improve security at our various facilities around the world in the wake of the October 1983 tragedy at the Marine barracks in Beirut. We all know that other painful attacks have occurred since that time. But I believe that our defensive preparations and tightened physical security have begun to pay dividends. Clearly, thought needs to be given to assisting U.S. businessmen to improve physical security at their facilities as well.

The risks and difficulties associated with terrorism are greatly diminished when regimes like those of Colonel Qadhafi's Libya and Ayatollah Khomeini's Iran actively support terrorist groups.

With the help of a sponsoring state, terrorist groups are able to use more sophisticated techniques because of state-funded training programs and technical expertise. Moreover, the groups can employ more deadly, more difficult to detect equipment and arms such as remotely detonated devices. They also receive intelligence, and get official travel documents — sometimes used as diplomatic cover — to hide their true identities. This support makes it easy for terrorists to mask movements and munitions deliveries — and then find safe haven in a sponsoring state after an attack. So the backing of governments enormously escalates the scope and power of even the smallest terrorist groups.

All of this is to say that improved physical security from terrorism, while important, is not enough.

Now I want to outline a strategy for dealing with this problem. Basically, there are three broad fronts on which we challenge the terrorist. First, we can improve our intelligence capabilities and work together more closely with other countries victimized by terrorism. Second, we can work toward a stronger legal framework to deal with terrorist acts and with prosecuting terrorist themselves. Third, the international community can work together to isolate terrorist gangs and the states that sponsor these gangs. Against a threat that observes no borders and respects no national flag — and which can move so quickly, widely, and quietly — it is immediately apparent that no one country can fight terrorism alone.

The first part of this strategy is to encourage the victimized countries to work more closely and to share vital information they have on terrorism. . . . Through intelligence exchanges, training and operational cooperation and technical support, we have, with the intelligence, security and police organizations of scores of countries around the world, developed a widespread counter-terrorism network which needs to be strengthened and improved upon. American intelligence, as the only worldwide apparatus other than the KGB, is at the heart of this. So far this year there were something like eighty terrorist acts around the world where preventive action was taken based on advance information from U.S. intelligence.

The second major part of our program is to continue working — as a community of nations subject to law — to construct a viable international legal framework for dealing with terrorists and their sponsors. This framework must be transnational in character and supported by vigorous legal action.

International law requires a state to control the activities of persons within its jurisdiction or territory which cause injury to the citizens of other states, and to punish any persons engaging in such activities.

During the last two decades, international agreements have repeatedly restated and expanded this basic duty of all countries. For example, the Convention for the Suppression of Unlawful Seizure of Aircraft, otherwise known as the Hague Convention, imposes obligations on states to establish criminal jurisdiction over the offense of air piracy, and requires that countries extradite hijackers or submit hijacking cases to competent authorities.

Despite such agreements, the existing legal obligations by themselves are insufficient to thwart terrorism: First, not all states are signatories to these conventions. Second, state signatories face little or no possibility of being penalized for failure to adhere to their international obligations. Libya, for example — one of the world's leading fomenters of terrorist violence — hypocritically is a party to the Montreal, Hague, and Tokyo conventions. And third, there has been no appropriate articulation of a formal definition of terrorism. Efforts to obtain general acceptance of the 1972 U.S. Draft Convention on Terrorism were linked to an intentional avoidance of the issue of definition and thus focused only on a narrow common interest among nations. However, even this focus has not led to formal adoption of the convention.

The legal framework is there. What is needed is the will to make use of it — the will to put teeth into these international agreements by severely punishing violations. Many nations have been slow on this. The current defaults on the part of the Egyptian, Italian, and Yugoslav governments can, if our public diplomacy and political action are vigorous enough, represent an opportunity to bring about a broader and stronger governmental will to deal with terrorism. . . .

The third major part of our program requires that all victimized governments should impose political and economic isolation on states like Iran and Libya that sponsor terrorism. I find it incredible that certain of our friends and allies still have dealings with terrorist atrocities cooked up in Teheran, Tripoli, and other such centers. And, as long as they permit Libyan and Iranian agents to move about freely — and indeed pay huge sums into the treasuries of those two countries — we have no leverage whatsoever. Simply put, states that sponsor terrorism must be quarantined from the rest of the international community until their behavior changes.

So far as the terrorist himself is concerned, we must take vigorous action to isolate him from his target — attacking the public mind. That is to say we must defeat the terrorists' strategy of manipulating public perceptions. We must deny the terrorist the fruit of his favors — namely, the ability to exploit the media to instill in the public feelings of uncertainty and fear. The media must play the leading role in this effort by treating news of terrorist incidents in a more reserved fashion, and by providing strong editorials that discredit the terrorists' actions. Imagine if you will the terrorist's reaction if he and his exploits were downplayed or even ignored.

In addition we should strive to instill in the terrorist those same pervasive feelings of fear that he seeks to instill in the public — the feeling of constantly being the hunted, rather than the hunter. The terrorist must at all times have the impression that his movements are known, his plans understood, and his cells penetrated. We can do this, as I mentioned earlier, by improving coordination of intelligence, police and counter-terrorist units, and especially by mobilizing media support to sustain the courage of the public and to convince the terrorist that his actions are repudiated by the public.

If we can do this, the terrorist will watch in frustration as his power over the media dries up and, with it, his power to assault the mind. If cut off from his sponsors, the terrorist will watch with growing apprehension as he learns that the costs and risks of his operations skyrocket while the impact of his actions plummets. In my view, the futility of terrorism will at last be made obvious to the terrorist himself, and his devastating war on the mind will slowly come to an end.

You might well ask the very pertinent question: but does all this work? I believe it does. And I can mention two success stories in war on terrorism.

It may surprise you to know that the country having the highest number of terrorist incidents during the late 1970s was not Lebanon or Israel, but Italy. The wanton murders of Premier Aldo Moro and the kidnapping of General Dozier galvanized the Italian government into action. Italian courts have stepped up their effort at prosecuting and convicting captured terrorists, and handing down stiff sentences. The Italian national police and security services have stepped up their activities targeted at penetrating terrorist units or otherwise spoiling terrorist operations. Moreover, European services have been active in sharing information on these terrorists, subsequently leading to the capture of some of those involved.

As a result of excellent intelligence work, vigorous police anti-terrorist activities, and increased court actions, Italy since the early 1980s has been one of the countries in Europe least affected by terrorism. A key factor in this effort was the turn-around in support for the Italian security services by most parties in the Italian Parliament and the general public. As a consequence of this, despite the current crumbling of political will at the top which may only be temporary, the Italian anti-terrorist forces now have the upper hand are doing excellent work in fighting terrorism in Europe.

Another success story is the Republic of El Salvador. That small country – the victim of both externally-supported aggression and terrorism – has risen to grave challenges posed by purveyors of violence who receive their orders from Managua and Havana.

In the past twelve months, we have witnessed an increase in Marxist-directed terrorism that had included bombings of civilian installations, the mining of public roads, armed robberies, brutal kidnappings, and assassinations. This increasing turn to terrorism has come about in part because of the growing popular support for President Duarte's government and in part because of the rapidly faltering political and military fortunes of the rebels. The insurgents increasingly have fallen back on dramatic acts of violence to draw attention to their cause, and force President Duarte's popularly-elected government to share political power.

You may recall that last June a gang of Marxist thugs staged a bloody machinegun slaying outside a sidewalk cafe of thirteen unarmed people, including four off duty U.S. Marines and two U.S. businessmen. The so-called Central American Revolutionary Workers Party – which claimed "credit" for the June slayings – is a member in good standing of the five-group Salvadoran Marxist Alliance and has its command headquarters in Managua, Nicaragua.

The Salvadoran government responded quickly and decisively to this urban terrorist threat. Since the June massacre, the Salvadoran army has launched operations against these terrorists and other Marxist base camps in the central and eastern mountains. The army's offensive has proved quite successful, as a large number of insurgents – including some field commanders – were killed, communication lines were disrupted, and supplies captured. Captured documents and prisoners provided valuable intelligence which the security forces promptly used in rounding up some forty urban terrorists, including two of the actual triggermen involved in the June killings. The triggermen will be tried for murder.

Let me give you one final thought on which much further study and work is needed. Dr. Yonah Alexander talked this morning about the terrorist network. This network may not be a component of but it works in unison with what the Soviets have developed into the most powerful weapons system the world has ever seen. This consists, perhaps not primarily, of the missiles capable of striking at the United States and most of its allies and the overwhelming conventional strength which can be projected into Europe and towards the Persian Gulf, but also of the weapons of aggressive subversion. It has succeeded in installing communist governments in Angola, Ethiopia, South Yemen, Mozambique, Cambodia, and Nicaragua, and resulted in sending its conventional forces for the first time over the border of the Soviet Union to occupy Afghanistan. It consists also of the system of the combination of active measures, political action, and propaganda which the Soviets use to influence and manipulate popular opinion and political processes in the open societies of the world.

The creation and training of terrorists is the primary measure of how severe this problem will be for us during the remainder of this century. This will be determined in part by the six hundred or so young men who are brought into Moscow every year to be indoctrinated to serve as organizers in other countries around the world, and by how many other young men are brought into terrorist and paramilitary training camps elsewhere. Where are these training facilities located? They are heavily concentrated in the Soviet bloc — in the Soviet Union itself, in Bulgaria, Czechoslovakia, East Germany, South Yemen, Cuba, and increasingly Nicaragua, and in the radical entente countries of Syria, Libya, and Iran. So, as we fight the terrorist threat directly on the ground we also need to bring out the ultimate source of much of this activity.

The reality — the bottom line — is that terrorism, in all its forms and all its sources, aims at the very heart of civilization. We have no realistic choice but to meet it, and that means head on. Nothing else will work. And the aim of the terrorists and the ultimate objective for those who sponsor, train, encourage, and supply terrorists, is to undermine our values, shatter our self-confidence, and ultimately destroy our way of life. In the absence of a national will to fight terrorism at its roots, we must be content only to cope with terrorism's effects, not its cause. And that will not be enough.

* * *

Chapter 8

Learning From History

THE LESSONS OF WORLD WAR II:
HELPING OCCUPIED NATIONS OVERTHROW
TOTALITARIAN REGIMES

Intelligence analysts working under Casey often found themselves involved in "lessons-learned" projects: team efforts that focused on a particular foreign event that caught U.S. intelligence by surprise or a particular analytic projection that turned out not to be accurate. The objective of these efforts was to develop some insight into just where CIA had gone wrong, or missed a signal, or been caught napping. To Casey it was forgivable to make a mistake provided one learned why and never made it again. And when things went right – that is, when the intelligence community called a shot accurately – Casey also organized "lessons-learned" projects, to assure that we learned the right lessons and thus would be more likely to replicate our success in future, similar circumstances.

In this speech, Casey offers a sweeping perspective of Allied resistance movements during World War II. His focus is on the proper role and function of external support to resistance movements – precisely the activity in which he himself was so deeply involved as a senior officer of the Office of Strategic Services (OSS). He then provides a "lessons-learned" perspective to relate the activities of these World War II movements, and the external support they received, to efforts against current totalitarian states.

Address to the OSS/Donovan Symposium, Washington, D.C., September 19, 1986.

Fellow survivors, it's great to gather this morning with so many old friends and comrades who share a pride and satisfaction in the work of OSS some forty to forty-five years ago. Thank God we're all here!

I'd first like to congratulate Max Corvo for conceiving this symposium on the history of OSS, and thank him for having the spirit and the will and persistence to bring us together for this occasion. We owe a debt of gratitude to Mim Daddario, Ray Cline, and others on the committee for putting the program together. We thank Jeff Jones for his diligence and leadership as President of Veterans of OSS.

My assignment is to provide an overview. I have puzzled a great deal at what that requires. It is not easy because OSS was such a far-flung activity. A great deal of new documentation about OSS has become available. There is in the historical work already done on OSS a wide range of opinion and interpretation. Even after two days of lively debate, these proceedings will not produce final answers to the questions of how OSS came to be created, what it did in the war, and how its experience has influenced the development of American intelligence since then. In these two days, one of the most useful things we can do is to identify the high points and the main gaps in our knowledge of OSS.

OSS was an extraordinarily well-documented organization and there are a lot of private papers around. In the past year, the U.S. Army's Military History Institute at Carlisle, Pennsylvania, has opened up to researchers the papers of General Donovan himself. While this valuable collection includes some microfilm of the wartime director's office files, the papers, naturally, mainly focus on General Donovan and not on OSS. The truth is that comprehensive and thoroughly documented studies of the history of OSS can't be done without substantial research in its official wartime records. Until recently, however, most of these records were still classified and researchers had no access to them except through the Freedom of Information Act. I'm glad to be able to report, however, that these records – around 4,000 cubic feet of them – have nearly all now been declassified, transferred to the National Archives and Records Administration, and opened to the public for research. The OSS records in the National Archives will eventually make over more than 100 million pages of OSS records available for historical research.

One of the great resources available to those interested in OSS history is John E. Taylor, who for many years has assembled and organized the OSS records at the National Archives. He certainly knows more about

OSS and its history than anyone else in the world and gladly will share this knowledge to help researchers find what they are looking for in this vast collection.

OSS was virtually worldwide, except that General MacArthur and Admiral Nimitz did not use OSS in their huge Pacific theater. Under Carl Eifler and Ray Peers, a large force of Kachins was organized and supplied to assist General Stilwell by fighting behind Japanese lines in Burma. Extensive intelligence operations were carried out in China, sometimes with and sometimes against Chiang Kai-shek's intelligence services. Toward the end of the war, OSS intelligence activities were carried on with Mao Tse-tung's communist forces in China, and OSS functioned in Indochina in support of and under the direction of General Mountbatten's headquarters in India and Ceylon. Other activities were carried on in Africa and the Middle East.

My own activity and knowledge was confined to General Donovan's headquarters in Washington and the war against the Nazis in Europe. The best way I can provide an overview is to discuss how OSS worked, and the range of its capabilities in the context of the war against Hitler. I want to emphasize that comparable activities were carried on in other theaters — Italy, the Balkans, the Middle East, Burma, China, and Indo-China.

OSS started with Bill Donovan's vision that intelligence, subversion, and psychological warfare could be our spearhead in the invasion of Europe. He created a novel instrument to serve the purpose. The thrust and cutting edge which intelligence and deception, and psychological and irregular warfare can give to a military command and troops in battle cannot be conjured up overnight. The foundations of the covert war against Hitler were built by the British when they stood alone. Its major achievements — their reading of the German communications, the writing of German intelligence assessments from London by their deception planners, the timely assessment and development of countermeasures against German secret weapons, and the early support of resistance forces in Europe — were almost entirely British. While this foundation was being built, America had little more than a volunteer one-man intelligence service in William J. Donovan, plus a few brilliant cryptographers hidden away, when Henry Stimson as Secretary of State declared that gentlemen don't read other people's mail. The organization which Donovan created had to be taught, trained, and built on the experience and professional expertise which had been built up in Britain – and in France and Poland, Belgium and Holland, Scandinavia, and Czechoslovakia.

You had only to be around OSS a few days in the summer of 1943 to realize how embattled an organization it was two years into the war, even after its mettle had been tested and proven in the crucible of the North African campaign. But to the entrenched Washington bureaucracies that cut little ice. It is no exaggeration to say that Donovan created OSS against the fiercest kind of opposition from everybody – the Army, Navy, and State Departments, the Joint Chiefs of Staff, the regular Army brass, the whole Pentagon bureaucracy, and, perhaps most devastatingly, the White House staff.

Everyone in Washington was trying to walk off with a slice of Donovan's franchise. J. Edgar Hoover resented a rival and fought for as much intelligence turf as he could get. He ended up in charge of secret intelligence operations in Latin America, an area from which OSS was totally excluded. Nelson Rockefeller hacked out an exclusive franchise to report and analyze political and economic intelligence there, as well as conduct propaganda. Byron Price headed the Office of Censorship; Lowell Millet the Division of Information of the Office of Emergency Management. Playwright Robert Sherwood edgily divided his time between writing FDR's speeches and running the Foreign Information Service under Donovan, while he was bucking for an independent information franchise. Archibald McLeish had the Office of Facts and Figures. It seemed as if anyone with access to Roosevelt could get a charter for himself.

That OSS operations in North Africa did not establish the organization more firmly as part of the Washington establishment must remain one of the minor mysteries of the war. Rarely had intelligence and diplomacy meshed as smoothly as they did in preparing Operation "Torch" and helping it achieve early victory.

North Africa was OSS' first testing ground. Donovan had pinpointed the area as a critical one in his report to Roosevelt eighteen months before the American landings in November 1942. That most remarkable of American diplomats, Robert Murphy, had given OSS a headstart in North Africa where he served as a kind of American pro-consul. In late 1940, he persuaded French authorities to let him bring in twelve observers, ostensibly to assure the British then blockading the African coast that food shipments allowed through did not get into German hands. These observers were also allowed to use secret codes and couriers with locked pouches. Able to send out uncensored reports, they became the nucleus for the first operating American intelligence network of the war, and Donovan wasted little time building on the base they provided. He named Marine Colonel William Eddy, English professor at the American University in Cairo and fluent in Arabic, as his chief in North Africa.

Large elements of the French army in North Africa and many French civilians were prepared for resistance to any German occupation. Eddy and his men helped organize and supply this resistance, while at the same time winning the support of native Moor, Algerian, and Tunisian leaders.

OSS research and analysis scholars under Bill Langer and Sherman Kent delivered studies of the French North African railways, the capacity of the rolling stock, the condition of the roadbed and track, terrain maps, charts of reefs, channels, and tidal tables – all assembled from manuals, engineering journals, and other sources available in the Library of Congress. In November 1942, the months of preparation paid off. As the ships approached their destinations along the coasts of Morocco and Algiers, Allied army, navy and air officers with the invasion fleet received – until the last minute of H-hour and beyond – detailed information on what to expect at every landing point. They were met and accompanied by OSS representatives who advised them on the terrain, on locations of French headquarters and German Armistice Commission offices, and on the officials whom they could rely on for assistance.

Squads of friendly Frenchmen, Moors, and Riffs were instructed to cut telegraph and telephone lines and to obstruct public utilities generally. Still others were to go just before H-hour to detonate mines on roads and beaches which the Allies would have to use. Groups were assigned to beachheads and landing and parachute fields, with flares to signal troops in from ships and guide them inland.

Bob Murphy's dozen and Donovan's OSSers had successfully prepared the way and almost entirely eliminated resistance to the landing of only 110,000 American and British troops along 1,200 miles of Atlantic and Mediterranean beaches. Military planning in Washington and London had estimated that they would need 500,000 men to take and hold French North Africa. The foothold in North Africa, which the military planners had estimated would cost 10,000 casualties, had been gained with less than a couple of hundred.

In February 1943, Donovan sent David Bruce to London to take over a small OSS headquarters. It was Bruce's task to sell OSS to the various organizations in wartime London, those building the invasion armada and those charged with directing three wars from London – the air war, the subversive war already under way, and the land war soon to be launched over French beaches.

We were the new boys on the team and the British were reluctant to risk what they had built up to let us show our stuff and develop our talents in areas where they were already active and successful. They preferred to engage OSS in new projects and to do that under British tutelage. Much to his later chagrin, Donovan agreed to do this.

Donovan soon regretted his commitment not to send American agents into Europe from Britain without British approval, but he could not change it. Moreover, even without such an explicit agreement, the British could easily have stopped any independent effort whenever they felt it risked their own operations. They controlled the air and the sea and all movements in and out of Britain.

We finally got the British to agree to a joint intelligence undertaking. The Sussex Plan called for dispatching 120 agents in teams of two, one observer and one radio operator, into France just ahead of the invading armies. They were to report from key points in France on German troop movements. It was a tripartite operation with French, British, and American agents in civilian clothes organized into thirty teams for the British combat zone in France and another thirty for the American battle area.

In the summer of 1943, Allen Dulles scored the first big OSS coup in Switzerland and we felt the repercussions in London. Fritz Kolbe, an official of the German Foreign Office charged with handling cable traffic with diplomatic posts all over the world, had made his way to Berne carrying sixteen telegrams taken out of the files of the Foreign Office in Berlin. Ultimately, Dulles received a huge amount of this information which we called "woods cables".

They stirred up a fierce storm in London. Sir Claude Dansey, the Deputy Chief of British Intelligence, had been in charge of intelligence operations from Switzerland before the war. He charged OSS with falling for an obvious plant. When our "woods cables" stood up as valid under comparison with the decodification of cables intercepted between the German Foreign Office and German embassies abroad, Dansey retreated grudgingly and Dulles's "woods" reports gained acceptance as perhaps the greatest espionage coup of the war.

In those early days, most of our intelligence came from the neutral capitals. In Switzerland, Istanbul, Lisbon, Madrid, and Stockholm, free of our British tutors, Donovan had created missions to develop contacts and sources, and the flow of American information from thee areas enhanced the OSS position in London's intelligence community. With direct air links via regularly scheduled passenger flights to both Berlin and London, the neutral capitals — Lisbon, Madrid, Stockholm, Berne, and Istanbul — served as windows on occupied Europe and meeting places for "our" and "their" people.

Gregory Thomas and Frank Schoonmaker built up extensive intelligence networks from Barcelona down San Sebastian into southwestern France. Henry Hyde from Algiers and Allen Dulles from Switzerland built agent networks into southern, eastern, and central France. When Calvin Hoover, who ran OSS operations in Stockholm, established that ball bearing exports were much larger than the Swedes admitted, a U.S. economic warfare mission won Swedish agreement to stop the shipments.

In London we worked closely with the Allied governments in exile, their contacts with the resistance in their homelands, and with the intelligence links they established back home. None were more important than the French. France was our invasion target. Though the regime was in exile and the resistance at home riven with factions, both were active, strong, and eager. By 1944, DeGaulle's intelligence, under Colonel Passy and Colonel Remy, was distributing reports to the entire London intelligence community twice a day. The monthly output of this information factory averaged 200,000 mimeographed sheets, 60,000 copies of maps and sketches, and 10,000 photographic reproductions.

The Poles in London ran one of the most efficient and ambitious of the exile intelligence services. Colonel Gano developed large networks both in Poland and in France where hundreds of thousands of Poles had found refuge. Belgian intelligence had eight to ten effective intelligence networks operating in Belgium and in that part of northern France which the Germans administered from Brussels. The Norwegians, the Danes, and the Dutch were similarly active.

The first of what would total some 150 messages that passed among Berne, London, Stockholm, and Washington clattered over the airways at the turn of 1944. It told us about a mushrooming conspiracy inside the Reich which Dulles called "breakers". The conspirators wanted to get rid of Hitler, form a new government, and bring the war to an end.

The British Joint Intelligence Committee and our Joint Chiefs urged a restatement of the unconditional surrender formula to encourage German commanders to lay down their arms. Roosevelt rejected these proposals but Eisenhower kept pressing all the way to the end, almost to the day of the invasion. At the end of April, he had Bedell Smith formulate a policy, which the German generals might be able to accept, to quit fighting; and in late May he got Bob Sherwood to draft a speech redefining unconditional surrender, intended to be delivered after the landing but apparently never approved.

When the attempt on Hitler's life came on July 20, 1944, the information Dulles provided caused Churchill to publicly encourage internal action against Hitler. Dulles's contacts with the German resistance resulted in Roosevelt having for some days earlier a paper from Donovan telling him that an attempt on Hitler's life was imminent and urging him to respond publicly.

Meanwhile, OSS was contributing heavily to the intellectual and strategic basis for the air war on German industry. This was done by the Enemy Objectives Unit developed in Donovan's Ivory Tower back in Washington by Ed Mason, an economics professor from Harvard, and brought to London under the leadership of Charlie Kindelberger.

The American talent working in this area was prodigious, as the future careers of those who took part would testify. Kindelberger's stars included: Walt Rostow, later to become Lyndon Johnson's National Security Advisor; Robert Roosa, a future Under Secretary of the Treasury for Monetary Affairs; Charles Hitch, who would become President of the University of California; Carl Kaysen, who was to head the Institute for Advanced Studies at Princeton; Chan Morse, Emil Despres, Harold Barnet, and others I cannot recall.

These OSS economists, applying economic analysis to strategic bombing, developed criteria and doctrine for target selection and carried out cost/benefit analyses on the relative merits of bombing factories that made aircraft engines, assembled planes, and produced ball-bearings.

In the spring of 1944, they lost a campaign to persuade Eisenhower to shift from the bombing of railroad marshaling yards, which they argued could be quickly repaired, to the destruction of synthetic oil plants which they felt could be kept out of action longer, and which would slow down German airpower and trucks more permanently and more valuably than damaging marshaling yards. They felt that any traffic delays resulting from the bombing of marshaling yards would slow down civilians more than military transport because the German military would have priority and get through.

Where and how and when supplies to the French resistance would be delivered was planned jointly by OSS and the British Special Operations Executive (SOE), already working in tandem as Special Forces Headquarters (SFHQ). Specially trained British and American crews flew modified planes to drop weapons to the resistance. With the French resistance leader in London we struggled with the American Air Force to get more air drops for the resistance, and with the British we trained and sent close to 100 young Americans as agents into France.

In those last weeks before the landings, the wireless reports received in London in increasing profusion created a growing sense of control over large areas of France. Our agents would find themselves surrounded by a large group of people as they landed with fires burning, autos on hand to divide them through villages and smaller towns under marquis control. Supply depots and hospitals for resistance fighters were functioning. German forces kept to the main routes and the big towns because they found the secondary roads too dangerous. By sticking to backroads it was possible for our agents to drive long distances with impunity.

Our planes were parachuting almost 100 tons of arms and ammunition a week, ten times what we had been doing two months earlier. The Royal Air Force was dropping even more, and still more came from Algiers. The radio sets in contact with London or Algiers had become the great sources of power in dealing with resistance factions and their leaders. The tapping of the Morse key could, like magic, bring them sten guns, grenades, bazookas, and explosives. A single radio could provide a center of communication for groups of hundreds and even thousands of resistance fighters extending over hundreds of miles of winding roads as their leaders came to request arms and propose or accept missions of destruction, interdiction, or preservation.

As the invasion drew nearer, resistance leaders operating behind the lines and officers commanding invading troops had to be able to communicate quickly and effectively if their operations were to mesh. Radio contact alone could not accomplish this. We needed men in Allied uniforms to advise the resistance on Allied needs. We needed specialists attached to the invading armies who understood the resistance, to advise Allied commanders on what French forces could deliver.

Teams of three — an American, British, and French officer or noncom — called "jedburghs" were air dropped into France starting a day or two before D-day. All in all we trained 300 volunteers and organized them into 93 teams. Virtually all were dispatched into France behind the lines. In addition, small special forces detachments, made up of OSS and SOE officers, were detailed to each army and army group headquarters. Equipped with direct radio links to OSS radio stations in England, they served as the European resistance's central nervous system in indirect contact with resistance forces.

Our counterespionage outfit, X-2, under Jimmie Murphy and Hubert Will, organized teams to join the army staffs and support them with data and files which, when they got to France, were used to apprehend the German spies that had been left behind or who had been captured. Donovan had turned to the American ethnic melting pot to organize operational groups, some twenty to forty of French, Italian, Scandinavian, and Slavic origins, who were to be dropped into France, Italy, Norway, and Yugoslavia to cooperate and support local resistance forces. Several of these operational groups went behind the lines in France and Italy. Toward the end of the war, Bill Colby, having finished his mission into France as a jedburgh, took an operational group into northern Norway near the Russian border.

On May 31, word reached us at Grosvenor Street that the Supreme Headquarters Allied Expeditionary Forces (SHAEF) had turned the policy for using French resistance upside down. We were told that instead of signaling the resistance to rise unit by unit and join the fighting on a gradual, as-needed basis, all action signals to resistance groups in every corner of France would be sent out simultaneously.

Most important, Eisenhower wanted to protect the deception campaign that had the Germans expecting the landings to come further to the north on the *Pas de Clais* and would keep Hitler's best divisions there, 100 miles from the Normandy beaches, for several weeks after the landings.

Our first reaction to the new order was one of gloom and foreboding. This could touch off a national uprising. The Germans would have little trouble drowning the revolt in a blood bath with grave, long-term political consequences. Finally, and perhaps most important, our troops moving across France would be deprived of military support from the FFI (*Forces Francaises de l'Interieur*, the French resistance groups unified under DeGualle). David Bruce went to argue this out with General Walter Bedell Smith, Ike's chief of staff, to no avail. The decision was firm. Eisenhower wanted all the help he could get when he needed it most, at the time of the landing.

On June 1, the first set of some 300 messages went out over the BBC alerting resistance leaders all over France that the landings were to come during that week. The action messages on the night of June 5 triggered the rail disruptions, wire cuts, and road and bridge destruction that had been targeted all over France. Trains and convoys carrying German troops and supplies to the bridgehead were delayed for days and weeks. Troops arrived at the front on bicycles and horse-drawn carts. German headquarters with their telephone lines cut had to communicate with radios which our codebreakers in England read with dramatic consequences.

In late May, a SHAEF assessment had found that bombing railroad marshaling yards had indeed failed to impair the enemy's ability to move up reinforcements and maintain his forces in the West. The Germans still had three times the capacity needed to support their military traffic.

After losing the fight to give priority to attacking oil facilities, the OSS economists had gone all out to refocus allied bombings away from marshaling yards to bridges, fuel and ammunition dumps, and tank and truck depots. They argued that it could take up to three weeks to repair a bridge but only hours to fix a track inside or near a marshaling yard or railroad center.

The OSS economists had been right and the Allied air marshalls — Tedder, Leigh-Mallory, Spaatz, and Arnold — authorized the attacks on bridges spanning the Seine, Oise, and Meuse. Success was spectacular. General Spaatz particularly went after the synthetic oil plants as Kindelberger had urged months earlier, and this contributed heavily in slow-ing down German air attacks, tanks, and transport for the duration of the war.

Now as the French bridges were hit, stone and masonry tumbled into the dusty rivers, forcing German soldiers off trains to trudge down a road toward the front lines.

In the week after D-day, resistance teams made 1,000 rail cuts, and 2,000 within three weeks. After June 7, not a single train crossed the area of Burgundy between Dijon, Besancon, Chalon, and Lous le Saunier, through which ran all the main and secondary lines between the Rhone Valley and the Rhine.

The German 11th Panzer Division took a week to get from Russia to the Rhine and three weeks to get across France to Caen. One of the oldest and probably the best of the Panzer Divisions, Das Reich, ordered to Normandy, which should have been a three-day trip, arrived fifteen days late.

After the landings, particularly during late June and July, we poured in a torrent of supplies. With the lift it gave resistance fighters, it paid off during August and September when resistance groups south of the Loire protected Patton's right flank as he raced across France from Brittany to Nancy and ultimately liberated all of France south of the Loire and west of the Rhone. East of the Rhone resistance forces, along Napoleon's route, the resistance protected the flanks of the American Seventh Army as it moved from its Mediterranean landing beaches to take Grenoble within nine days after landing on the coast. The Seventh Army operational plan had figured it would take much longer to take Grenoble.

While this was going on, OSS jedburghs from Algiers ranged as far north as Dijon and as far west as Vichy, rallying resistance forces to disrupt Germans, with some seeking to provide reinforcement and others retreating. The military command in Algiers had remarkably accurate intelligence on German dispositions in France of which, a British G-2 officer estimated, 50 percent came from OSS.

This brilliant result came from intelligence networks in France launched when Henry Hyde persuaded the British to allow him to send a two-man team he had recruited in Algiers from England. The year this gave Hyde to develop his networks before any other agents could be dropped from England paid enormous dividends.

Hyde's team had quickly built a tight espionage network through southern France that had 2,500 agents and 337 radios transmitting intelligence to Algiers. Complimenting Hyde's Algerian effort was OSS in Madrid, putting agents across the Spanish border; and Allen Dulles, in Switzerland, pushing agents down through the Alps towards the Mediterranean coast.

When British and American armies approached the Belgian border, the Port of Antwerp was a great prize. When Belgium was liberated in September, the Belgian secret army had prevented the Germans from carrying out orders to destroy it. The port was handed over to us intact. One of the great foul-ups of command in World War II was the failure to cross the Albert Canal to seal off the German 15th Army in its retreat from the channel coast. The result was that substantial elements of that army survived to defeat Montgomery's thrust to cross the Rhine at Arnheim and that we had to sit until November to clear the approaches to Antwerp so that supplies could be brought to the front by the shortest and fastest route. The war would have lasted a good deal longer if we had not been able to use those port facilities in the late fall of 1944.

During September and October, with France liberated, everyone from the British Joint Intelligence Committee to the high command to the lowest GI thought the war was virtually over, the Germans licked. OSS almost dismantled itself. Everybody had hustled to Paris in order to be in Paris. London was denuded. Neither office was really functional. OSS detachments with the armies in the field had little work to do since contacts with the resistance and the local population either were non-existent or had to be rebuilt from scratch. We had staff and organization but few functioning agents, and no air lifts nor communications on the continent.

The surprise and power of Hitler's counterattack through the Ardennes changed all that. Donovan must have reached for an airplane the moment he heard about Hitler's drive into the Ardennes. He was in Paris a few days before Christmas. Intuitively, Donovan sensed both failure and opportunity.

He knew, too, that neither OSS nor the British were producing enough intelligence from behind German lines. He named me chief of secret intelligence for the European theater with blanket authority to preempt people from any part of OSS, and concentrate all of its resources on prying fresh intelligence out of the Reich. Bitterman reinforced me by bringing Milton Katz up from Italy to be my deputy and Dick Helms, Mike Burke, and Hans Tofte, who had completed missions in France and Yugoslavia, to run our operations into Germany.

I have wondered how he picked on a young naval lieutenant for that task. I may have found the answer quite recently when a friend poking through the OSS files in the National Archives, sent me a copy of a paper I had sent to Donovan in the fall of 1944. It laid out that we had to change gears. In part it read:

> It must be assumed that the Germans will be able to maintain resistance throughout the winter and that the allied forces will be forced to drive slowly, taking important centers in Germany at well spaced out intervals. As long as organized resistance is maintained, the intelligence on order of battle, defense installations, air targets, morale, military plans, and other conditions inside Germany will carry the highest priority.

> Controls over movements and eating are now so tight that the establishment of agents inside Germany is likely to be an extremely slow and uncertain process. However, if and when controls begin to break down, OSS must be ready to step up the placing of agents within Germany. Moreover, it is likely that controls will break down locally in areas in the line of advance of allied forces. OSS must be ready to seize the opportunity to send agents through the lines if and when they become fluid and to take advantage of local collapse of controls in areas up to 25 and 30 miles behind the front lines.

We had men and women beating at our doors to jump into France. Now all we were hearing was how risky, even foolhardy it would be to try putting agents into the darkness of Germany. Our British partners and tutors had decided long ago that odds against agents sent to Germany were stacked too high. This shook me, but we had to try. The Battle of the Bulge was proving how much punch the Wehrmacht had left. The men who would have to lay their lives on the line were entitled to better information than we had been getting them.

Between October 1944 and April 1945, we sent more than 150 agents, mostly Belgians, Dutchmen, Frenchmen, and Poles, into Germany with identification as foreign workers, together with anti-Nazi prisoners of war in German uniform. They were sent to transportation centers with radio sets or new equipment we developed to enable them to hold a conversation with an airplane sent out for that purpose. These brave men went into Germany blind and it was remarkable that over 95 percent of them came out alive.

In the few months, and in some cases only weeks, that these agents had to operate inside German, and with the war drawing to a close, the intelligence produced was of marginal value, but the experience and confidence it gave us was invaluable.

OSS operated under its own steam in a way it never really had, even during the latter phase of the French campaign. Then, we had been dependent on the French for cover story, intelligence, and creativity, and on the British for document manufacture and agent equipment. Now, in Germany, the British came to us for the help. The painstaking research and assembly, the endless classification of information had finally paid off. Our work met the acid test of German inspection with flying colors. Only two sets of documents failed to pass inspection and twice the Germans issued warnings that American agents in southern Germany were equipped with papers too good to spot as false.

Donovan's insistence in 1942 and 1943 that the American armies should have their own independent, self-sustaining intelligence sources had finally been vindicated in Germany.

Donovan promised to send our German team to China to do a repeat performance against the Japanese, and we were ready and eager, but the Japanese surrender saved us that trouble.

Finally, let me have a brief word on what the OSS experience means to us today and for the future. It provides the tradition, doctrine, skills, and many of the people who built the CIA. For one-half of the life of the CIA its director has been someone who worked under Bill Donovan in the OSS. What we face today has much in common with what we faced in 1944.

The West again has totalitarian states using force and violence against its interests. Marxist-Leninist policies and tactics have unleashed the Four Horsemen of the Apocalypse — famine, pestilence, war, and death. Throughout the Third World we see famine in Africa, pestilence through chemical and biological agents in Afghanistan and Indochina, death everywhere with over 300,000 Soviet, Vietnamese, and Cuban troops in savage military operations directed at wiping out national resistance in Afghanistan, Kampuchea, Angola, Ethiopia, Nicaragua, and several other countries.

What is the purpose of all this carnage, this creeping imperialism? In my view, there are two primary targets: the oil fields of the Middle East, which are the lifeline of the Western alliance; and the isthmus between North and South America. Afghanistan, South Yemen, Ethiopia, as well as Cam Ranh Bay in Vietnam – and Mozambique and Angola in southern Africa –bring Soviet power much closer to the sources of oil and minerals on which the industrial nations defend, and put Soviet naval and air power astride the sea lanes which carry those resources to America, Europe, and Japan.

Another phenomenon dominating the landscape during and after World War II was the tragic plight of refugees escaping totalitarianism. Totalitarian aggression since then has produced additional waves of refugees from Eastern Europe in the 1940s and 1950s from Castro's Cuba, from the communist takeovers in Vietnam and Cambodia. One-quarter of the population of Afghanistan has fled into Pakistan. Already hundreds of thousands of Nicaraguans and Salvadorans have fled their countries and headed north. Can anyone doubt that as soon as it becomes apparent that the communists are about to complete their conquest of Nicaragua another signal will be flashed and millions of people will leave Central America, and ultimately Mexico, to cross the border of the United States?

This recurring refugee phenomenon is an eloquent indictment of the nature and dimension of what is happening from Ethiopia to Afghanistan to Cambodia, and in our own hemisphere. In addition to the millions voting with their feet, however, Moscow's surrogate totalitarians are facing a new phenomenon – the rising up of hundreds of thousands of ordinary people who are volunteers in irregular wars against the Soviet army or Soviet-supported regimes. Whereas in the 1960s and 1970s anti-Western causes attracted recruits throughout the Third World, the 1980s have emerged as the decade of freedom fighters resisting communist regimes. Today in a very real way, the occupying forces are besieged much as the Nazi army and puppet rulers were by the French, Belgian, Dutch, and Norwegian resistance in 1943 and 1944.

We hear it said that these Contras, *mujahideen*, and tribesmen led by Dr. Jonas Savimbi can't win. Who would have thought that George Washington's rag tag army, down to 3,000 men at some points, could have, with covert assistance from France, thrown out of North America the British with the largest and most powerful army in the world? Who would have thought that the Vietcong, with Soviet covert aid, could have forced out of Indo-China an American army of half a million?

The truth, as revealed in our World War II experiences and numerous struggles in the Third World since then, is that far fewer people and weapons are needed to put a government on the defensive than are needed to protect it. A resistance movement does not seek a classic definitive military victory. External support is almost always a key factor in resistance success. A progressive withdrawal of domestic support for a government accompanied by nagging military pressure largely against economic targets is what helps being down or alter a regressive government.

The small and weak countries that are combatting Soviet inspired subversion, and the resistance movements that are combatting Marxist-Leninist repression do not need and cannot handle a lot of sophisticated military hardware. What they need is what always has been needed in these kinds of situations: small arms and training in their use in small unit actions, good intelligence, and good communications. We helped provide this with effect to the resistance against Nazi Germany and if we can muster our resolve and act before resistance assets are allowed to wither away, we can put these tactics to good use today.

In conclusion, ladies and gentlemen, it's still worth talking about how the OSS and the British SOE helped the French resistance forces and contributed to the defeat of Nazi Germany because I'm convinced that our success in that work can teach us something about how we can meet our global responsibilities today. With a relatively few skilled officers and a tiny fraction of our military budget, we can introduce new elements of stability into the Third World and check Third World Marxist-Leninist regimes that are stamping out democratic liberties and human rights, and posing a threat to our own national security.

◆ ◆ ◆

HISTORICAL PERSPECTIVES ON CONTEMPORARY RESISTANCE MOVEMENTS

Here's Casey the historian at work again, describing what was learned during World War II about resistance movements and relating this knowledge to events in Vietnam, Central America, and elsewhere in the Third World.

I am delighted to be here this evening with the Society for Historians of American Foreign Relations. I'm glad that you invited me to join your discussions. I'm glad that the Conference on Peace Research in History and the American Military Institute are both with us, since intelligence is a function that is as essential for the conduct of foreign policy. Foreign policymakers need the best intelligence possible if they are to spend a $300 million Defense budget wisely, and if they are to shape a sound American policy to preserve the peace. Modern arms control agreements, for example, are only feasible because of the effective technical means of verification that our intelligence community works to provide.

Research into the relationship between intelligence and history is much easier than it used to be. As a result of Senator Durenberger's initiative, and with the encouragement of the Senate Intelligence Committee, CIA took steps to transfer to the National Archives and Records Administration its entire holdings of declassified OSS paramount records. This large and important collection has been transferred in increments over the past two years, and almost all of it is now open to the public at the National Archives on Constitution Avenue. The opening of this collection for the first time permits well-documented studies of the role of American Intelligence in World War II.

I have built on this transfer of OSS records to establish an Historical Review Program to review and release records of CIA itself for historical research. In organizing this new program we had invaluable help from consultations last year with Robert Warner, then Archivist of the United States; John Broderick, Assistant Librarian of Congress; and three distinguished American diplomatic historians, John Lewis Goddis, Richard Leopold, and Gaddis Smith. With additional resources from Congress we have organized a concerted effort to declassify and trans-

Address to the Society for Historians of American Foreign Relations, Washington, D.C., June 25, 1986.

fer to the National Archives the greatest feasible volume of historically important CIA records, beginning with our earliest holdings. I might add that in connection with Historical Review Program, Ken McDonald and the CIA History Staff are cooperating with the Department of State Historian's plan for publishing supplements to early volumes of the *Foreign Relations of the United States*, which will contain material declassified since these volumes first appeared. I have also pledged my strong support for President Reagan's directive last November that necessary measures be taken to ensure the publication by 1990 of the *Foreign Relations* volumes through 1960. CIA will do everything it can – especially in declassification review – to help State meet this accelerated schedule.

Now let me turn to the interplay between history and intelligence during our lifetime. We had substantially demolished our intelligence capabilities in the years leading up to World War II. When a New York lawyer, Bill Donovan, was pressed into service by President Roosevelt in 1940, the whole United States intelligence apparatus was down to something like 100 officers in Army and Navy units. Upon his return from a fact-finding mission to Europe and the Middle East, Donovan told the President that America needed an intelligence and covert operations capability. Roosevelt didn't need much persuasion. Six months before Pearl Harbor, Donovan was in business as head of what would become the OSS.

In World War II we were amateurs and learned about intelligence from the British. We also learned that when people are deprived of civil liberties they fight. Guerrilla movements in Yugoslavia, Greece and Albania were a major factor in keeping some forty German, Italian, Bulgarian, and Croatian divisions in Southeast Europe far from the arena of decision. Resistance armies in Norway, Denmark, Holland, and Belgium tied up other German forces and delayed their movement to reinforce fighting in Europe.

After the fall of France in 1940, Great Britain found itself alone, with most of its army's guns, armor, and transport left behind on the continent. Fearing invasion of its own island, Britain could only wage a war of attrition against the economy and morale of the victorious Germans. Britain had to use the only weapons it had left – the Royal Navy to blockade, the Royal Air Force to bomb, and the people of Occupied Europe to sabotage and undermine.

To mobilize resistance in the vanquished nations, Winston Churchill created SOE, the Special Operations Executive, and issued the memorable orders, "set Europe aflame." Many brave Britons were ready to become commandos and many brave Europeans eager to risk their lives to inflict damage on the conqueror and redeem their national pride and honor. Europeans at large cheered them on until they discovered what the occupier would do in reprisal, like wipe out an entire village. German reprisals turned the SOE and the resistance groups that sprang up all over Europe largely away from of one-shot sabotage and hit and run raids. Rather, they began carefully and slowly to organize, train and equip specialized groups and networks that could get intelligence, spread propaganda, do quiet and difficult-to-detect sabotage, and develop paramilitary units capable of striking when the time came. A long slow process, some three to four years, of building skills, support structures, training capabilities, organization and relationships set in.

There were three separate but loosely tied together organizations which guided and supported this process from outside France. SOE, the Free French in London and Algiers, and during the last two years, the OSS from Washington, London, and Algiers. Separately led and frequently rival resistance forces inside France developed from five principal strands. Indigenous resistance groups sprang up all over France and consolidated into some half a dozen movements, more or less focused in particular regions of the country. When the Germans attacked Russia, French communists and far left groups which had largely supported the occupiers went into resistance and began to form their own units. SOE and General De Gaulle's intelligence and action service separately sent organizers and radio operators all over France to recruit resistance groups and provide them with communications, training, and weapons. Finally, when the occupier imposed a labor draft, thousands of young men left their homes to hide in the hills and forests and ultimately formed themselves into military units seeking arms from London directly or through one of the earlier resistance networks.

Before D-Day and during the Allied advance from Normandy to the Rhine, the French resistance provided invaluable intelligence about the situation and activities of German forces in France. In World War II this kind of intelligence, collected by old-fashioned espionage – human intelligence, or "humint" in today's jargon – was enormously important. Although getting similar information for our advancing armies from inside Nazi Germany proved a much tougher proposition, in the last six months of the war we managed to infiltrate some 150 American agents into the Third Reich — and to get almost all of them out again alive. The other two principal sources of intelligence about the German war machine were aerial reconnaissance and code-breaking, the forerunners of our great technological intelligence gathering capabilities today. Aerial reconnaissance was of key importance both for ground forces and air operations. Research and analysis on the German economy laid the basis for the great strategic bombing offensive. The breaking of German high-grade ciphers and the operations and strategic use of these breaks — evoked by the single word "Ultra" — is one of the most exciting stories of the war. Beyond this, OSS and British counterintelligence worked together in deception operations that badly misled the Germans about both the time and place of the cross-channel invasion.

When the Americans of OSS arrived on the scene in London and Algiers early in 1943, our new and senior partners of SOE and the Free French had been supporting resistance forces for some three years and had become proficient and confident in sending organizers and saboteurs into France and keeping them there. They had performed sabotage jobs, established resistance organizers and communications, built up caches of weapons, and organized resistance bands and formed them into networks. But using these scattered and irregular forces in support of large-scale military operations in France was a new problem. It had to be worked out with military planners and commanders skeptical about the value of resistance forces. We were in something of a vicious circle. We needed to satisfy ourselves about the reliability of resistance forces, and persuade the arriving American military to provide the plans and equipment they would require to have any value. Yet we found that the military commander's coming over from the U.S. were schooled and geared to secure their objectives by the application of overwhelming firepower, and they believed they had it. For the most part, they knew little and cared less about French resistance or guerrilla warfare.

For the generals at SHAEF, the French resistance movement might be as good and as important as OSS and SOE said it was. On the other hand, the resistance might be an illusion and not materialize in the crunch. Sure, there were thousands of Frenchmen eager to fight the occupier, as many as 150,000 by some estimates. But they had to be organized, armed, and directed. Could the still nascent and loosely knit resistance movement quickly become a cohesive striking force that was sufficiently under our command and control to make a military contribution to the invasion? To answer yes required an act of faith. OSS and SOE officers in Grosvenor Street and Baker Street who had worked with General De Gaulle's intelligence service and with the men going in an out of France were willing to make that commitment.

Selling the idea to our generals and their planners wasn't easy, but in March 1944 the Supreme Commander, General Eisenhower, came down on our side and ordered a new Special Forces Headquarters to implement plans for resistance activities in support of the invading armies. Beginning 1 June, some 300 messages went out over the BBC alerting resistance leaders all over France that the Normandy landings would come during the week. The French resistance made 950 cuts in French rail lines on 5 June, the day before D-Day, and destroyed 600 locomotives in ten weeks during June, July and August of 1944. Our greatest debt to the resistance fighters is for the delay of two weeks or more which they imposed on one Panzer division moving north from Toulouse, two from Poland, and two from the Russian front as they crossed France to reinforce the Normandy beachhead. We'll never know how many Allied soldiers owe their lives to these brave Frenchmen.

The French resistance forces continued their magnificent work throughout the liberation of France, and when it was all over, General Eisenhower said:

> . . . In no previous war and in no other theatre during this war have resistance forces been so closely harnessed to the main military effort. . . I consider that the disruption of enemy rail communications, the harassing of German road works, and the continual and increasing strain placed on the German war economy and internal services throughout occupied Europe by the organized forces of resistance, played a very considerable part in our complete and final victory. . . .

At the end of World War II President Truman was persuaded that in peacetime the United States would not need the kind of central and strategic intelligence that OSS had provided. He therefore dissolved OSS in October 1945, soon after V-J day.

The Soviet seizure of Czechoslovakia and threats to Iran, Turkey, and Greece showed that Harry Truman had acted too quickly. After a long debate, in which General Donovan and others who had served in OSS played an important part, the Central Intelligence Agency was established in September 1947, by the same National Security Act that created the Secretary of Defense, an independent Air Force, and the National Security Council. CIA's origins in the wartime OSS were evident in its leadership, which had been dominated by former OSS officers, by its functions, which are largely the same as those that OSS performed in World War II, and by its role in the government, which is close to the vision that General Donovan had for OSS.

Yet while CIA's legacy from OSS is large and important, CIA today is very different from OSS in World War II. As one who served in OSS in the second war and in CIA since 1981, I am keenly aware that the world CIA lives in, and the problems it deals with, are infinitely more complex, variegated and difficult than those we faced in World War II. Signals intelligence has come a long way since "Ultra" and "Magic," and we have capabilities in overhead reconnaissance today that could not even have been dreamed of forty years ago. Constantly developing technical systems that cost billions of dollars now produce enormous amounts of intelligence.

In the World War II emergency we did a remarkable job of transforming talented and patriotic amateurs into competent and effective intelligence operators whose sole mission was to win the war against the Axis powers. Today CIA has developed a highly training and disciplined corps of career intelligence professionals who can cope with vastly more complicated and diffuse challenges. We have a host of new missions in such areas as international debt, technology transfer, gauging foreign industrial competition and the implication for US security, helping to stop the international flow of narcotics, and fighting against terrorism. Even in our central traditional role of assessing our potential adversaries' strategic capabilities we find counting Soviet mobile intercontinental ballistic missiles a very different and more complicated enterprise than tracking Wehrmacht divisions.

But we can perhaps make too much of these differences. There are still lessons to be learned, and insights to be gained, from the World War II experience of OSS. During the Vietnam War, I'm afraid we forgot our World War II experience in resistance warfare. There we took over a losing war from locals, ready to fight for their homeland, who might have won it if intelligently supported and directed and if the external support provided the invaders had been effectively restricted.

In the aftermath of Vietnam, the challenge that we failed to handle effectively there has only proliferated. The Soviet Union soon began to test whether the U.S. would resist foreign provoked and supported instability and insurgency elsewhere in the Third World. Fully aware of the political climate in this country, it developed an aggressive strategy which avoided direct confrontation and instead took maximum advantage of Third World forces or surrogates to obtain Soviet objectives. This enabled Moscow to deny involvement, label such conflicts as internal and warn self-righteously against "outside interference."

Over the last several years, the Soviets and their allies have supported, directly or indirectly, radical regimes or insurgencies in more than a dozen countries in every part of the Third World. It is also no coincidence that these subversive efforts supported by the Soviets and their allies are occurring close to the natural resources and the choke points of sea lanes on which the U.S. and its allies must rely to fuel and supply their economic life. Time and time again we have watched the Soviets and their surrogates move in to exploit and instigate social and economic discontent. They gain an insurgent base, expand it with trained men and military arms, sabotage economic targets, drive out investment, and wait for another plum to fall. Since 1972 five nations have extricated themselves from Soviet grasp and 25 nations have fallen under a significantly increased degree of control by the Soviets or their proxies.

And now we have begun to witness a new phenomenon. Moscow now finds itself supporting high cost, long-term efforts to maintain in power the regimes they have installed or coopted in places like Afghanistan, Angola, Ethiopia, Cambodia, or Mozambique, Yemen, and Nicaragua – a reversal of the roles played by the United States and the communists in Vietnam. In my opinion, this amounts to something of an historical turning point in the last half of this century the significance of which has not yet been fully appreciated and assessed by informed public opinion or, perhaps, even by historians.

In seeking to stem subversion in the Third World and in attempting to help local populations resist Soviet-backed repressive Third World regimes, the United States and its allies can indeed apply our historical experiences in supporting resistance forces. El Salvador is a good example of how these old lessons can be successfully applied to help a beleaguered nation defend itself. The successful free elections that have been held in El Salvador were made possible largely by our help in developing new intelligence sources and showing the El Salvadoran army how to use intelligence to break up guerrilla formations before they could attack provincial capitals in order to disrupt voting. The dramatically improved security situation there has been due largely to a relatively modest training effort on our part which has imparted new capabilities to the government army. Today El Salvador has a popularly elected government and a population that has overwhelmingly rejected insurgents organized, supplied, and directed from Cuba and Nicaragua.

And what about Nicaragua? In my opinion Nicaragua can and should be a perfect example of how some of our experiences in World War II can be applied with great effect in support of a resistance movement. During the debate on the renewal of United States aid to the Nicaraguan resistance, a number of misconceptions about the nature and effectiveness of resistance to oppressive governments have surfaced. For example, it been said that there is no way the hundreds of millions of dollars the Soviets are providing the Sandinistas could be matched, or that the insurgents will never have the military power to match the governments' might. We hear that a resistance movement should be totally self-sufficient and that external support would undermine its legitimacy. These arguments, of course, ignore our experiences with the resistance in World War II and reflect a basic misunderstanding about the way insurgencies and resistance movements work.

◆ ◆ ◆

THE ORIGINS OF AMERICAN INTELLIGENCE

Here is Casey-the-scholar at full throttle. Casey concludes this remarkable analysis of the American Revolution by noting the lessons that contemporary policymakers can learn by studying the defeat of the British.

Address to the Sons of the American Revolution, Palm Beach, Florida, February 21, 1983.

How did Washington's ragtag army, some 6,000 to 8,000 men for most of the war, defeat what was then the most powerful nation in the world?

Second only to Washington's qualities as a leader in this achievement were his natural aptitude as a director and practitioner of intelligence and special operations, and a master of what we know today as guerrilla warfare.

Washington's early training and experience developed the instincts of an intelligence officer. He began as a surveyor's helper, and at the age of 16 was appointed assistant to the surveyor who was to lay out the town of Alexandria at the top of the Potomac. By the time he was 19, Washington was an explorer and surveyor in his own right, picking up work as he scouted the wilderness.

 In 1973, reports had been received that Royal territorial claims were being ignored by the French as they edged into Pennsylvania and Ohio. His Majesty's government directed the Lieutenant Governor of Virginia to send an agent to see if the French were, indeed, building forts on British soil. George Washington was chosen for the task.

His orders were to enter the wilderness, attempt to locate such forts and gather clandestinely as much intelligence as possible. Further, he should make contact with the French to establish their intentions. The pretext for contact was to be delivery of a polite warning that the French evacuate. With this courageous and foolhardy mission, Washington became, as he described the task in his journals, an "intelligencer."

Washington did as he was ordered, locating and returning with a far more detailed description of Fort LeBoeuf and its troop strength than anticipated – the French had permitted him to wander around the fort while they considered the British demand. He also carried the French rebuff to the eviction notice.

As an adjutant in the French and Indian War, he created light horse units for such assignments as reconnaissance, the capturing of prisoners for interrogation, and for what today would be called harassment and diversionary operations. He made full use of sources behind enemy lines, secret patriots who remained behind when we were forced to withdraw – so-called "stay-behind agents" dispatched there for the collection of intelligence, and the many travellers and refugees crossing into American-controlled territory with information concerning denied areas.

Washington's military performance in the late 1750s with British-Colonial forces around what is now Pittsburgh promised little of the leadership and insights he was to demonstrate twenty years later. Still, he garnered more military experience than all but a handful of the colonial leaders on hand when the shooting started, and the disasters he encountered in the west in service under the British generals Braddock and Forbes are likely to have contributed to the military prudence he demonstrated, and the value he placed on intelligence in his conduct of the Revolutionary War.

Perhaps more important, there is some evidence that these early experiences led Washington to read and think a lot about the art of war during the intervening twenty years. In his library or among books he recommended to his officers were three French military works: Count de Crisse's *Essay of the Art of War*, dealing heavy in spies and intelligence, Dejeney's *The Partisan*, dealing with the use of small detachments to reconnoiter, hit outposts, ambush convoys, exploit surprise and harassment of the enemy, and Marshal Saxe's *Reveries, or Memoirs upon the Art of War*. These works appeared in English during the 1760s with analysis and advice still sound today in the practice of the American Revolution and other little wars down to Vietnam and Afghanistan.

Even before Washington came to Boston to take command of the patriot forces there, vigilance groups like the Committee of Safety and Correspondence and individual patriots like Paul Revere had mounted intelligence operations.

It was this gathering of bits and pieces of information that enabled the patriots in Boston to see through the British cover story that royal troops were on the Common only to learn new military drill routines. Intelligence that sent Revere on his ride, is an example of the "early warning" which is so vital today when nuclear missiles can arrive in half an hour.

When Washington took command of the Continental Army he soon discovered that he was fighting the strongest nation in Europe virtually barehanded – without sufficient guns, ammunition, even clothing for the men willing to fight. He pleaded for help anywhere it could be found, and Britain's rivals abroad were the best prospects.

Congress responded by creating committees – in September 1775, for example, the Secret Committee – for covert and open procurement of arms and ammunition. To this Committee the Continental Congress appointed its strongest members –Benjamin Franklin, Robert Morris, Silas Deane, John Jay, Benjamin Harrison, Richard Henry Lee, and John Dickinson. But is was Morris, Franklin, and Deane who did the vital work. The Secret Committee regularized prior secret contracts for arms and gunpowder negotiated by Robert Morris and Silas Deane without the formal sanction of Congress.

Before returning to American from his early work in London, Franklin had talked to munition makers and merchants from England, Holland, and France about supply and transport of guns and ammunition to the Colonies. The key player was one Pierre Augstin Caron de Beaumarchais. Trained in Paris by his father as a watchmaker, he developed into a hanger-on at Versailles. He seems to have made his initial mark by making and presenting to Madame de Pompadour a watch small enough to fit into a finger ring. Handsome, articulate, with many talents –playing the flute, harp, and violin – he was soon giving music lessons and teaching watchmaking to princes at the court. Before long he was engaged in literary work, culminating in writing the comedies "Marriage of Figaro" and "Barber of Seville." He travelled to London, Madrid, and Amsterdam, sometimes as confidential agent for Louis XV or his foreign minister Verennes.

Beaumarchais sold the French foreign minister on secretly providing arms and funds to American colonies, skillfully playing on the French desire to weaken Britain and their fear that the defeat of the rebellion would free British troops to seize in the West Indies. By the time Beaumarchais completed his preparations, the Secret Committee of the Congress had sent Silas Deane to Paris as an agent to arrange financing, shipping, and purchasing of guns, ammunition, and uniforms.

Deane and Beaumarchias worked well together and accumulated enough war supplies to fill eight ships. In a mere three months, huge shipments of goods were arriving to be loaded on chartered ships at Nantes, Marsailles, Bordeaux, Havre, and Dunkirk –clothing, powder, guns, bullets, cannon balls, and tents. Nobody has ever figured out who got how much of whose money for this. But seven of the eight ships arrived safely with guns and powder which pulled the Americans through the most critical years of the Revolution.

As Washington besieged the British in Boston, he got all the intelligence he needed with his spy glass from Cambridge and the Bostonians who were allowed to pass through the British lines as General Gage ran out of food. But it was a different thing when Washington came to New York and found himself faced with a British army which could hop by sea or land between Long Island, Staten Island, Manhattan Island, and the mainland on either side of the Hudson River. He sent out a plea for men who would go behind British lines. His first volunteer, Nathan Hale, after crossing Long Island Sound from Connecticut to Long Island and returning to Manhattan by land going along Long Island and across the East River in a small boat, was caught as he tried to walk through British lines and executed as he proclaimed, "I regret that I have only one life to give for my country."

After his retreat form New York through New Jersey and across Delaware, Washington first displayed his genius as a master of hit-and-run guerrilla warfare in recrossing the Delaware to surprise the German garrison at Trenton, outflank the force under General Cornwallis which had pursued him from New York, and again surprise the British at Princeton.

In winter quarters at Morristown, Washington's army had sunk to its lowest point. He had saved it from extinction by his daring and successful moves in Trenton and Princeton and by pledging his own personal fortune.

In New York City, Howe had at least 27,000 troops under his command and could easily have marched through New Jersey to Philadelphia in the spring of 1977. Yet, with only 3,000 men at the end of March, Washington was able to carry on raiding and deception activities that had Howe imagining huge American forces ready to pounce on his army, should it move through New Jersey.

Colonel Elias Boudinot, who worked with Washington on intelligence and deception, left a journal that reveals how assiduously and ingeniously Washington labored to impress on Howe an exaggerated estimate of his strength. Washington distributed his men "by 2 and 3 in a house, all along the main road around Morristown for miles." This persuaded local observers that the Americans were several times their real strength. As Washington wrote to Congress: "We are deceiving our enemies with false opinions of our numbers."

This was only the beginning. When a New York merchant showed up in Morristown claiming to be a refugee but suspected of being a British agent, Washington saw an opportunity. He told the adjutant general to become friendly with the New Yorker. He ordered each of his brigadiers to prepare a false strength report, adding up to a force of 12,000 – triple the actual numbers. These reports were sent to the adjutant general and kept on his desk. Then the New Yorker was invited to supper, and left alone with the phony strength reports when his host was "called away." Washington knew that his strategy had worked when the New Yorker left town the next morning. In fact, this misinformation so strongly impressed Howe that he angrily rejected more accurate reports that came in subsequently. Washington was a born intelligence officer, and he continuously reinforced the initial impression he had planted in Howe's mind by staging a series of hit-and-run raids at scattered points along the British lines.

Watching General Howe in New York, Washington expected him to move up the Hudson to split New England from the other colonies or move south to take Philadelphia, seat of the Continental Congress. He sent General Thomas Mifflin to Philadelphia in April of 1777 to set up a spy system, in case Howe should succeed in occupying Philadelphia. When Howe did march into Philadelphia in September 1777, a spy network under the direction of Major John Clark was in place waiting for him.

To preserve the Continental Army and protect his supply source, Washington had to keep British forces holed up in Philadelphia and New York. General Clinton in New York had to be made to think that General Gates, fresh from his victory at Saratoga, was preparing to attack New York City, and Howe in Philadelphia had to be made to believe that Washington at Valley Forge represented an imminent threat to him.

Clark was able to plant one of his men on Howe, who enticed the British general into expressing an interest in documents from Washington's headquarters. Washington prepared a highly exaggerated strength report and a few notes outlining some future plans, and these paper reached Howe, along with reports that Gates was planning to attack New York with the large force that Dickinson was preparing to attack Staten Island. Shortly thereafter, Clark was able to report to Washington that Howe believe the American order of battle to include 8,000 men from Gates's army.

Intelligence reports flowed by small boats up the Schuylkill and along the roads out of Philadelphia to alert the Americans to British plans for a night march on Washington's headquarters at Whitemarsh and the Delaware forts, of foraging raids into the countryside and, most critically, of General Howe's almost sure-thinking, all-out, three-pronged effort to surround Lafayette at Barren Hill. The most intriguing channel for communication intelligence reports was used by Quakeress Lydia Darragh. Mrs. Darragh dictated to her husband the intelligence she collected, who would get it into shorthand on bits of paper small enough to be hidden inside coat buttons; and their fourteen-year-old son wore them when he walked out to the American Camp to visit his older brother, a lieutenant in the Continental Army. Lieutenant Darragh was able to transcribe his father's shorthand notes for General Washington. Later, carrying in her head the British plan to march on Washington's headquarters at Whitemarsh on the night of December 4, Mrs. Darragh walked five miles to a flour mill on Frankford Creek, and was allowed to pass by British sentries, who saw nothing wrong in a little old lady going out into the country to fill the empty flour bag she carried.

As he gradually created a working intelligence network, we see Washington developing as his own intelligence chief.

The intelligence process consists of three broad steps: collection, which is the identification and collection of the information relevant to planning decision; production, which is the evaluation and analysis of information, drawing inferences and conclusions from it, and relating it to planning and decision; and finally, dissemination, which is conveying facts and conclusions to commanders and policymakers needing them.

It is no exaggeration that Washington performed all of these functions. In his letters time and again he specifies and pleads for the kind of information he needs to estimate the enemy's plans and intentions. The analysis and interpretation of the facts collected for him takes place in his own mind, and his massive correspondence was a major means of conveying relevant information to his commanders and the Congress.

Here is an example of the detail in which Washington specified to his agents in British-occupied New York the facts he expected them to collect for him:

> How their transports are secured against an attempt
> to destroy them – whether by armed vessels upon
> the flanks, or by chains, booms, or any contrivan-
> ces to keep off fire rafts.

The number of men destined for the defense of the
city and environs, endeavoring to designate the particular corps, and where each is posted.

To be particular in describing the place where the
works cross the island in the rear of the city – how
many redoubts are upon the line from river to river,
how many cannon in each, and of what weight and
whether the redoubts are closed or open next the
city.

Whether there are any works upon the island of New
York between those near the city and the works at
Fort Knyphausen or Washington, and if any,
whereabouts and of what kind.

To be very particular in finding out whether any
works are thrown up on Harlem River, near Harlem
Town, and whether Horn's Hook is fortified. If so,
how many men are kept at each place, and what number and what sized cannon are in those works.

To enquire whether they have dug pits within and in
front of the lines and works in general, three or four
deep, in which sharp pointed stakes are fixed. These
are intended to receive and wound men who attempt
a surprise at night.

The state of the provisions, forage and fuel to be attended to, as also the health and spirits of the army,
navy, and city.

Washington recruited and operated his own agents until he settled
upon Major Benjamin Talmadge to develop a real intelligence network
for him in 1777. Talmadge went to work establishing a spy ring in Manhattan and Long Island Sound, through Connecticut and Westchester
County to Washington's various headquarters across the Hudson.

Talmadge established code names for the agents in his major network.
"Samuel Culper, Sr." was Abraham Woodhull, "Samuel Culper, Jr."
was Robert Townsend, and Talmadge was known as "John Bolten."

Woodhull lived in Setauket, Long Island. He worked out of his sister's
boarding house in Manhattan, recruiting helpers to pick up what British

soldiers were saying in the coffee houses and taverns of New York City. The operation became more sophisticated as journalists and rebel sympathizers working at British headquarters were recruited.

Robert Townsend was a classmate of both Talmadge and Nathan Hale at Yale. To cover his intelligence work, Townsend became a partner in a dry goods business in New York. He also cultivated the friendship of James Rivington, a Tory newspaperman, and even went so far as to finance Rivington's attempt to open a coffee house. Once this refreshment establishment was on a going basis, Townsend, posing as a Loyalist gentleman, would frequently visit the house and listen to the gossip of British officers.

Setauket, Long Island became the nerve center of this American intelligence network reaching into New York City. Caleb Brewster, with a helper or two, would row from Fairfield on the Connecticut coast to Setauket Beach, and their whaleboat would be pulled across a couple of hundred yards of sand into Conscience Bay without alerting the British lookouts watching the channel into Port Jefferson Harbor.

Austin Roe, who operated a local tavern, would ride the 110-mile round trip between Setauket and New York City through territory patrolled by British troops and marauded by bandits, to carry intelligence reports. Written in invisible ink, the reports enabled Robert Townsend, the head of Washington's tight little intelligence network in New York, to communicate with the commander chief.

At Setauket, Roe would leave these reports in a letter drop at Abraham Woodhull's house, across Little Bay from the home of Ann Strong. She would signal a code based on a petticoat and six handkerchiefs on her clothes line, where to find Brewster's whaleboat and deliver the papers. Brewster would row back across the sound, the message would be taken to Major Benjamin Talmadge, and a series of mounted messengers posted every 15 miles would take the report across Connecticut and Westchester to Washington.

Washington himself was assiduous in using Talmadge's network to get the specific facts he needed to assess the strength and probable movements of British forces; in suggesting ways to get reports to him more quickly; in insisting that their reports be in writing and specific and precise; in watching over them to assure their personal cover and security, and the security of their messages through the use of invisible ink — which his letters always referred to as "stain"; in limiting intelligence to those who had a need to know; and in insisting that no expense be spared to get necessary information, while watching closely that too much was not being paid. All this, as his extensive correspondence clearly shows, he attended to personally, plying this network with demands and instructions.

On August 8, 1778, Washington wrote to Caleb Brewster, who rowed among the British ships moving between New York and Newport on Long Island Sound:

> Let me entreat that you will continue to use every possible means to obtain intelligence of the enemy's motion, not only of those which are marching eastward, upon Long Island, but others. In a more especial manner, I have to request, that you will, by every device you can think of, have a strict watch kept upon the enemy's ships of war, and give me the earliest notice of their sailing from the Hook. To obtain speedy and certain intelligence in this matter may be of great importance to the French fleet at, and the enterprise on, Rhode Island; for which reason, do not spare any reasonable expense to come at early and true information; always recollecting, and bearing in mind, that vague, and uncertain accounts of things, on which any plan is to be formed is more distressing and dangerous than receiving none at all. Let an eye also be had to the transports, whether they are preparing for the reception of troops. Know what number of men are upon Long Island; whether they are moving or stationary; what is become of their draft horses; whether they appear to be collecting of them for a move; how they are supplied with provisions; what arrivals, whether with men or provisions; and whether any troops have imbarked for Rhode Island or elsewhere within these few days.

Realizing and stressing the need for promptness in acquiring intelligence information, Washington lamented over the fact that the long route of delivery – from New York City to Setauket, across the Sound in Brewster's boat, and then through a portion of Connecticut, across the lower portion of New York state (just above the city), and finally across the Hudson River to New Jersey — was simply too long and too slow. This represented a major intelligence problem that the commander was long to face. It was hoped by the anxious commander that a much shorter route, possibly by way of Staten Island, could be developed. In late April he again wrote to Talmadge on this matter:

> I have been duly favored with your letter of the 21st instant and its enclosures. The plan for opening the communication by way of Staten Island may be delayed till C hears from me on the subject. However, I would have him to keep his eye upon such persons as he may think worthy of confidence.
>
> Should Brown be released from the Provost, and returned to Bergen, and appear fully adequate to such a conveyance, as has been proposed, C may make the experiment by way of Bergen, as this will be nearer to Head Quarters than the route at present made use of; at any rate let him be regular and frequent in his correspondence by the old conveyance.
> . . .

We find Washington meticulous on matters of tradecraft, security and precision in reporting, and protection of tasking of agents as to their objectives and operating methods. Witness these instructions in February of 1789:

> Secrecy in the business you have been requested to put in train is so essentially necessary that those who are willing to embark in it may rest assured that not even a whisper shall be heard from hence.
>
> It is to be presumed that every circumspection and caution that the case will admit of will be used to prevent a discovery of any of the agents; but if, notwithstanding, the one at Secaucus should be suspected and prosecuted, I must, in behalf of the public, stand between him and the consequences of a prosecution. It may not be amiss however to observe, by way of caution, that the great pursuit of those who heretofore have been employed in this business, is traffic, and this being carried on with

avidity the end for which they were engaged was
defeated, because suspicions on our part, and a
desire of rendering themselves useful to the enemy,
to accomplish with more ease their own lucrative
plans, gave a turn to the business which operated
much to our prejudice.

I do not know how easy it may be for the agent at
Secaucus to obtain free access to the intelligencer at
New York; but it is absolutely necessary he should.
It is the hinge on which the whole turns and without
it, nothing can be done to effect. Hence, is it not
necessary to have a person on the No. River, at or
near Bergen town, who can, at all times, have equal
access to the City and Secaucus unsuspected? It is
not necessary also to have some person between
Second River and Head Quarters? These matters
you will consider, and determine on. I need not add
that the fewer hands a business of this sort is in, the
better it will be executed, and less risk there is of a
discovery.

Verbal accounts in passing through several hands,
and some heads which may not be very clear, are li-
able to such transmutation as serve to confound and
perplex rather than inform; for this reason the Agent
in New York should give all his intelligence in writing which may be done fully and with security (even
if the letters should fall into the hands of the enemy)
in the manner I shall hereafter communicate. His letters may be addressed to the Agent at Second River,
or any other (more proper) person, if one can be
thought of; but whether he will write in his own
name, or under an assumed one, must be left to himself to determine when he comes to understand the
mode for communicating the intelligence.

The persons intermediate between him and me (serving as mere vehicles of conveyance) will know
nothing of the contents; consequently the avenues
leading to a discovery of the person in New York

(who should be shielded on all sides) will be much
lessened and guarded.

The compensation for these services had better be
fixed, beforehand, because loose agreements are seldom rewarded to the mutual satisfaction of both
parties. I shall be glad to see you tomorrow morning that I may have some further conversation with
you on this subject. With esteem, etc.

In 1780, the war shifted to the south when Clinton sailed from New
York with a large force. In May of 1780, the colonists suffered the worst
defeat of the war in the surrender of 5,500 men to Clinton at Charleston. Thereafter, the fight was carried on with irregular modes of war,
more deadly than the conventional American military power which had
been surrendered at Charleston, launched under the leadership of three
guerrilla fighters of genius, Brigadier Generals Francis Marion, Thomas
Sumter, and Andrew Pickens.

Small guerrilla bands, sometimes a hundred men or more, sometimes
a dozen, harassed British and Tory forces and kept the flames of resistance glowing throughout the South. They would hit an enemy outpost
or cut off a detachment or seize a supply train, melting away afterward
into the swamps or forests and emerging again to fight another day.

Francis Marion was a lowland planter of Huguenot origin. He had
fought the Cherokees, been a captain of militia and member of the
Provincial Congress, and later formed his own partisan regiment. His
fighting style was to move fast with small bands on little-known trails,
attacking with only a few rounds of ammunition per man, relying heavily on homemade cutlasses. Marion himself carried only a cutlass, which
seldom got out of its scabbard, and gave his orders with blasts of a
whistle. His men acquired their provisions and powder by raiding the
British. On the march, they carried baked sweet potatoes and lean beef
in pockets or saddlebags and drank water mixed with vinegar, the drink
issued to Roman Legions on the march. When hard pressed, Marion's
forces would simply disperse and fade away among the local farmers.
Tarleton, the British cavalry leader, gave him his nickname: Once,
trying to corner Marion and losing him in watery trails and deep swamps,
he exclaimed, "This damned swamp fox, the devil himself couldn't catch
him!"

Thomas Sumter, 41 years old when the Revolution broke out, raised and commanded his own crops of irregulars as a brigadier general. Not as cautious or as thoughtful as Marion, he took greater risks and his tactics were characterized by boldness in attack with larger forces and more sustained fighting. His personal qualities were reflected in the nickname "Carolina Game Cock."

Virtually by themselves, Marion and Sumter kept a rebel force in being throughout the state. Later, Nathanael Greene, who understood how to fight a hit-and-run war, used them along with a great militia leader, Andrew Pickens, and his two great cavalry leaders, Light Horse Harry Lee and William Washington, to range far and wide and ultimately take both Carolinas away from the British. Cornwallis and Benedict Arnold, now commanding a British force, battered a small Continental force under Lafayette and chased Jefferson, then governor, out of the capitol and pursued Virginia militia into the western hills of that state.

Meanwhile, in the north another of Washington's deception operations proved successful in shielding the newly-arrived French forces from attack. In late July, 1780, a message in secret writing was received from New York and developed by Washington's *aide-de-camp*, Colonel Alexander Hamilton. It carried an alert that Admiral Graves's British fleet had sailed for Rhode Island with some 8,000 troops. General Rochambeau's forces were only then debarking and regaining their land-legs at Newport. Hamilton conveyed the agent report to Washington, who recognized that only an immediate offensive, or the appearance of one, would abort the British mission. The British troopships were under sail when a Tory farmer arrived at a British outpost with a packet of letters he claimed to have found along the highway. The documents disclosed that Washington was on the move with twelve thousand men for the long-awaited invasion of New York. Signal fires were lighted and the British fleet returned to New York to undertake its defense.

The deception permitted the French troops to complete the landing without Royal interference. They would be better prepared to fight another day.

Washington's crowning achievement was bringing his dwindling army and troops sent from France under General Rochambeau, under the nose of the main British army in New York, from Rhode Island and White Plains down to Virginia to corner Cornwallis at Yorktown.

Washington himself described how he had led General Clinton to believe he was preparing to attack New York as he and Rochambeau started out on their march to Virginia. He wrote:

> It was determined by me, nearly twelve months beforehand, at all hazards, to give out, and cause to be believed by the highest military as well as civil officers, that New York was the destined place of attack, for the important purpose of inducing the eastern and middle states to make greater exertions in furnishing specific supplies than they otherwise would have done, as well as for the interesting purpose of rendering the enemy less prepared elsewhere.

> It was never in contemplation to attack New York, unless that Garrison should first have been so far degarnished to carry on the southern operation as to render our success in the siege of that place, as infallible as any future military success can ever be made.

> That much trouble was taken and finesse used to misguide and bewilder Sir Henry Clinton, in regard to the real object, by fictitious communications, as well as by making deceptive provision of ovens, forage, and boats in the neighborhood, is certain. Nor were less pains taken to deceive our own army; for I had always conceived, where the imposition does not completely take place at home, it would never sufficiently succeed abroad. . . .

Washington planted reports and double agents on Clinton in New York and filled his mail pouches with false information. In April 1781, the British captured a patriot courier, Montaigne, leading one of Clinton's generals to note: "I am confirmed in my idea from reading the intercepted letter from General Washington. . . he will never venture to move southward." As Montaigne recalled after the war, Washington personally gave him the pouch and dictated the route to be taken. When Montaigne protested that taking the specified route would result in certain capture, Washington stiffened and said, "Your duty, Sir, is not to talk, but to obey."

A British agent, James Moody, was allowed to capture a mail pouch containing a letter from Washington to Lafayette which said: "Upon full consideration of our affairs in every point of view – an attempt upon New York. . . was deemed preferable to a southern operation."

There were also many agent reports advising of specific elements of the New York attack plan, properly attributed to loose-lipped American officers. American patrols were exploring all the side roads. Cannons were emplaced. Officers scouring the Jersey shore for small boats were jubilant and boasted openly of certain victory in New York.

We know that all this deception worked from a letter Clinton wrote on June 8, 1781, to Cornwallis in Virginia which said:

> I enclose to your Lordship copies of some inter-
> cepted letters; by these your Lordship will see we
> are threatened with a siege....Your Lordship will
> see by Lafayette's letter that you have little more op-
> posed to you than his corps and an unarmed
> militia....Your Lordship can, therefore, certainly
> spare two thousand, and the sooner they come the
> better....From all the letters I have seen, I am of the
> opinion...the enemy will certainly attack this post.

Major Benjamin Talmadge, Washington's intelligence chief, described Washington's ploy:

> General Washington entirely deceived the British
> general by marching his combined forces down New
> Jersey opposite New York, as if he intended invest-
> ment of that city. After maneuvering a few days in
> September opposite Staten Island [all] of a sudden
> whole armies were found in full march for the
> Delaware River, which they crossed at Trenton, and
> then proceeded on to the head of the Elk, where they
> embarked to move down the Chesapeake Bay for
> Yorktown, where Lord Cornwallis had taken his sta-
> tion.

Washington put together the fundamental ideas of modern revolution-ary warfare. He won the war without winning a major battle, just as

Nathanael Greene liberated the Carolinas while losing every battle he fought. For seven years Washington kept the main British force bottled up in New York or Philadelphia. The two armies which did venture into the countryside, Burgoyne's and Cornwallis's, were cut up and devastated as they were lured farther and farther from their seaport bases and their supplies and troops became more and more exhausted. The defeat of Burgoyne's army generated the political decision in Paris to get into the war, and the defeat of Cornwallis's army at Yorktown destroyed the political will in London to continue the war.

The British were never able to comprehend that a defeat in the field did not mean the end of the resistance in the American countryside. To Cornwallis, when Gates's army was demolished at Camden, all that remained was the simple task of occupying conquered territory. Slowly it sank into the British military mind that whether they won or lost a particular battle, their very presence in the countryside stirred Americans to activity, which British forces could not match, let alone overcome. As long as Washington and Greene kept an army in being to prove that the British were not overrunning the country, recruits would flow in to replenish American losses, and militia and guerrilla bands would keep Loyalists out of action and whittle away at British regulars. Greene, in the Carolinas, demonstrated how occupation of the countryside could be converted into continuing revolt. Partisan bands were integrated into his army organization, which adopted their tactics. What Cornwallis called "the hornets" never permitted the British to relax in their supplies or their position, and Greene never gave the British a chance to destroy his little army.

As British expeditionary forces, huge for the time, stayed locked up in New York or stumbled inconclusively around the countryside, other voices – the great Lord Chatam, Edmund Burke, Charles James Fox, Lord Amherst, and Lord Barrington, the Secretary of War – stressed the folly, the humiliation and the cost of carrying on a land war across an ocean against an armed population. Just as in 1954 the French defeat at Dien Bien Phu reverberated in Paris, when Washington, Rochambeau, and de Grasse converged at Yorktown and forced Cornwallis, battered by Greene and Lafayette, to surrender, the political will to fight a war 3,000 miles away was broken in London.

Two hundred years later, another American army committed across an ocean and, fighting in the style of earlier European wars like the

British in 1776, was unable to cope with the irregular, guerrilla tactics
of an indigenous force backed by the Soviet Union which, like France
in 1776, was able to inflict defeat on its militarily stronger rival by
providing supplies, money, and ships, while conserving its manpower.

◆ ◆ ◆

KNOWING YOUR ADVERSARY

In this speech, Casey discloses a vital tidbit of U.S. intelligence his-
tory about the Soviet Union's postwar drive to build an atom bomb and
the U.S. effort to find out about it. It becomes clear in reading this speech
that Casey was a serious student of nuclear strategy. As Director of
Central Intelligence, he devoted an astounding amount of time to master-
ing the technology and capabilities of nuclear weapons.

Casey closes this speech, again, by applying to current U.S. global
responsibilities the lessons learned from history.

I am greatly honored to receive the Brian McMahon Award and most
grateful to you for bestowing it on me. As I look at the distinguished list
of those you have honored in previous years I feel most privileged to
join their ranks although I must tell you I didn't vote for any of them except Malcolm Wilson. The Brian McMahon Award has a special significance for me. Brian McMahon ranks in the annals of Fordham greats
with Frankie Frisch, Zev Graham, Ed Danowski, Vince Lombardi, and
the Seven Blocks of Granite. I remember Brian McMahon as lawyer, as
Assistant Attorney General, and as a Senator who looked like a Roman
head and didn't need a toga to create that effect.

When he graduated from Fordham in 1924 at the tender age of 20, his
classmates demonstrated the perspicacity, for which Fordham men are
known the world over, by nicknaming him "the Senator." It took him
twenty years to ratify their judgment by becoming, in 1945 the first
Fordham alumnus to sit in the United States Senate.

He defeated a one-term Senator named John Danaher, an Irishman,
Catholic, and Republican. One of the stories that came out of that cam-

Address to the Fordham University Club, Washington, D.C., May 21, 1981.

paign was about the two ladies standing in front of the Church. One of them pronounced that she would not vote for Senator Danaher because he was a Republican. Whereupon the other said, "Glory be to God, that can't be true. I just saw him come out of confession."

I have been collecting McMahon stories. During 1944 he was with a friend in the Mayflower bar and shook hands with a little man who passed by. Said McMahon to his friend, "That's the nicest guy in the United States Senate — but he won't amount to anything." Within a year the little guy was President of the United States and McMahon was in the Senate, and they were to make history together.

Senator McMahon had been sitting in the Senate for barely one-half year when an event occurred which made an indelible impression on his mind and plunged him into leadership in an area of public policy which dominated his all too brief career in the Senate. It gave him a stature and a relevance which carries on to this day and which few, if any, have equaled in so short a time. That event was the use of the first atomic bomb to kill 66,000 people in Hiroshima.

McMahon was one of the first to see clearly and broadly the sweeping implications of this event for the hope of world peace, for military strategy, foreign policy, and world living standards. Galvanized by what he saw, McMahon leaped into a role unprecedented for a freshman. In his first year in the Senate he introduced the legislation that created the Atomic Energy Commission, and a resolution calling for a Senate committee, which under his chairmanship, got deeply briefed on nuclear physics and conducted a sweeping investigation of the implications of atomic weapons and nuclear power. McMahon was soon Chairman of the Joint Congressional Committee on Atomic Energy and the predominant voice in the land on matters nuclear. Indeed, I recall Jim McInerny, then Assistant Attorney General, President of his club and unrivaled in his day as a toastmaster, introducing Senator McMahon in 1951, only a year before his untimely death. He brought down the house by hailing McMahon as having made the first peacetime use of atomic energy — in winning his 1950 campaign for re-election in his home state of Connecticut.

The bare facts about Senator McMahon's career are exciting enough to give a special distinction to the award you've given me. But I'd like to take a few more minutes to recall both the quality of Senator McMahon's statesmanship and the special role that he played in preserving our national security and world peace during the last quarter of a century.

He was profoundly shocked by the slaughter at Hiroshima and thoroughly appalled at the horror an atomic war could inflict on the world. Yet, he saw clearly that our own national security and the hope of world peace demanded either international control with inspections and with teeth, or that America maintain its leadership in nuclear technology and nuclear weaponry.

He led the way to the great decision to seek an international system for the control of atomic power. The U.S. went to the United Nations and offered to share with other nations the good in atomic energy. In return, we asked that other nations join with us to curb its power for evil. By this offer, all nations were asked to diminish their own sovereignty in the interests of world security – just as each of us gives up some degree of personal independence when communities establish laws and set up police forces to see that they are carried out.

Unfortunately, as we all know, the Soviet Union has thus far refused to join in a workable system. The reason is obvious: To be effective, such a system would require United Nations inspection; and the Kremlin fears to open up the windows and doors of its giant prison. It fears to have the rest of the world learn the truth about the Soviet Union. It fears even more to have the Russian people learn the truth about the rest of the world.

In 1947 the experts for the most part believed that the construction of an atomic bomb was simply beyond the immediate competence of Russian science or the capability of existing industrial organization in the Soviet Union. The majority opinion estimated that Russian achievement of nuclear weapon capability was a remote concern.

Senator McMahon, with his friend and colleague Lewis Strauss, before there was a CIA, performed one of the most important intelligence missions in the history of our nation. Together, they insisted that we had to develop a program to monitor and detect all large explosions that occurred at any place on the earth. We had to have that intelligence.

The first chance to perfect such a system was offered by tests which we were planning to conduct in the vicinity of Eniwetok in the spring of 1948. A detection system was devised by the end of 1948 but the Air Force found itself short of funds to procure instrumentation for the monitoring program – about one million dollars would be required to complete it. Contracts had to be let at once if the instruments were to be ready in time. Lewis Strauss, a great patriot and Chairman of the Atomic Energy Commission, volunteered to obligate himself for the one million so that the contracts could be made firm immediately. This effort was launched in the nick of time and in September it established that an atomic explosion had occurred somewhere on the Asiatic mainland at some date between August 26 and 29, 1949.

Had there been no monitoring system in operation in 1949, Russian success in that summer would have been unknown to us. In consequence, we would have made no attempt to develop a thermonuclear weapon. It was our positive intelligence that the Russians had exploded an atomic bomb, which generated the recommendation to develop the qualitatively superior hydrogen weapon – thus to maintain our military superiority. And *that* recommendation nearly failed because of determined opposition to it. The Russian success in developing thermonuclear weapon capability in 1953 would have found the United States hopelessly outdistanced, and the Soviet military would have been in possession of weapons vastly more powerful and devastating than any we had.

From quite early days in the Manhattan Project, several of the scientists speculated on the possibilities of producing a bomb which would derive its force not from "fission" – the splitting of the heavy elements (uranium and plutonium) – but from "fusion" – the coalescence of nuclei of light elements at the other end of the atomic table (for example, hydrogen and its isotope, deuterium). Those of you who took physics from Father Joe Lynch will understand this perfectly.

When Admiral Stauss learned that the Soviets only three years after us had exploded an atomic weapon, he was among the first to express grave concern that Russia might be giving top priority to the development of a thermonuclear bomb. When he asked the Atomic Energy Commission to join him in a recommendation that we undertake development of what became known as the hydrogen bomb, the Commission voted against him four to one. Then, the clear mind of Brian McMahon, the leading advocate of international control of atomic weapons, weighed in. He wrote President Truman to make the point that there was no moral distinction between the use of a single weapon causing great loss of life and heavy damage, and the use of a series of smaller weapons with the same aggregate result in death and destruction. He pointed up the fact that the raids on Hamburg, reported to have killed over a hundred thousand persons, and the fire raids on Tokyo, had been no less lethal than the raids on Hiroshima and Nagasaki.

He reasoned that the argument that we should indicate our unwillingness to develop a super bomb if the Russians would pledge themselves to refrain was totally meaningless without inspection and control to ensure compliance. The Russian attitude toward the Baruch proposal for the control of atomic energy had indicated how far we would be likely to get with any proposition for foolproof inspection and control. McMahon pictured what in his opinion would be the effect if the Russians were able to develop a thermonuclear weapon before we should succeed in doing so, expressing the apprehension that they might be attempting to leapfrog our development by going directly from their first fission weapon test into the development of thermonuclear weapons.

He concluded by pointing out that, if the Russians should produce the thermonuclear weapon first, the results would be catastrophic, whereas if we should produce it first, there was at least a chance for protecting ourselves.

This is a long story about the absolutely critical role Brian McMahon played in the history of the post-World War II world. His support of Admiral Strauss was the turning point. His friend, Gordon Dean, a member of the Atomic Energy Commission, changed his vote to come to the support of Strauss. In December of 1949 Klaus Fuchs, a physicist who had been sent to the United States with other British physicists to work at the atomic weapons laboratories during the war, confessed that he had regularly communicated to Russian agents particulars concerning such work on the hydrogen bomb as had been done at Los Alamos.

On January 30, 1950, President Truman, McMahon's little friend from the Mayflower bar, made the decision to build the bomb. We were able to test our first hydrogen bomb in November 1952. The Russians tested their first weapon involving a thermonuclear reaction the following August.

The President's decision was not only sound but in the very nick of time. By so close a margin did we come to being second in armament, not only in the eyes of the world, but in fact, had we begun our development after the successful Russian test, there is no reason to believe that we would have been accorded time to equal their accomplishment. Thus the decision, made when it was, provided us with the time and posture with which we have sustained our national security up to this time.

This little bit of history illustrates the need to know what our adversaries are doing and keep one jump ahead. That's what the American intelligence community is all about.

◆ ◆ ◆

ALGER HISS AND BENEDICT ARNOLD: THE AGENT OF INFLUENCE

His public image as a Cold War Spymaster notwithstanding, Casey understood that there is much, much more to intelligence than merely stealing secrets. (Casey never read spy novels, by the way, and efforts to interest him in one or another "good read" met with withering contempt. "Life is short. I've got more important things to read, and so do you," is among his gentler responses.)

An invitation to be the guest speaker at the 1984 Halloween Dinner of the Pumpkin Papers Irregulars – an informal, free-wheeling group of people bound together by their continuing interest in the Chambers-Hiss affair – provided a good opportunity to expound on the crucial but little-understood difference between the spy and the agent of influence.

At the dinner, Casey was presented with a book called The Documentary Life of Nathan Hale, _by George Dudley Seymour. The book became one of Casey's prized possessions because of the following handwritten inscription:_

> _For Bill Casey: Because you personify the qualities articulated in Nathan Hale's lesser-known, but equally profound, expression of patriotic commitment:_
>
> _"I wish to be useful, and every kind of service necessary to the public good becomes honorable by being necessary."_
>
> _With warm regards, Ronald Reagan._

Address to the Halloween Banquet of Pumpkin Papers Irregulars, Washington, D.C., October 31, 1984.

Although Casey enjoyed writing speeches, especially those in which he was able to talk about history, he usually left the chore for the last possible moment and would be angry with himself for doing so. In this case, he wrote the entire speech on the very day of delivery. At the dinner itself, few attendees expected such a serious and scholarly speech from Casey. They were visibly stunned, and when Casey concluded his remarks there was a long silence, followed by a thundering, standing ovation. An adviser to Casey happened to be sitting (and standing) next to Norman Podhoretz, the distinguished editor of Commentary. *Straining to be heard over the applause, Podhoretz fairly shouted into the adviser's ear: "That was incredible, just incredible! Who wrote it for him?"*

As I look around and think of all the years many of you have poked into that pumpkin and how loaded you are with trivia about the papers and all that surrounded them, I am reminded of a fellow who loved to talk about the Johnstown flood. There came a time when he passed away, he was received by St. Peter, who found him a pretty good fellow, heard he loved to talk about the Johnstown flood. The fellow gathered a group of people around him up there and he started out telling how the waters had gathered and came crashing down. He was just about reaching his finale when St. Peter reached over, tapped him on the shoulder and he said, "By the way, I forgot to tell you that Noah is in the audience."

I am grateful that I was forced to delve again into the Chambers affair and reflect on its implications. If I have any theme, it is that it is not quite accurate to think of Alger Hiss as a mere Russian spy. His role as an agent of influence is far more meaningful to us. He did steal and pass along through Colonel Bykov, his Soviet handler in New York, some information about Japanese troop movements to Manchuria, French military supplies to Rumania, and such things in the late 1930s. How trivial this seems compared to the Soviets having, at the end of World War II, an agent of influence close to the major policymakers in Washington.

Hiss was a close and trusted colleague of the American Secretary of State. At Bretton Woods he worked with Harry Dexter White in the shaping of the post-war economic world. He was at the side of President Roosevelt at Yalta and, as Secretary General, welcomed President Truman to the first convocation of the United Nations in San Francisco.

How the KGB must have preened itself at the photos of the smiling Alger Hiss standing behind Roosevelt, Stalin, and Churchill at Yalta and welcoming Harry Truman to the podium for the first address of an American President to the U.N. How trifling the theft of some papers passing over his desk when matched up against the opportunity to whisper into the ears of American leaders and counsel them on their policies. I have often marveled at how Hiss deftly moved from the office of Secretary of State Stettinius to the side of John Foster Dulles. How lucky, or possibly how shrewd a move, as the long reign of the Democrat Administration seemed to be entering its final stages, to position one's self near the ear of the prospective Republican Secretary of State.

Even today when American intelligence is so good at obtaining the information we can see and hear and sense, it is still so difficult to get actual knowledge of the plans and purposes of the other side. How we would love to have someone positioned in Moscow right now as Alger Hiss was positioned in Washington at a critical point in world history, or as Kim Philby was in London.

One of the remarkable aspects of the Hiss penetration was how broad-reaching it was, how easily it was accomplished, how early it was achieved, and how long it was known about and ignored. Hiss came out of Harvard Law School to be a law clerk to the Supreme Court Justice Oliver Wendell Holmes, Jr. When Jerome Frank became General Counsel to the Agricultural Adjustment Administration, the famous AAA perhaps best remembered for its slaughter of little pigs, he hired such young stars as Adlai Stevenson, Thurman Arnold, Abe Fortas, Lee Pressman, and Alger Hiss. Pressman, a classmate of Hiss at Harvard Law School and a self-confessed communist, was, Jerome Frank noted in a letter, brought "onto the staff at the insistence of Mr. Hiss who has the highest regard for Mr. Pressman's character." Pressman, together with John Abt, Nathan Witt, Nathanel Weyl, and Julian Wadleigh, later either admitted or indicated clearly enough by their activities their close communist ties. In the AAA, these young staffers came under the leadership of Harold Ware, an acknowledged communist and the son of "Mother" Bloor, revered in those days as the matriarch of communism in the United States.

By 1934, Hiss was counsel to the famous Nye Committee of the Senate, muckraking among the defense contractors of those days and labeling them the "merchants of death." He went on to the Department of Justice to argue cases before the Supreme Court of the United States, and then to the State Department to become Director of the Special Political Affairs Division, before going public at the great international conferences at Dumbarton Oaks, Yalta, and San Francisco.

As smooth and shrewd as Hiss's fast shuffle from Acheson to Dulles in 1946 was his ability to sail onwards and upwards in Washington while his communist affiliation became increasingly well known. Milton Gould, author of that brilliant article in the *New York Law Journal* spelling out how Hiss victimized himself by his hubris, told you a year or two ago how, in drifting into a Washington cocktail party of AAA staffers in early 1935, he found the communist interest well represented and well recognized.

In 1939, Whittaker Chambers went to Adolph Berle, then Assistant Secretary of State, with the information that Hiss, then a trusted officer of the Department of State, was a communist and "underground espionage agent for the Soviet Union." Berle passed this to the Federal Bureau of Investigation in a memorandum which lay smoldering in FBI archives as Hiss marched forward to Dumbarton Oaks, Yalta, San Francisco, and the Carnegie Endowment. It wasn't until nine years later that FBI agents first interrogated Hiss on Chambers' charges.

Still, information kept piling up. In 1940, Isaac Don Levine, told the House Committee on Un-American Activities that Hiss was a Communist agent. William Bullitt, American Ambassador to France, told Stanley Hornbeck at the State Department that French Prime Minister Edouard Daladier had warned him about Hiss as early as 1940. This information circulated around town, even reaching the ears of President Roosevelt who, along with J. Edgar Hoover, dismissed it as loose talk. In 1945, on the eve of the San Francisco U.N. meeting, Raymond Murphy, a high State Department official, was warned about Hiss. A month or two later, investigations by the FBI and State Department were triggered by Igor Gouzenko, a code clerk at the Soviet Embassy in Ottawa who defected and disclosed that the Soviets had an agent in Washington who was an assistant to then Secretary of State Edward Stettinius. Canadian Prime Minister MacKenzie King wrote in his diary that the Soviets had an agent "close to Stettinius."

Sometime in 1945, J. Edgar Hoover asked Attorney General Tom Clark for authority to install a wiretap on Hiss's Washington home, to intercept his mail, and keep him under physical surveillance. In a report to President Truman on "Soviet Espionage in the United States," J. Edgar Hoover devoted several pages to the evidence that had accumulated on Hiss. By March of 1946, a new Secretary of State, James Byrnes, together with the Attorney General and the Director of the FBI, had concluded that there was enough negative information against Hiss to justify his dismissal from the State Department. Hiss' security clearances were lifted but still the State Department protected him for seven months until December 10, 1946, when he resigned to accept the post offered him by John Foster Dulles as President of the Carnegie Endowment for International Peace. Before accepting this lofty post, Hiss went to Dean Acheson to say he didn't want to leave the government until the charges against him had been cleared up. He got typically Achesonian clear and sound advice. Acheson said: "This kind of thing rarely ever gets cleared up. The government has to protect its sources of information. There is no way of final adjudication of this matter. People will continue to raise these doubts about you as long as you are in a position where you are subject to attack, and if I were you I would leave and go to New York." That's what Hiss did.

Still, he came close to getting away with remaining in public service. In September 1945, Stettinius conferred in London with Andrei Gromyko, the Soviet Ambassador to the United Nations. Stettinius's diary reflects that he asked Gromyko if the Russians had thought about who should be Secretary General of the new U.N. Gromyko said: "We would be very happy to see Alger Hiss appointed temporary Secretary General as he had a very high regard for Alger Hiss, particularly for his fairness and impartiality."

If Hiss had been appointed to this critical post, what would have happened to the material piled up in the State Department's security file? It was not until two years later, in 1948, that Chambers brought his charges to the public before the House Committee on Un-American Activities. It would be interesting to know what kind of an investigation the trustees of the Carnegie Endowment for International Peace made before selecting Hiss as the man most eligible to be president of that venerable institution.

The story becomes even more bizarre after Hiss left public service. During the period of his investigation and trial, some very strange events occurred. The Justice Department lawyer and friend who notarized Hiss's signature on the transfer of title for an automobile which became an issue in the case, W. Marvin Smith, was pushed to his death down an office stairwell. Harry Dexter White, the former Assistant Secretary of the Treasury and a principal figure in the apparent communist penetration of the United States Government, died suddenly. Herbert Norman, Canadian Ambassador to Egypt, discovered to be a communist and about to be exposed, fell, jumped, or was pushed from a window in Cairo. Harvard Professor F. O. Mathiessen, communist sympathizer, recently returned from Czechoslovakia and due to be questioned, plunged to his death from a rented hotel room in Boston. Lawrence Duggan, a former State Department official and friend of Hiss, jumped or fell from a Wall Street law office, wearing one galosh. The other galosh was found on the floor in his office, certainly suggesting a quick exit.

It was almost like the Wall Street crash of 1929. Which reminds me of the two brokers who saw a body hurtling by as they looked out a 26th-floor window. One of them turned and said to the other, "Do you suppose he knew something we don't know?"

Americans have from the very beginning been singularly vulnerable to people working for the enemy getting close to our leaders. Tom Murphy, in summing up the case against Hiss, compared him to Benedict Arnold. This comparison of Hiss with Arnold would not have withstood scrutiny in the Second Circuit in the times in which we live. It would have been dealt with as prosecutorial misconduct and the case would have been remaned for retrial. I leave it to you whether this is progress or not.

George Washington thought well of Benedict Arnold. Arnold had led 600 men in that amazing 500-mile march through Maine to assault Quebec. His dash and valor had turned the tide at Saratoga. But something had happened to him in some months of social whirl with a new wife in the capital of the young nation at Philadelphia. For over a year he bargained with the British General Clinton about how much he would be paid for every American soldier he succeeded in surrendering to them. There were 4,000 troops in the Hudson highlands under the commander of West Point. When Arnold asked Washington directly for that command, Washington told him that he was too good in battle to waste on the garrison soldiers at West Point, but rather should have command of light troops. When Arnold pleaded the bad leg he got at Saratoga, saying he couldn't serve in a more active command, Washington relented and gave him West Point. This put Arnold in a position to turn over to the

British control of the Hudson River and the entire supply line between New England with its ports and Washington's army, something which Arnold agreed to do for 20,000 pounds. Only the accidental interception of a message between Arnold and the British Command averted that disaster.

Another example: When you enter the American Embassy in Paris, you see on the wall in the lobby the list of distinguished Americans who have represented us in the French capital. Benjamin Franklin heads the list. As he labored in Paris to get the essential supplies without which the revolution could not have been fought let alone won, and the critical French alliance from Louis XIV, Franklin was surrounded by British agents. Edward Bancroft, an American in British employ, lived in as his secretary. Spies must have been running into each other in Franklin's hallways. Copies of his correspondence arrived in London on an almost daily basis. When a friend warned Franklin of all this, his response was an all too typically American casual concern about this threat. He replied:

> As it is impossible to discover in every case the falsity of pretended friends who would know our affairs; and more so to prevent being watched by spies when interested people may think proper to place them for that purpose; I have long observed one rule which prevents any inconvenience from such practices. It is simply this: to be concerned in no affairs that I should blush to have made public, and to do nothing but what spies may see and welcome. When a man's actions are just and honorable, the more they are known, the more his reputation is increased and established. If I was sure, therefore, that my valet was a spy, as probably he is, I think I should not discharge him for that if in other respects I liked him.

This attitude, understandable in a Pennsylvania politician, but potentially disastrous in running a war and conducting foreign affairs, guided more than one desperately needed shipload of supplies into the hands of the British.

We haven't improved. In our lifetime, Soviet agents have succeeded in getting hold of detailed data on everything from the nuclear bomb to the MX, including a real Sidewinder missile, Stealth bomber technology, vast amounts of computer methodology, and buckets of information about our satellites, both reconnaissance and communications.

Still, I think even today as it was in the time of Alger Hiss, the Rosenbergs, and the others who stole our nuclear technology for them in the middle 1940s, the Soviets see and get more mileage in influencing our policies and lifting our technology than they get from political and military espionage. After all, they roam freely among us, read uncensored technical publications, use a legal right to request documents from our files, profit from a flood of leaks used as weapons in policy struggles, and attend the debates that we conduct in public and that they conduct among a handful of men behind closed doors. That is how they get most of the political and military intelligence we work so hard to pry out of their closed society with our multi-billion dollar technical marvels. This leaves more KGB case officers to troll for agents of influence among those who tend to favor Soviet objectives, using false flags and false masks against those who can be manipulated.

At times, the Soviets have been dazzling at penetrating high places where they have a shot at influencing policy as well as producing intelligence on policy objectives and initiatives: witness Hiss at State, Dexter White at Treasury, Laughlin Curry at the White House, Philby and Maclean in Britain, Charles DeGaulle's and Willy Brandt's personal intelligence advisors in Paris and Bonn.

But even these dazzling penetrations pale into insignificance when compared to the concerted assaults which the Soviets have learned to make on public opinion in free countries. I have time only to mention their success in getting President Carter to reverse field on deploying the enhanced radiation weapon in 1978 after he had persuaded our European allies to commit to it at great political risk. We figure that the Soviets spent on the order of $100 million to pull that off. Now, just recently we read in the press complaints that we may have spent a few million to counter that massive Soviet effort. I found one of the best summations of their advantage in influencing policy in Leslie Gelb's article on what we know about the Soviet Union in last Sunday's *New York Times Magazine*. He quotes a Soviet arms negotiator this way:

> We know so much about how you make decisions. Americans are talking about this and writing about this all the time. It is more than we can swallow. But

> you know little of how we make decisions and we
> are not going to tell you. Because we do know, we
> have some chance of influencing your decisions. Be-
> cause you don't know, your chances of influencing
> ours are limited, and we intend to keep it that way.

The Soviets, the Cubans, and their followers take great pains to conceal their involvement in other countries to destabilize, subvert, influence policies, defame, and so on. In our seeking authority to respond,
we are called upon to "prove" the existence of their hidden hand.

Providing "proof" is likely to involve the unacceptable risk of drying
up our source of information. At the same time, policy motivated disclosure of classified information and sometimes reckless investigative
reporting gives too many free rides to the other side. To handle these
multiple dilemmas, we need broader public understanding of what we
face, a restoration of discipline and indeed, secrecy in our public officials, and a better understanding from and closer collaboration with the
media. All of us will have to break new ground to counter a more aggressive, more sophisticated, and more subtle Soviet expansionism.

We continue to face today the kind of struggle between those with faith
in our society and its values and the will to defend them and those who
believe us to be sick. In many ways our side has been gaining. Where in
the 1960s and 1970s communist causes were attracting recruits
throughout the Third World, the 1980s has emerged as a decade of
people rising to resist communist regimes – in Afghanistan, Angola,
Cambodia, Ethiopia, and Nicaragua, to mention only the most prominent
areas – with hundreds of thousands of ordinary people going into armed
resistance against communist oppression. Right here, while the communists continue to go to extraordinary lengths to keep faith with Alger
Hiss with endless efforts to redeem his reputation, an American President is bold enough to call Communism what it is and to preach the sus-
taining faith of our own heritage as he stands up to award the Medal of
Freedom posthumously to Whittaker Chambers.

* * *

Chapter 9

To Those Who Serve

THE PURSUIT OF EXCELLENCE

As even a cursory perusal of the press will show, no senior Reagan official was subjected to such a sustained barrage of criticism as was Casey. It often seemed as though the Washington Post *felt itself in competition with* Pravda *to publish disinformation about the U.S. Intelligence Chief. (The* Post *was usually ahead.) Casey's good humor while under attack from those who professed to be on our side was not merely a source of inspiration to those of us who worked with him, but a source of amazement. "It only hurts for a day," he used to say, with a wink and a shrug. That wasn't true, of course, but Casey understood the importance of being optimistic to achieving one's objectives.*

Good afternoon to all of you. There is no more pleasant duty than to congratulate outstanding young men and women on their achievements. I am especially gratified and take pride in the work recognition of Sandra Kruzman as I am sure, other agency heads take pride in the achievements of those in their organizations who are being recognized today.

Sandra and all of you deserve a hearty congratulations for a job well done.

You are a distinguished group, representing several different federal agencies, specialties, and academic backgrounds. Yet despite these surface differences, you all share an important characteristic – a commit-

Address to the Fleming Awards Ceremony, Washington, D.C., April 22, 1983.

ment to excellence. This basic orientation has never been more important to the future of this country as we face together the multiple social, economic, technological, and political challenges of an increasingly complex world. Today we are indeed living in interesting times that tax our combined talents. To navigate safely through the present challenges, we must all be committed to doing our best. So I would like today to focus on the ingredients of excellence which you all personify, and give some thoughts on federal service in general.

Commitment to excellence means the willingness to take risks, not necessarily physical risks, although that can also be required, but the risk of putting one's professional reputation, and maybe even one's personal reputation, on the line. To pursue excellence, you must risk new solutions – more effective methods to old problems. Without the ability or willingness to take risks there can be no creativity – a badly needed quality in our organizations today, public or private. The pursuit of excellence also means cultivating a basic optimistic outlook on life. You have to believe things can be better, that one person's performance can make a difference, before you can begin to improve your office, agency, or the world around you.

Without optimism, temporary detours appear to be road blocks, and small fences become high walls. With optimism, failures never lead to quitting. A short-sighted man once asked Thomas Edison how it felt to be a failure after trying 25,000 times to invent the storage battery. Tom replied, "Failure? I'm not a failure. I now know 25,000 ways not to make a storage battery!"

Finally, all of you are already managers or may be presently under consideration as a manager. The excellent manager, the exemplary leader, must have a quality I define as congruence of character. What does this mean? It means that an individual's actions match his or her beliefs. Those you are trying to lead, to motivate, will quickly perceive any divergence between what you fundamentally *believe*, *say*, and *do*.

Keeping an optimistic outlook and cultivating the other qualities I have mentioned today can be difficult. I know that there are many federal workers who feel they are under attack and unappreciated. Nobody joins the federal government to make their fortune. Most new applicants desire to serve – to work for something larger, more important than one company's narrow concerns. I know it is true of many of the CIA's new employees. They want to contribute to this country's security. I am sure that the desire to serve is found in you and among others in the agencies you represent. In my own experience in government, I have been fortunate to know many dedicated, honorable fellow civil servants. I am reminded of Napoleon's advice to his housekeeper at St. Helena when she asked a group of people with heavy loads on their backs to clear the way for the emperor. He said to her: "Madam, respect their burden." I respect the load all federal workers carry and I think the majority of Americans do also. Never let anyone tell you you're second best!

So congratulations! Now that you have won this award and after the applause dies down — what next? The hardest part will be maintaining your commitment to excellence for the next ten to twenty years. I think you are equal to the task. There will undoubtedly be times of great frustration. Take a vacation, a long walk, go into a private room and yell — but don't give up! That is the greatest challenge.

◆ ◆ ◆

THE CONTRIBUTION OF JOHN A. McCONE

Casey had a special respect and affection for John A. McCone, the California industrialist and public servant who served as CIA Director from 1962 through 1964. McCone was Casey's sort of man: smart, successful in business and in government, devoted utterly to serving the country. By the time Casey became Director of Central Intelligence in 1981, McCone had long since retired. But although his body had become frail, there was nothing wrong with his brain; McCone visited Washington often, and spent far more time with Casey than most Agency employees realized. More than once a (junior) employee would ask, "Who's that old guy sitting in the Director's anteroom?" McCone considered his meetings with Casey to be an obligation, albeit a pleasant one. Casey considered McCone's willingness to meet with him — despite the obvious physical toll — an honor. And he found McCone's advice to be invariably sensible.

In this tribute to McCone, on the occasion of his receiving the William J. Donovan award, Casey notes a characteristic common to both men:

Address to the Veterans of the Office of Strategic Services, San Francisco, California, May 22, 1982.

"The most surprising and significant quality that these two remarkable men share is that, though primarily perceived as doers and men of action, Donovan was and McCone is a true scholar. Their most critical and lasting contribution was to establish scholarship as the highest virtue, the heart and core, the quality which most distinguishes the American intelligence system. "

Of course, this description applies equally well to Casey himself.

It is a real privilege for me to join you tonight in honoring John McCone. I plan to say a little about General Donovan and more about John McCone than he would want me to say, but I don't think more than you should hear on this occasion.

John McCone is a particularly fitting recipient of an award created to recognize and foster the kind of continuing dedication and contribution in both private and official capacities to country, and the cause of freedom which characterized Donovan's career. It was created to recognize the citizen statesman and the citizen soldier. Bill Donovan demonstrated those qualities beginning with World War I, moving in and out of a law office to serve as soldier, as intelligence officer, as statesman, and as private citizen acting on his own and always on call when our national interests were at risk.

When World War II loomed on the horizon, Donovan was among the first to see it. As a private citizen, he left his law office time after time to watch military exercises in Germany and to visit battle fronts in Spain, Libya, and Ethiopia. It's hard for us to realize today that there was a time when William J. Donovan was a one-man CIA for President Roosevelt. Donovan was sent to England to make an assessment as to whether England could survive and what it would take. He came back with the conviction that Britain had the will to survive no matter how overwhelming the odds. He persuaded Franklin Roosevelt to provide destroyers to keep the Atlantic sea lanes open and to lend-lease planes, tanks, and guns to replace those which Britain had lost on the Continent and in the great air battle raging over the British Isles.

At about the same time, John McCone focused his great managerial and engineering skills on providing major support to the war effort. He built *Liberty* ships, that ungainly bulwark of the Allied supply lines, at a pace unprecedented in the shipbuilding industry. He directed the final modifications of B-24 and B-29 bombers before they went into combat.

He was instrumental in the establishment and maintenance of a tanker fleet to fuel the U.S. Navy in the Pacific Ocean. McCone did all this with a verve and distinctive quality that set him apart.

After World War II, John McCone served as Under Secretary of the Air Force when this service first emerged as a separate branch of the armed forces. He ensured a correct understanding of the role of the U.S. Air Force in an era where the potential for the uses of air power were subject to wild surmises. When the conflict in Korea began, John Mc-Cone applied his managerial talents to the production of fighter aircraft, and his efforts produced the required flow of these weapons to the Allied forces. John McCone also served as Deputy Secretary of Defense when the Department of Defense was a new and untested outfit. He prepared and presented the first ever Department of Defense budget.

As Chairman of the Atomic Energy Commission, McCone played a key role in assuring an adequate arsenal of weapons to deter Soviet aggression and also in developing International Atomic Energy agreements to introduce some sanity and reason into the handling of nuclear materials. His was the strongest voice in persuading the Soviet Union to sign such agreements and, thus, make international inspection of nuclear facilities a reality.

During the closing days of World War II, Donovan saw clearly that Soviet behavior in Poland, Romania, and Hungary constituted a threat to European and American security. When this materialized in the Cold War, he preached that the way to avoid a hot war was to win the Cold War. In his work for the Air Force and the Atomic Energy Commission, John engaged directly with top Soviet officials, and he measured them carefully. He found them to be dedicated to the single goal of world domination and willing to use any and all means to achieve their aims. John McCone concluded that the United States and its allies had to be prepared to take extraordinary measures to combat the extension of Soviet power and communist principles and practices into the free world. He recognized that a clear understanding of Soviet capabilities and intentions was essential and that because the Soviet Union was a closed society, the responsibility for obtaining this essential knowledge would fall heavily on the U.S. intelligence community.

When President Kennedy summoned John McCone to return to public service in 1961 as the Director of Central Intelligence, McCone made it clear to the President that he viewed the Soviet Union as a dangerous and devious adversary. He noted that this view was not shared by all the President's colleagues, and insisted on direct access to the President as the only means of ensuring that the objective judgments of the nation's intelligence professionals received an unbiased hearing.

Both Donovan and McCone were innovators with the force and courage to fight for their ideas. When Donovan recognized that the great American melting pot could produce courageous young Italian Americans, Greek Americans, Slavic Americans, Norwegian Americans, and Oriental Americans to fight behind enemy lines with resistance forces in Italy and France, Burma and China, Norway, Greece and Yugoslavia, the Pentagon fiercely opposed what they disparagingly called Donovan's "private army." Donovan prevailed and operational groups of the OSS greatly strengthened and focused resistance forces to save much time, blood, and treasure in liberating Europe and the Asiatic mainland.

When McCone became Director of Central Intelligence, he quickly recognized that the time had come to bring American intelligence into the space age. He had to overcome heavy opposition in the Pentagon to establish the battery of satellites which today count and measure, locate and warn against the missiles and other weapons which the Soviets keep most secret but, as we saw in the SALT debate, the American public know and discuss in great detail.

The most surprising and significant quality that these two remarkable men share is that, though primarily perceived as doers and men of action, Donovan was and McCone is a true scholar. Their most critical and lasting contribution was to establish scholarship as the highest virtue, the heart and core, the quality which most distinguishes the American intelligence system.

Donovan's talent and interest in intelligence came out of his experience as the outstanding investigative lawyer of his time. In the *Madison Oil* case, in the *Appalachian Coal* case, in nationwide investigations of bankruptcy practices and public utility regulation, and in Senate hearings on the munition makers, he had learned how to gather a huge array of facts, sift and analyze them, assess their meaning, arrive at a conclusion, and present it vividly. He persuaded President Roosevelt that it would be critical in fighting a war and preserving the peace to develop and apply this ability on a worldwide scale. For the OSS, Donovan scoured our campuses and gathered hundreds of the finest scholars in America to process geographic, scientific, political, and military information, and analyze every military, political, economic, and technological aspect of the war and the preparations for peace.

Kenneth Strong, General Eisenhower's G-2 in the European war, rated McCone at the top of the world's intelligence chiefs in his book, *Intelligence at the Top*. Of McCone, he wrote: "It was widely assumed that in view of his previous experience he would concentrate on management. In actual fact he became particularly distinguished among his professional intelligence associates for his work in substantive intelligence. . . . " John McCone saw the primary mission of CIA and the intelligence community to be the production of sound and relevant national intelligence estimates. These were to be based on the best analytical talent available and to be supported by the best collection systems that human ingenuity could devise.

McCone devoted as much personal attention to the writing of national intelligence estimates as any Director of Central Intelligence has ever done. He took full advantage of his direct access to the President and his senior national security advisers to ensure that these estimates were given full consideration in U.S. policy decisions.

McCone gave CIA analysts a sense of purpose and accomplishment in knowing that their judgments were heard. He set the National Intelligence Estimate firmly in its rightful place as a means of providing advice directly to senior policymakers.

McCone quickly established a reputation for resisting the conventional wisdom and for having the personal courage to make his convictions known. Soon after becoming Director of Central Intelligence, he worried about the size of Soviet military aid to Cuba, and ordered increased intelligence coverage. This soon disclosed that surface-to-air missiles were being deployed to the island. What are they there to protect, he wondered, not sugar plantations or rum mills. There are no targets there now, he concluded, so they must intend to bring something there. Perhaps they are being deployed to prevent our U-2s from detecting something yet to come or to defend something to be brought in which we would have to attack. Thus, he was many months ahead of anyone in Washington in predicting that Moscow might base offensive missiles in Cuba. When Cuban refugees brought reports that large missiles were being landed and installed in Cuba, everyone else in Washington dismissed them. To a man, the experts said they could not be offensive weapons. The Soviets would never do anything so foolish. McCone's break with the conventional wisdom was vindicated when a U-2 airplane returned with pictures of Soviet missiles in Cuba which could not be denied.

John McCone looked at the situation as Khrushchev might view it. The Soviet leaders were well aware of the U.S. edge in intercontinental ballistic missiles; the Soviets had a large number of medium and inter-mediate range missiles which could not reach the United States. If these missiles were deployed to Cuba and made operationally ready with nuclear warheads, then the strategic advantage would shift in favor of the Soviet Union.

The strength and clarity of the McCone approach to intelligence was again illustrated by his role in Vietnam. The intelligence community's estimates on communist reactions to U.S. courses of action in Vietnam were accurate. It is a great credit to their integrity that they stand today, inadvertently disclosed, as a testament to the ability of the intelligence professionals to foresee an unfavorable outcome long before our senior policymakers did.

McCone was disturbed by the tendency of senior officials to discount distasteful intelligence findings, and he made a point of urging his own views and the judgments of the intelligence community on the top leaders. McCone's view of the communist actions in Vietnam was clear and steady, and he displayed the courage of his convictions. His final act as Director of Central Intelligence was to hand the President per-sonally – minutes before the new Director of Central Intelligence was sworn in – his unequivocal views on the Vietnam issue. He warned that the decision to put U.S. forces into a direct combat role would involve the United States in a land war in Asia, a situation against which our most respected military authorities had also repeatedly warned. Such a conflict would be unwinnable, and it would become increasingly dif-ficult to extricate ourselves. If infantry operations were to be confined to South Vietnam, then the scale of air warfare against North Vietnam should be intensified. If the conflict became prolonged, world opinion, including the American public, would turn against the U.S. role in Viet-nam, and he would be under relentless pressure to settle on terms not of our own making. On this prophetic note, John McCone retired from ac-tive government service.

I cite these highlights not as a summary of McCone's accomplishments as the Director of Central Intelligence (this would require volumes), but to underline his evaluation of intelligence to its highest role as a major contributor to policy consideration. When national intelligence is objective — and honest in recognizing gaps in our knowledge and differences of opinions — and when it is relevant to the issues facing our nation's leaders, then it is doing what its founder, William J. Donovan, intended that it should do. When there is a sense of national urgency and need, then the intelligence community needs to work together in a way which overrides bureaucratic parochialism and jockeying for position.

When John McCone returned to private life in 1965, he left a legacy of accomplishments worthy of emulation by all future Directors of Central Intelligence. Whatever changes have been brought about by the passage of time, by managerial restructuring, and by the forays of self-serving investigative bodies and individuals, the need for a strong intelligence organization persists, and the need to identify and understand the major threats to our security has increased.

When John McCone left the government, his direct involvement may have diminished somewhat, but his concern for our national security and his dedication to preserving and strengthening our intelligence functions have not waned. He has continued to act as a sage counsel to the leaders of our nation and, in particular, to successive Directors of Central Intelligence. I have sought his advice; I have tried to model myself as Director of Central Intelligence on John McCone. I shall continue to call on him for counsel.

Bill Donovan would have been extraordinarily proud of the way John McCone put substance into the concept of an American national intelligence service.

◆ ◆ ◆

THE COMMITMENT OF VERA ATLINS

Casey always responded when his old buddies from the OSS asked him to help host an event. His willingness to lend a hand — and the prestige that came with his position — fueled criticism that he lived in the past and that his views on how to manage the U.S. intelligence service were outmoded. Of course, as his speeches make clear Casey didn't live in the past — or even in the present. He lived in the future, but never forgot the past.

Sir William Stephenson, he of the golden troops, fondly known as the Bard of Rockefeller center, Minister Jerry Regan, Ambassador Gotlieb, all the other distinguished guests on this ship, including the veterans of OSS. This is a happy occasion, honoring Sir William with the medal which commemorates his wartime partner, Bill Donovan, and getting together with so many friends and fellow intelligence officers who have come across from Europe and down from Canada.

Today the Free World has a highly sophisticated intelligence apparatus to watch for signs of danger. It was not always so. When Hitler was building his war machine and planning his aggression, Bill Stephenson, along with Winston Churchill, were lonely voices sounding the warning bell in England, and Bill Donovan was a one-man CIA, roaming Europe for Franklin Roosevelt.

Sir William saw that Donovan got a thorough knowledge of the intelligence service that England had developed over five centuries, and the way Britain was nourishing resistance in the occupied nations of Europe pursuant to Winston Churchill's dramatic order to "set Europe ablaze." Donovan in turn was to tell Roosevelt that intelligence, psychological warfare, and irregular forces drawn from the great ethnic melting pot which is America would be the spearhead to liberate occupied Europe. Out of this came the OSS. Today, OSS stands for Old Soldiers Society. In 1941, Bill Donovan assembled what had to be the most diverse aggregation ever assembled of scholars, scientists, bankers and foreign correspondents, tycoons, psychologists and football stars, circus managers and circus freaks, safe crackers, lock pickers and pickpockets.

Address to the Veterans of the Office of Strategic Services, New York, New York, September 23, 1983.

On this dais and scattered around this ship are the remnants of that collection. We have to admit that this was a bunch of amateurs. It was Sir William who provided the know-how and the training which made it possible for them to develop into an effective intelligence service. Sir William brought experienced intelligence officers over from London to assist in developing the structure and procedures of a professional organization. Early recruits to the OSS were trained in camps which Bill Stephenson had established in Canada. He then provided trainers for OSS to develop its own training schools in the United States. General Donovan said it all after the war. He said: "Bill Stephenson taught us everything we ever knew about foreign intelligence operations."

But there was still a lot of polishing to do. A British intelligence officer, who became a renowned writer and pundit, Malcolm Muggeridge, described it vividly. He said, "Ah those first OSS arrivals in London! How well I remember them, arriving like young girls in flower straight from a finishing school, all fresh and innocent, to start work in our frowsty old intelligence brothel."

The seasoning came with on-the-job training obtained by working daily with people like the comrades of those days who came across the Atlantic to be with us on this occasion. Here on the dais is Pierre Fourcaud who was the first of General de Gaulle's followers to parachute back into France to become a leader of french resistance forces. I see down there Flemming Juncker who brought the Danish railway system to a grinding halt to delay German troops in coming down from Norway to reinforce Hitler in the Battle of the Bulge.

It's a special pleasure to have Vera Atlins here on her first visit to the United States. I can only describe her special war time role by saying that in a very real sense she was the heart of allied support to French resistance. It was she who saw that every agent who went into France to organize, train, or communicate back to London was prepared, briefed, encouraged, calmed down, and made to understand that those of us who stood behind them really cared and could be counted on.

There came a time, after the landing in Normandy, when General Eisenhower decreed that a French general should head up a new organization to continue support of French resistance forces. We Americans and the British, who were engaged in this work, were to go to a new headquarters and become part of this new outfit. We all went except Squadron Officer Atlins who announced that she had sent hundreds of men and women to parachute into France from British special forces headquarters at Baker Street, and they would find her there when they returned – and they did until France was liberated. Then, she went over to find and help those who had survived the risks they had taken to help British and American forces land and fight their way through France – and, indeed, the families of those who had not survived.

So, all of us tonight salute you Pierre and you Flemming and you Vera, as well as you Sir William.

◆ ◆ ◆

THE VISION OF LEO CHERNE

Casey's first real job after completing law school was with the Research Institute of America, founded and run by Leo Cherne. In addition to being Casey's first boss, Cherne – a New York lawyer, business executive, and public servant extraordinaire – also became one of Casey's closest friends and confidants.

It was as Cherne's right-hand man at the Research Institute of America, in 1938, that Casey got his first taste of how Congress manages national-security affairs. The law required that in 1938-39 our country's Industrial Mobilization Plan be updated. But Congress, having passed the law, refused to allocate any money for the update. The executive branch officials charged with implementing the Plan, should that become necessary, asked Cherne if the Institute would undertake the massive project pro bono. Cherne agreed, and he in turn brought Casey into the project. The result was a 3,000-page report which Cherne and Casey delivered to the U.S. government on September 1, 1939 – the day World War II started.

Casey left the Research Institute shortly afterwards to join the OSS and General William Donovan. At war's end Casey rejoined the Institute briefly before moving on to other ventures, but he and Cherne remained close. When Cherne was named Chairman of the President's Foreign Intelligence Advisory Board by Gerald Ford, he

Address to the State Dinner in honor of the Honorable Leo Cherne, New York, New York, September 29, 1983.

engineered Casey's appointment to PFIAB. Cherne remained on PFIAB, as its vice chairman, during Casey's tenure as Director of Central Intelligence.

With overwhelming generosity Warren Meeker has allowed me five minutes to do justice to the multiple facets of Leo Cherne in a friendship which is now dangerously close to half a century in duration. I can only mention that I owe him so much for kindness, insights, lessons, inspirations and, above all, happy memories over a long and close association.

Watching this man in action, being associated with him, reacting to him, being challenged by him, I count as one of the joys of my life.

He hasn't changed much since the first day I met him when he hired me. He doesn't look very much older to me. After all those years he wrote those reports — it was a weekly struggle over the outlook and philosophy they reflected — he was the boss and had the last word but he gave me a lot of room and I used to get a lot of points in.

The big memory of those years was the quadrennial debate to which the institute staff would be treated. Casey for Wilkie and Dewey and Cherne for Roosevelt and Truman. As I recall it, I would win the debates but Leo always won the election. As he grew in wisdom, we found ourselves supporting the same presidential candidate.

For a decade we found ourselves engaged in publishing activities which were somewhat competitive. Whenever I got into a fight or a pickle, Leo would be the first to rush to my support.

We shared many other interests — the International Rescue Committee, encounters with a Russian tank in Czechoslovakia in 1968, visits to Indo-China, and concerns and worries about refugees from Eastern Europe, Cuba, Africa, India, and Pakistan.

Today we find ourselves engaged together with intelligence work which is in a very real sense a return to the beginning when Leo took me aboard. I was taken on in a private intelligence institution which he created and which he guides even to this day.

It is now close to ten years ago when President Nixon appointed him to his Foreign Intelligence Advisory Board and then a couple of years later President Ford appointed him chairman of that body and appointed me a member.

For close to ten years the American intelligence community has carried Leo's imprint with a much greater focus on economic intelligence and competitive analysis and in many other ways. For the last two and one-half years I can testify personally to his unbelievable commitment and dedication to the creative recommendations, the prodding, and the challenging stimulation that flows from his arduous study, application, and his ever fertile mind.

Any recitation of Leo's accomplishments, of what Leo has done and how he has done it, will not capture the style and the vision which makes him so special. Anyone who has had the privilege of hearing or reading his eulogy to his secretary of so many years, Liz Paul, would see there how deep his sentiments and feelings run. The kind of vision which makes his so special is clear when you think about his pioneering work, his industrial organization, when very few people understood the meaning of that term, which a few years later became so vital to the nation's life when bombs fell on Pearl Harbor. His advice to General MacArthur contributed so much to the economic vitality which Japan has since developed, and the book, *The Rest of Your Life*, which he wrote in 1946 charting the direction of post-war America. The qualities of sentiment and vision are beautifully captured in his dedication to that book to his then very young daughter Gail with these words:

> "To Gail:
>   With the deep hope that the rest of
>   her life will be linked to the possibilities,
>   not chained to the probabilities."

◆ ◆ ◆

THE CHARACTER OF SENATOR BARRY GOLDWATER

Here, Casey pays tribute to Senator Barry Goldwater, a personal friend and long-time supporter of U.S. intelligence.

Last year I was privileged to speak before the Security Affairs Support Association's first William Oliver Baker award to its namesake. Once again we gather here to commemorate the achievements of another

Address at the Presentation of the Security Affairs Support Association's Medal of Achievement to Senator Barry Goldwater, Washington, D.C., July 30, 1985.

great American who has made major contributions to the national security of the United States.

This evening we honor a man who has made great contributions to our American intelligence community through his unflagging support in the United States Congress, and his uncompromising public stand that U.S. intelligence should be the best in the world.

We know that Senator Barry Goldwater has been an elemental force in our nation for more than a quarter of a century, shaping and articulating a philosophy of peace and progress through strength and freedom. We know that his wisdom and eloquence, his statesmanship and political skills have played a historic role injecting this philosophy into the laws of our land and the hearts of our people.

But there is much about Barry Goldwater that is not so well known and I intend to take this occasion to tell you a little about the private Barry Goldwater. He is a man of amazing versatility. A man of many parts. An aviator, starting with the Army National Guard in the 1930's, he served as a pilot with the U.S. Army Air Corps in World War II, flying the hump between China and India. He kept on flying and he has flown every known type of airplane, and just recently qualified for a license as a helicopter pilot. A musician, he plays a lousy trombone. His trombone is known as the Goldwater deterrent. This comes of threatening his friends that if they don't behave, he will play his trombone.

He is a gadgeteer, skilled in electronics. If you invite him to your house for the weekend, he is apt to install a doorbell playing 20 different tunes before he leaves. His automobile has so many gadgets and gauges you think you are in the cockpit of a 747.

He is an avid ham radio operator. One year he gave his wife a $10,000 radio antenna as a Christmas present, but Mrs. Goldwater has had lots of experience in handling Barry. The next year for Christmas she gave him a sable coat.

He is an accomplished photographer with professional skills sufficient to qualify him as a member of the Society of American Photographers.

He is a scholar, a historian with deep knowledge of the American Civil War and the history of Arizona; a geographer who knows the state of Arizona like the back of his hand.

I can tell you that the gruff Barry Goldwater is a facade. Behind that stone face is a heart of putty. Barry is generous and always ready to reach out and help a friend or acquaintance in trouble. During the dark days of the Vietnam War Barry was on the air night after night working his shortwave radio, taking hundreds of calls from American soldiers in Vietnam every week and patching them through to their parents and sweethearts at home – all at his own expense.

Beyond these elements of personal charm and accomplishment, what brings us here to do honor to Barry Goldwater tonight is his distinguished decade of services on committees appointed to oversee the intelligence efforts of this country. In this capacity, Senator Goldwater proved himself time and again to be a vigorous defender of the intelligence family. For example, when hysteria was sweeping the country about alleged intelligence improprieties, Senator Goldwater was one of only three courageous and farsighted members of the Church Committee to firmly oppose the release of that committee's report on the National Security Agency. Later, he fought vigorously to prevent the budgetary cutbacks and hiring freezes that he saw were aimed squarely at paralyzing the nation's intelligence capabilities.

His tenure as Chairman of the Select Committee on Intelligence, which began in 1981, was marked by a continuing improvement in the intelligence community's ability to do its work. Largely as a result of his efforts, the slow but steady recovery and build-up of our capabilities has enabled us to better track Soviet weaponry and activities around the world. Senator Goldwater let it be known on Capitol Hill and on Pennsylvania Avenue that he considered intelligence to be America's first line of defense, and vital to our ability to meet the challenges of a complex and dangerous world.

Senator Goldwater backed up his words with deeds, including solid legislation that greatly benefitted the intelligence community. His leadership was crucial in securing the passages of the 1982 Intelligence Identities Protection Act that protects our intelligence officers and sources overseas. He personally introduced other legislation in 1983 that led to the eventual passage of the Central Intelligence Agency Information Act of 1984. This legislation safeguards our operational and technical files from unwarranted search. Moreover, he played a vital role in securing the enactment of a series of intelligence community budget authorizations that were essential to the rebuilding of the intelligence capabilities of the United States.

Senator Goldwater's stewardship of the Select Committee on Intelligence has shown that Congressional oversight of our nation's intelligence activities can be both tough and fair, responsible and supportive, rigorous yet secure.

One final personal note. I cannot let this occasion go by without expressing my personal appreciation and that of our intelligence officers working around the world for the many times Barry dropped in on our missions in his travels around the world. I can't tell you how many times I heard how important those visits were, how much his talks with our officers encouraged and inspired them and contributed to their understanding of the importance of their work to our national security and an increasingly dangerous world.

I am now greatly pleased and honored to present this second William Oliver Baker award to a distinguished member of Congress, military officer, traveller, author, public servant, all around good fellow and one of the great patriots in our history. Senator Goldwater, I salute you and ask you to step forward to accept this medal and certificate.

♦ ♦ ♦

THE SILENT SERVICES

In this witty and sensitive speech, Casey pays tribute to the men and women who serve without public recognition.

The speech reveals a warm, personable William Casey that the public never knew. It includes one of the all-time funny war stories. In fact, Casey did not keep the medal he talks about receiving.

It is a special pleasure and a distinct honor for me to be with you submariners this evening for your 85th birthday party. There are many reasons for this, not the least of these reasons is a certain nostalgia. It's a truly rich experience for me right now to have this opportunity to imbibe some of the culture and spirit which characterize the submarine service. I have always had deep feelings of affection and loyalty for the Navy despite the somewhat abbreviated and spotty nature of my naval career. I started out in 1942 with one-and-a-half stripes sailing a desk on Constitution Avenue. I thought that was no way to fight a war and it

Address to the 85th Submarine Birthday Ball, Arlington, Virginia, April 13, 1985.

took me about six months to escape into the OSS. That finally got me out of the country, but the closest I got to naval action was a billet in what was then the flagship of the Navy of the Seine. It was called the Royal Marceau Hotel in Paris. It lived up to the finest Navy tradition: in the cold winter of 1944, it was the hotel in Paris with hot water. A naval officer could trade a half-hour of shower time in his bathroom for bottles of whiskey, cartons of cigarettes, and all sorts of things. As I look back, I have to admit that it was the perks that won my heart for the Navy.

There came a time toward the end of 1944 when the Allied Command was forced to recognize that it was not going to win the war in France and would have to fight in Germany. I was told that it was my job to get people inside Germany in the hope that we wouldn't be surprised again as we had been by Hitler's counteroffensive, which became known as the Battle of the Bulge. By that time I had gotten another half stripe, but in this assignment I would have opposite numbers in Allied intelligence who wore two stars. The ranking naval officer in OSS, Captain Armour, walked me across Grosvenor Square to Admiral Stark's office, explained the problem to him, and said I would need more rank. Admiral Stark listened, took one look at me, and said, "The best thing we can do for him is get him a gray suit." Captain Armour walked me around the corner to Selfridge's and I bought two gray suits. The deal was that I was to get the same pay as a civilian as I had been getting in the Navy. A little later, David Bruce, then an Army colonel and Commanding Officer of OSS in Europe, asked me what my civilian pay should be. I dutifully added up my salary, per diem, overseas allowance, and perhaps another item or two, and gave the number to Bruce. David Bruce was a mild man but he exploded at this, saying, "Hell, that's more than I am getting paid and I am a full colonel in the Army." I said, "That's no surprise, Captain Armour is probably getting almost as much as General Eisenhower." All that left me with a keen appreciation of the way the Navy takes care of its own.

As long as I have started to tell war stories, there is another one that comes to mind. It is how I got my *Croix de Guerre*. One day, in July of 1945, the war was over and I was sitting at Headquarters with Colonel Forgan, who succeeded Bruce in commanding the OSS in Europe. A liaison officer from French military intelligence came by with a brown paper bag. He dropped the bag on Colonel Forgan's desk and said the

French wanted officers in our Headquarters to have these five *Croix de Guerre* medals. Forgan opened up the bag, looked at the medals, and turned to me and said, "Who should we give the other three to?"

In my present incarnation, I have developed a deeper and more profound appreciation of the Navy, and particularly of the submariners. You submariners and we intelligencers both do our work quietly. Both of us are sometimes known as the "silent service." Beyond that, the way the world has developed in a geostrategic sense, the multiplication and ramification of threats that have been generated from so many directions, have made both of us, in a very real sense, the nation's first line of defense, the sentries of freedom. Your service has seen our principal adversary, the Soviet Union, develop in less than a quarter of a century from a continental power, virtually landlocked, to a global power with bases on all continents and sea power which can be deployed on all the oceans of the world. Perhaps even more important, as the land-based strategic deterrent, which has kept the peace for forty years, becomes increasingly vulnerable and less survivable, the sea-based deterrent, which your service has developed with such vigor and creativity, seems likely to become the main guarantor of peace and the main deterrent against the use of nuclear weapons for the remainder of this century.

There are still other threats. We have witnessed the perpetrators of totalitarian aggression who tend to telegraph, if not announce, their intentions. Some of us can remember how the democracies refused to believe Hitler's *Mein Kampf*, which described how he would conquer Europe. Twenty-four years ago, Nikita Khrushchev proclaimed Communism would win not by nuclear war which might destroy the world, nor conventional war which might lead to nuclear war, but by national wars of liberation.

We have seen it happen again — how the Soviet Union has transformed itself from a continental to a global power, acquiring bases and partners in Asia, Africa, and Latin America, with access to all the oceans of the world.

We have seen the Soviets move aggressively with a mix of propaganda, economic and military aid, diplomacy, subversion, terrorism, and insurgency to destabilize, overthrow, or otherwise gain a dominant influence over Vietnam, Cambodia, Laos, Angola, Ethiopia, Mozambique, Afghanistan, South Yemen, and Nicaragua.

Afghanistan, Angola, and Cambodia are kept under control by more than 300,000 Soviet, Cuban, and Vietnamese troops. Half a dozen other countries – Nicaragua, Ethiopia, Mozambique, South Yemen, Vietnam, and Cuba – are controlled by committed Marxist-Leninist governments with military and population control assistance from the East bloc. It costs the Soviet Union some ten billion dollars a year to keep 120,000 Soviet soldiers in Afghanistan; to enable Vietnam to maintain the fourth largest army in the world on China's southern flank; to provide Ethiopia with the largest army in Africa; to maintain Cuba as the second most powerful military force in the Western Hemisphere; and to give Nicaragua a military force more powerful than all of its Central American neighbors put together.

At the same time, we see radical states – Iran, Libya, and Syria – aided and abetted by the Soviet Union and its proxies – North Korea on its eastern border, Bulgaria and East Germany on its western border, and Cuba in our own backyard – use terrorism as an instrument of foreign policy. All over the world these forces are targeting and threatening American embassies and military installations, American diplomats and soldiers, and American citizens in all walks of life.

Another ominous threat is that of strategic surprise arising from scientific and technological breakthroughs. We see the Soviets rapidly enhancing this potential by working all over the world to steal technology, and by their own persistent commitment to apply the technology they develop and steal to enhance their military capability. You have seen them develop four new submarines in the last few years. In doing this, they have come up with an impressive ability to develop titanium hulls, dive deeper, and cruise faster and more quietly – all of which will challenge to the utmost the young officers whom you are developing. In dealing with these quiet threats – creeping imperialism around the world, international terrorism threatening our installations, and scientific and technological breakthroughs which threaten to erode our qualitative edge, which has been and must continue to be the basis of our national security – the silent services – you submariners and we intelligencers – must continue to work together quietly, closely, and assiduously. I look forward to that challenge.

It is particularly gratifying, as I look around the room, to see so many distinguished submariners who understand this world so well and contributes so valuably in developing the understanding and capability we

will need to meet the intelligence challenges of the future — Admiral Bob
Long with his seminal report on the Marine tragedy in Beirut and his
ongoing work on the Intelligence Community's Scientific and Technical
Advisory Panel; Admiral Al Burkhalter for his contribution in the full
range of intelligence challenges in his capacity as Director of the Intelligence Community Staff; Admiral John Butts with his long and varied
career in intelligence culminating in the enormously creative contribution as Director of Naval Intelligence, those submariners who built the
foundation which supports our efforts today; my distinguished predecessor, Red Raborn, and Fritz Harlfinger, and so many others.

Finally, I want to salute the quality and professionalism which are the
hallmarks of your service and which distinguish you submariners in both
wartime and peace. The capabilities that you provide in the pursuit of
intelligence are unparalleled, and it would be my strongest desire that
in the future the Navy continue to place high emphasis on these qualities
which are unique to the submarine platform. I have been tremendously
impressed with your professionalism and your dedication.

In closing, let me say that I look back fondly on my brief time as a
naval officer, and I am proud to be present tonight on such a happy Navy
occasion and to join in saluting all submariners wherever they may be
— whether on land or under the sea.

I yield the rest of my time to you submariners here to take all these
lovely ladies to the dance floor.

◆ ◆ ◆

RECALLING OLD FRIENDS

*Opportunities to review past work came along only rarely, but
when they did Casey took advantage of them and enjoyed himself.*

This 50th anniversary is a splendid occasion to reminisce about a great
institution that has left its mark on each of us. But as I see so many old
friends I just can't resist the opportunity to dispel the vicious rumor that
I mumble. You know it was the *Washington Post* that launched the

Address at the United States Securities and Exchange Commission Golden
Anniversay, Washington, D.C., June 29, 1984.

canard that Ronald Reagan appointed me to the CIA as an economy measure. He figured I would be the first Director of Central Intelligence for whom it would not be necessary to buy a scrambler. From personal experience I can tell you that mumbling is more in the mind of the listener than in the mouth of the speaker. There are people who just don't want to hear what the Director of Central Intelligence sees in a complex and dangerous world.

In contrast, Wall Street knew that I, as Chairman of the Securities and Exchange Commission, had two not secret weapons at the SEC. Their code names were Irving Pollack and Stanley Sporkin. As a result, when I spoke then, Wall Street listened and they damn well understood.

It was at the SEC that I made my first political master stroke. I inherited from my predecessor, Judge Budge, a very bright and able young legal assistant named Max Baucus. It wasn't long before he came in to tell me that he was leaving the Commission to return to his home state of Montana where he intended to run for the state legislature. When he got back home and announced his candidacy I sent him a campaign contribution of $100 with a note which read: "Dear Max, investing $100 in a future United States Senator is like buying Xerox at 10." Max turned out to be one of those slow growth investments. It took him seven long years to get elected to the United States Senate.

As I look around the room I get the feeling of a class reunion or alumni homecoming. This is quite natural because the SEC is, among other things, a great educational institution. The agency has for decades conferred honorary doctorates in high and low finance on departing commissioners.

Some laugh at those doctorates. But I submit that an SEC degree gets at least a slight semblance of "de facto legitimacy" from the many distinguished academics and ex-academics who figure so prominently in the Commission's history: Jim Landis, Bill Douglas, Abe Fortas, Bill Cary, Louis Loss, Homer Kripke, Andy Barr, and Sandy Burton are among the names that come to mind.

On a more personal note, the SEC certainly taught me some law. I remember quite a bit of what I learned from the elaborate staff memoranda, from the interminable discussions at the Commission table, and from studying the scholarly briefs submitted in the Commission's name. My rough, unaudited estimate is that I remember about half of it. Unfortunately, the half I retain is the half that the Supreme Court has since thrown out of the window.

Still, my years at the corner of North Capital and E Streets gave me a rich, informal education that has since stood me in good stead. I give my on-the-job, clinical training at the SEC full credit for my success in dealing with congressional committees and with the press. Also valuable to me was the excellent course in state secrets and how to keep them. In addition, I learned something about Judge-designate Sporkin and how to get along with him. If I appear nervous this evening it's because I'm wondering who's going to keep me out of trouble when Stanley puts on those judicial robes.

Stanley taught me two basic principles of SEC administration and law. The first one was: "Yes, you do have to register," and the second was "It sounds like 10(b)5 to me." That's all you have to know. If one of these principles doesn't work, you just use the other and you've got them.

The most unique and indispensable element in the SEC's half century is the spirit, the drive, and the commitment of its staff, which is so marvelously and so regularly renewed and reinvigorated year after year and decade after decade. I've always thought that the creativity and resourcefulness of the staff had its genesis in a story that may be apocryphal but I prefer to believe it happened. Joe Kennedy, upon being appointed Chairman, asked a young professor from Yale Law School to come down to help him. His name was Bill Douglas. He reported to Kennedy Monday morning and said, "Sir, what are your instructions?" Kennedy looked at Douglas and snorted, "If I knew what to do why the hell would I ask you to come down here. Now get going." And the staff has been going ever since.

With less warmth I recall those SEC watchers in the law reviews and elsewhere. They would spray you with cold showers of knowledgeable, uninhibited critical comment. And they don't stop after you are gone.

I was reminded of that just the other day when I glanced at the current issue of the *New York University Law Review*. In that issue Professor Homer Kripke reviews a history of the SEC. It was written by Professor Joel Seligman and it's called *The Transformation of Wall Street* with a subtitle, *A History of the Securities and Exchange Commission and Modern Corporate Finance*. And it is 700 pages long. Can you think of any other specialized government agency about which *anybody* (even a law professor) would want to write a 700-page history? And actually sell the book. That says a lot about the significance of the SEC.

In his review, Professor Kripke says that Seligman's book focuses on SEC chairmen and that this "inappropriately inflates the importance of a single official, ignoring the fact that the chairman has only one vote and that the SEC has always been a . . . Body whose permanent staff members retain strong abilities to survive and effectuate their policies, notwithstanding revolving-door chairmen and commissioners." Kripke is fond of this point. He returns to it at the end of his review when he says that the book gives unwarranted attention to "personalities of bygone worthies" and that "its emphasis on SEC chairmen, *including undistinguished ones now forgotten,* slights the importance of many commissioners and leading staff members."

After I read that, I scrapped my prepared lecture about my many noteworthy accomplishments at the SEC. I did this with real regret because I had taken great pains with that speech. At the last moment, I decided not to inflict even greater pain on you by delivering it.

But I do want to celebrate with you the enormous contribution the fifty-year legacy of the SEC has made and is still making to the bounce which the American economy is demonstrating today and which the rest of the world so envies. It is the integrity of our financial system and the depth and liquidity of our capital market which has attracted from all over the world the investment funds that make it possible to fuel economic growth while carrying a large deficit. It is the ready access to that capital market which has become available to new ventures and growing companies that has made possible the development and application of so many new technologies and the creation of twenty million new jobs in the United States while Europe has been losing two million jobs. All of that would not have been possible without the assurances of integrity and fairness, of competence and efficiency provided by the collaboration of the SEC and the self-regulatory bodies.

Today, the traditions and standards developed over the past half century are carried on and adapted to a rapidly evolving economic and financial environment under the first chairman since Joe Kennedy to come out of the financial industry. It is something of a commentary on American public life that it took almost one-half a century after Joe Kennedy to bring to the SEC someone else with actual knowledge and experience in the securities market who actually proved it by making some real money there.

I salute you, John Shad, for the way you've brought your knowledge and experience in Washington to give leadership in preserving what has been accomplished in these past fifty years and adapting it to this era of the takeover and the leveraged buyout, of multi-purpose financial institutions and the financial department store, of instant communications and worldwide capital markets.

In conclusion, I would like to thank all of you for this welcome and pleasant opportunity to express this old alumnus's affectionate esteem for the SEC and for the many dedicated and gifted people who served it during his tenure and before and since.

◆ ◆ ◆

AN EPITAPH

Robert C. Ames was among those CIA officers killed in the terrorist bombing of the U.S. Embassy in Beirut on April 18, 1983. In this testimonial – Casey's last public speech – the Director pays tribute to a trusted, sorely missed, and much beloved colleague. His description of Bob Ames is striking, not only because it so accurately captures that officer's essence but because it serves so well as an epitaph for Bill Casey: "He had enough confidence in himself and his judgments not to worry about his 'image,' which helps explain why, in retrospect, his image is so impressive."

It's a great privilege for me to be here with you Brother Patrick, members of the faculty, alumni, students, and guests of La Salle University, and, in particular, members of the family of Robert C. Ames. I offer my gratitude on behalf of all employees of the Central Intelligence Agency for the opportunity to join La Salle in paying tribute to Bob Ames.

I am particularly grateful to you Brother Patrick, not only for the testimonial dinner and this handsome bronze plaque, but for holding the symposium on Middle East issues. No one should expect that a single

---

Address to the La Salle University Testimonial Dinner in honor of the Late Robert C. Ames, Philadelphia, Pennsylvania, December 11, 1986.

day's discussions can produce satisfactory answers to the vexing problems in that region, but it is reasonable to believe that at least the participants raised some of the right questions. In any case, no worthier compliment can be given the mind of Bob Ames than to assemble the best talents available to focus their intellectual energies on topics that commanded his attention.

In addition, I wish to thank your staff for their courtesy and competence in arranging today's events and welcoming all these visitors from Washington. Members of my staff are particularly appreciative of the role of your Associate Director of Alumni Edward Turzanski.

First, let me share with you two letters I've brought from Washington. They are addressed to Brother Patrick, and they were written and signed by two of the strongest and most fervent friends and admirers of Bob Ames.

At CIA, most of us who knew Bob Ames regarded him as about the closest thing to the irreplaceable man because he not only had great knowledge, but exceptional poise and an authoritative presence. As Secretary Shultz has pointed out, he had perhaps the keenest insights into the Arab mind of any individual in government, an asset which, when combined with years of experience in the area, made him a very special contributor in Washington. His warm personal relationships with many Arab rulers — so critical to understanding the region — helped guide our policies in this enormously complex and troubled part of the world. And, that "can-do" spirit that Secretary Shultz mentioned helped keep U.S. policy dynamic at a time when hostile forces in the area conspired to drive us out.

These qualities made Bob just as comfortable sitting cross-legged in the Arabian desert with Bedouin sheiks as he was in the White House briefing Presidents. He had enough confidence in himself and his judgments not to worry about his "image," which helps explain why, in retrospect, his image is so impressive.

While that confident image reflected on kings and presidents, its impact was also felt by Bob's colleagues in CIA. Young professionals remember how quickly Bob sought them out to welcome them and to offer ready words of advice and encouragement. Older hands remember how effortlessly Bob would come to them to try out his ideas as well as to elicit new thoughts. Bob was equally at ease in his intellectual surroundings at the Agency. Always attuned to the importance of protocol and stature in the Arab world, at home he never let an employee's rank or age stand between him and a good idea or an encouraging word.

One of his closest colleagues at the Agency believes that this poise and presence — as well as Bob's perseverance — were initially developed during his years at this University. She remembers his fond and grateful attitude toward La Salle. He talked to her many times about how much he had gained from his experiences there that helped him in his career. He felt that as a member of the school's championship basketball team he had learned how to manage pressure successfully, how to deal with losses as setbacks, not defeats, and how to give that extra measure when you think you are already at 100 percent effort.

Moreover, everyone who worked with Bob felt he was a real team player, and that too must have been developed at La Salle. He was quick to give others credit even when much of the work was his. He worked to cultivate the strengths of others, and was always open to their ideas. He accepted criticism with grace and handed it out gently.

And as a great team player I think Bob Ames would be particularly pleased that the plaque La Salle has designed takes note of his "colleagues" who fell with him that awful day in Beirut. Some of these Americans were fellow Agency employees. On a wall in the CIA headquarters building are stars honoring Agency personnel who died in the service of their country. A book of honor below the stars displays those whose names in death can be revealed, and Bob is among them. But the names of certain Agency employees can never be revealed, and they have only the stars. Some of those who died with Bob are in that category. Bob would be grateful that La Salle also honors the rest of the team.

This past Veterans' Day some Agency employees visited the grave of Bob Ames in Arlington Cemetery. They laid at the gravestone a wreath made in La Salle's blue and gold. Then, knowing that one of the other Agency employees who died with him was also buried in Arlington, they found that gravestone too and left a red rose. For Bob and those united with him in death, the words (of the poet, Laurence Binyon) often recited on Veterans' Day seemed fitting:

> They shall not grow old,
> As we that are left grow old:
> Age shall not weary them,
> Nor the years condemn.

> At the going down of the sun
> And in the morning
> We will remember them.

Thank you, La Salle, for remembering them with us.

William J. Casey was taken ill in his office on December 15, 1986. He resigned as Director of Central Intelligence on January 31, 1987, and died in Glen Cove, New York, on May 6, 1987.

* * *

A Eulogy for William J. Casey

by Jeane J. Kirkpatrick

"Bill Casey is a controversial man," a liberal journalist said to me last week. You have to face that."

But, of course, I said, he was a bold committed man in an age rent by controversy.

In *Paradise Lost*, Dante reserved the lowest rung of hell for those who do not care — for those who, confronted by great questions, are uninterested; who, faced with great needs, are unmoved; who, offered great opportunities, feel no challenge; who, endowed with freedom and power, make no use of it; the kind of man who, observing a battle between tyrants and those who would be free, remains indifferent.

Bill Casey was no such man. And, he knew it.

In one of his last public speeches, he quoted Theodore Roosevelt:

> Far better it is to dare mighty things, to win glorious
> triumphs, even though checkered by failure, than to
> take rank with those poor spirits who neither enjoy
> much nor suffer much, because they live in the gray
> twilight that knows not victory nor defeat.

"A lawyer," Casey once said, "has a ringside seat at the human comedy." But this lawyer was not content to merely observe his times.

"Casey is a real warrior," a CIA colleague told me...because, one might add, he decided to be.

He had a choice.

Before he was a warrior, Bill Casey was an intellectual, a man of letters, a bibliophile, prodigious reader, researcher, writer, editor.

Jeane J. Kirkpatrick served as United States Ambassador to the United Nations.

"During my entire working life," he wrote, "my activities as a lawyer, author, editor have involved the gathering, analysis, and evaluation of information and applying it to practical purposes."

This penchant for gathering, analyzing, and evaluating information made Bill Casey a superb Director of the Central Intelligence Agency where, insiders understand, his greatest interest and most outstanding contribution was to strengthen the skill and confidence of the CIA's analysts.

The same commitment to gathering, analyzing, and evaluating information led Bill Casey to the conclusion that our violent century is dangerous for Americans, that the stakes are very high, and that we no longer have a comfortable margin for error. These views were the spur to action.

Watching the Soviet Union shoot down KAL 007 on the mere *suspicion* that it *might* have been engaged in espionage (as he put it), observing the framing and arrest of Nicholas Daniloff (hostage taking, he called it), Casey concluded that in the Soviet government, we are dealing with men who have "a fundamentally alien and totally unpalatable value system."

He believed on the basis of vast information collected and reflected on, that the Soviet leadership is "committed to building a military force that could fight and win a nuclear war."

He was deeply concerned with growing U.S. vulnerability to the highly accurate Soviet mobile missiles which "promise to make deterrence through offensive missiles increasingly uncertain in the years ahead." He worried about the long Soviet lead in research on high laser particle beam weapons, radio frequency and kinetic energy weapons. He ardently supported SDI against a relentless Soviet propaganda campaign.

He was also concerned, for both human and strategic reasons, about the Soviet "creeping imperialism" in the Third World.

They had, he said, unleashed the Four Horsemen of the Apocalypse – famine, pestilence, war, and death – in Ethiopia, Cambodia, Afghanistan, Mozambique – devastating people and moving relentlessly toward "two primary targets" – the oil fields of the Middle East (the lifeline of the Western Alliance) and the isthmus of Panama, which separates North and South America.

No one welcomed signs of Soviet liberalization more than Bill Casey. But *glasnost* ' has not come to Afghanistan, Nicaragua, or to Soviet Jews.

These people will one day be free from force, Casey believed, because "the pendulum of history is slowly but surely swinging away from Soviet Marxism...toward democracy and free market economics."

"The Soviet Union may have a proven recipe for subversion and an undiluted willingness to use raw power to shore up its unpopular clients, but we in the West have an infinitely more powerful weapon – the promise of long-term prosperity."

"I am high on the free market," Casey told the *Washington Post*, and many others. Freedom, he believed, worked for him, for us, and for every people who tried it. It is the alternative and the antidote to tyranny, stagnation, and starvation.

In addition to doing what we can to support indigenous freedom fighters, Casey wrote, we need to bring to bear the West's technological ingenuity, entrepreneurial talents, and free markets on the core problems of development and "piece by piece, technique by technique, country by country" eliminate hunger and raise Third World living standards.

"All we have to do is muster the courage and resolve to use our enormous advantages." He had the courage and resolve. He could barely stand it when we missed an opportunity to protect the United States and promote freedom. Bill Casey was a man of passionate convictions, willing to work long hours, make hard decisions, and endure criticism.

He dared to take a big step where one was required, understanding, like David Lloyd George, that you can't cross a chasm with two small jumps. He did not take to unnecessary risks, and he was not daunted by difficulties or difficult people. He worried quite a lot about America's growing incapacity to act with discretion and dispatch.

Most of all, Bill Casey had a passionate commitment to preserving the independence and freedom of the United States – from terrorists, nuclear blackmail, and isolation. Because he saw them as directly relevant to American security, developing a defense against incoming nuclear missiles and supporting Nicaraguan freedom fighters had special priority for him. There is no question about it. But they had no more priority than law.

Bill Casey was one smart lawyer who understood politics and history as well. He was a savvy, sometimes sassy, always feisty guy – and a fighter.

Some mean spirited, ill-informed comments have been written and spoken in the last days, reminding us as Marcus Aurelius said, "There is no man so fortunate that there shall not be by him when he is dying some who are pleased with what is going to happen."

These unpleasant comments would not have overly disturbed our friend. "The CIA is (not) the place for tender egos and shriveling violets." He told a university audience last fall, "The debates and clashes of ideas can get rough."

Casey could take the guff required to support unpopular ideas – like the free market – and controversial causes – like the contras – because he had studied the evidence and thought through his positions.

He could take the guff and not give up because he had built his life on solid foundations.

Plato and St. Augustine tell us one knows a man by what he loves. We know Bill Casey through his loves – of Sophia, Bernadette, his church, his country, his books, his freedom.

Bill Casey's inspiration was Greek in the cultivation of his capacities, Roman in his love of law, Christian in his love of God and the Church, American in his love of freedom.

He lived his life to the hilt and left it in the spirit of the man who said, "I am perfectly resigned. I am surrounded by my family. I have served my country. I have reliance upon God, and am not afraid of the Devil."

Bill Casey, with his intelligence, courage, wit and zest, contributed enormously to his family, his country, his President, and his friends.